# The Canterbury and York Society

*GENERAL EDITOR: DR P. HOSKIN*

ISSN 0262–995X

## DIOCESE OF CARLISLE

CANTERBURY AND YORK SOCIETY VOL. XCVI

# The Register of
# Thomas Appleby

BISHOP OF CARLISLE

1363–1395

EDITED BY

## R.L. STOREY

The Canterbury and York Society

The Boydell Press

2006

First published 2006


A Canterbury and York Society publication
published by The Boydell Press
an imprint of Boydell & Brewer Ltd
PO Box 9, Woodbridge, Suffolk IP12 3DF, UK
and of Boydell & Brewer Inc.
668 Mt Hope Avenue, Rochester, NY 14620, USA
website: www.boydellandbrewer.com


ISBN 0 907239 66 8


A CIP catalogue record for this book is available
from the British Library


Details of previous volumes are available from Boydell & Brewer Ltd


This publication is printed on acid-free paper


Printed in Great Britain by
Athenaeum Press Ltd, Gateshead, Tyne & Wear

# CONTENTS

# PREFACE

Professor Robin Storey had almost completed this edition when, sadly, ill-health prevented him continuing with the work in its final stages. Through the kindness of Dr Sheila Storey I was able to take away his files and prepare the volume for publication.

This present volume completes the publication of the surviving medieval episcopal registers of Carlisle and tribute must be paid to Professor Storey for his tireless work over the last decade since his retirement to Carlisle in tackling the registers of Bishops Ross, Kirkby, Welton and Appleby for this Society. Unfortunately I cannot know what Robin Storey intended to say in the introduction he never had time to write before the onset of illness and for my part I will confine myself to brief biographical details of the bishop and a description of his register.

## BISHOP THOMAS APPLEBY

Thomas Appleby was an Augustinian canon of Carlisle cathedral before his elevation to the bishopric. It is not known when he entered the community but he was obviously a trusted member of the chapter by 1353 when, as their envoy, he fell foul of the diocesan, Bishop Welton.[1] On the death of that same Bishop Gilbert Welton in late 1362, the cathedral chapter proceeded to an election and after royal licence to elect was granted on 18 January 1363 Thomas Appleby was chosen. Pope Urban V, who had reserved the see, quashed Appleby's election but appointed him as bishop by papal provision. He was consecrated at Avignon on 18 June 1363, and received the temporalities by royal grant of 10 August. His episcopate turned out to be the longest of any bishop of Carlisle to date and he ruled the border diocese for well over thirty years before his death on 5 December 1395.[2] His register, though incomplete, gives ample evidence of his careful administration of the diocese and also reveals his political involvement as a warden of the West March, frequently involved in negotiations with the Scots.

## THE REGISTER

Appleby's register forms part of the second composite register (DRC/1/2) in the Cumbria Record Office at Carlisle, containing the fragment of bishop-elect

---

[1] *Reg. Welton*, nos. 525–6.

[2] These details are taken in from the *Oxford Dictionary of National Biography* (2004) R.K. Rose, 'Appleby, Thomas'; *Fasti*, VI.97; *BRUO*, III.2144. See also R.K. Rose, 'The bishops and diocese of Carlisle: church and society on the Anglo-Scottish border, 1292–1395' (University of Edinburgh Ph.D. thesis, 1983).

John Horncastle's acts 1353, the register of Bishop Gilbert Welton 1353–62, a
copy of diocesan statutes attributed to Bishop Chaury 1258 × 1259, and the
register of Thomas Appleby 1363–95.[3] The composite volume has been paginated but each register retains its individual foliation as well, and both num-
bering sequences have been noted in the calendar. Appleby's register, foliated
1–136, covers pages 141–367 of the composite register. Its parchment quires
are in general of regular size, averaging 33.5 × 24 cms, the only exception
being fos. 107–121 which are slightly smaller (32 × 23 cms). The area for text is
normally delineated by ruled lines; there are brief marginal summaries as is
common with most episcopal registers and pointing fingers are also used in the
margin to 'highlight' particular entries. It is written in a variety of hands, not
particularly carefully it must be admitted, but then it is a working register. As
mentioned before it is incomplete and there are no entries after 1392. Even
within the chronological structure up to that date there are gaps and clearly
there are missing folios (and probably quires). Many of the current quires have
stubs indicating the removal of sheets. The current foliation of the register
runs 1–19, 21–31, 33–58, 60, 69–70, 72–3, 75–7, 78–80, [81–86 not numbered],
88–90, 92–5, [96 not numbered], 98–110, 113–15, 118–21, 123–4, 127–36. The
register comprises nineteen quires as follows:

| | | |
|---|---|---|
| Quire 1 | fos. 1–4 | (pp. 141–8) |
| Quire 2 | fos. 5–10 | (pp. 149–60) |
| Quire 3 | fos. 11–19 | (pp. 161–80) |
| Quire 4 | fos. 21–31 | (pp. 181–201) |
| Quire 5 | fos. 33–8 | (pp. 202–13) |
| Quire 6 | fos. 39–48 | (pp. 214–31) |
| Quire 7 | fos. 49–54 | (pp. 232–43) |
| Quire 8 | fos. 55–77 | (pp. 244–65) |
| Quire 9 | fos. 78–[83] | (pp. 266–77) |
| Quire 10 | fos. [84–6] | (pp. 278–83) |
| Quire 11 | fos. [88–9] | (pp. 284–7) |
| Quire 12 | fos. 90–2 | (pp. 288–91) |
| Quire 13 | fos. 93–106 | (pp. 292–317) |
| Quire 14 | fos. 107–8 | (pp. 318–21) |
| Quire 15 | fos. 109–10 | (pp. 322–5) |
| Quire 16 | fos. 113–18 | (pp. 326–33) |
| Quire 17 | fos. 119–21 | (pp. 334–9) |
| Quire 18 | fos. 123–30 | (pp. 340–55) |
| Quire 19 | fos. 131–6 | (pp. 356–67) |

[3] A brief description of this composite volume is in D.M. Smith, *Guide to Bishops'
Registers of England and Wales: a survey from the middle ages to the abolition of episcopacy in
1646* (Royal Historical Society guide and handbook 11, 1981), pp. 256–7.
Horncastle and Welton are printed in *Reg. Welton*, and the Chaury statutes in *English
Episcopal Acta 30: Carlisle 1133–1292*, ed. D.M. Smith (British Academy, forthcoming
2005), appendix I.

EDITORIAL METHOD

The calendar shows all persons and places in the manuscript. Footnotes giving further details about individuals and benefices are mostly attached to their first reference cited in the index. Place-names are given in their present form; for the first time each occurs, the form in the manuscript is next given in round brackets. Square brackets are used for editorial insertions. As recent scholars have sometimes in their references to the Carlisle registers cited folio numbers and page numbers, in this volume both folio and page numbers are quoted.

ACKNOWLEDGEMENTS

Thanks are due to the Right Reverend Graham Dow, Bishop of Carlisle, and to the staff of the Cumbria Record Office at Carlisle.

David M. Smith

# ABBREVIATIONS OF SOURCES

| | |
|---|---|
| *Accounts*, ed. Lunt | W.E. Lunt, *Accounts rendered by papal collectors in England 1317–1378*, ed. E.B. Graves (Philadelphia, 1968). |
| *BRUC* | A.B. Emden, *A Biographical Register of the University of Cambridge to A.D. 1500* (Oxford, 1963). |
| *BRUO* | A.B. Emden, *A Biographical Register of the University of Oxford to A.D. 1500* (Oxford, 1957–9). |
| *CCR* | *Calendar of Close Rolls.* |
| *CFR* | *Calendar of Fine Rolls.* |
| *Complete Peerage* | G.E.C., *Complete Peerage of England, Scotland, Ireland, Great Britain and the United Kingdom* (1910–98). |
| *CPL* | *Calendar of Papal Letters.* |
| *CPP* | *Calendar of Papal Petitions.* |
| *CPR* | *Calendar of Patent Rolls.* |
| *CWAAS* | *Transactions of the Cumberland and Westmorland Antiquarian and Archaeological Society.* |
| CYS | Canterbury and York Society. |
| *EPNS* | *Publications of the English Place-Name Society.* |
| *Fasti* | *John Le Neve: Fasti Ecclesiae Anglicanae 1300–1541*, 12 vols., 1962–7. |
| *Fasti Parochiales* | Yorkshire Archaeological Society Record Series 85, 107, 129, 133, 143, 1933–85. |
| *Foedera* | *Foedera, Conventiones, Litterae [etc.]*, ed. A. Clarke, F. Holbrooke and J. Caley (Record Commission, 1816–69). |
| *HBC* | *Handbook of British Chronology*, 3rd edn., ed. E.B. Fryde, D.E. Greenway, S. Porter and I. Roy (Royal Historical Society, 1986). |
| Hist. Man. Comm. | Historical Manuscripts Commission. |
| Lunt, *Financial Relations to 1327* | W.E. Lunt, *Financial Relations of the Papacy with England to 1327* (Cambridge, Mass., 1939). |
| Lunt, *Financial Relations* | W.E. Lunt, *Financial Relations of the Papacy with England, 1327–1534* (Cambridge, Mass., 1962). |
| Nicolson & Burn | J. Nicolson & R. Burn, *The History and Antiquities of the Counties of Westmorland and Cumberland* (1777). |
| *Reg. Halton* | *The Register of John Halton, bishop of Carlisle, 1292–1324*, ed. W.N. Thompson (Canterbury and York Society 12–13, 1913). |
| *Reg. Kirkby* | *The Register of John Kirkby, bishop of Carlisle, 1332–1352, and the register of John Ross, bishop of Carlisle, 1325–32*, ed. R.L. Storey (Canterbury and York Society 79, 81, 1993–5). |
| *Reg. Langham* | *Registrum Simonis Langham, Cantuariensis Archiepiscopi*, ed. A.C. Wood (Canterbury and York Society 53, 1956). |

| | |
|---|---|
| *Reg. Welton* | *The Register of Gilbert Welton, bishop of Carlisle, 1353–1362,* ed. R.L. Storey (Canterbury and York Society 88, 1999). |
| *Rot. Parl.* | *Rotuli Parliamentorum* (Record Commission, 1783–1832). |
| *Rot. Scot.* | *Rotuli Scotiae,* ed. D. Macpherson, J. Caley, W. Illingworth and T.H. Horne (Record Commission, 1814–19). |
| Summerson | H. Summerson, *Medieval Carlisle* (CWAAS extra series 25, 1993). |
| *Test. Karl.* | *Testamenta Karliolensia,* ed. R.S. Ferguson (CWAAS extra series 9, 1893). |
| *VCH* | *Victoria County History.* |
| Wilkins, *Concilia* | D. Wilkins ed., *Concilia Magnae Britanniae et Hiberniae, A.D. 446–1718* (1737). |

# OTHER ABBREVIATIONS

| | |
|---|---|
| BCnL | bachelor of canon law |
| bp | bishop |
| BTh. | bachelor of theology |
| card. | cardinal |
| coll. | collated, collation |
| dau. | daughter (of) |
| DCnL | doctor of canon law |
| DDec. | doctor of decrees |
| dioc. | diocese |
| DTh. | doctor of theology |
| Fr. | brother |
| kt. | knight |
| M. | Master |
| n. | note |
| n.d. | no date, undated |
| OCarm. | Carmelite |
| OFM | Franciscan |
| OP | Dominican |
| ord. | ordination(s) |
| OSA | Austin friar |
| tit. | title(s) [to major orders] |

# THE REGISTER OF THOMAS APPLEBY

[Fo.1; p.141] REGISTRUM VENERABILIS IN CHRISTO PATRIS ET DOMINI DOMINI THOME DE APPILBY DEI GRACIA KARL'N EPISCOPI

**1** Commission to the prior of Carlisle,[1] and Masters John de Appelby, rector of Kirkoswald,[2] and Adam de Caldbek',[3] to act as the bishop's vicars-general whenever he is absent from the diocese, with powers to correct and punish subjects, admit and institute presentees to benefices, compel those contumacious and disobedient by ecclesiastical censures, appoint and replace deans and other ministers, proceed in causes in the bishop's jurisdiction and all other business, excepting collations to benefices in the bishop's gift.[4] York, 13 August 1363.

**2** (i) Form of letter inviting a lord and friend (*precarissime domine et amice*) to attend the bishop's enthronement in Carlisle cathedral on Sunday, 26 November, together with prelates, lords and friends. (ii) The like (in French) to magnates and (iii) knights. Gateshead (*Gatesheved*) by Newcastle upon Tyne, 12 October 1363.

**3** (i) Commission of John [Thoresby], archbishop of York, to Brother Thomas, bishop of Carlisle, for an exchange of benefices between John de Marrays, [vicar] of Morland, and William de Laysingby, rector of Welbury (*Welbery*; dioc. York), sending the report of an enquiry by the archdeacon of Cleveland's official. Cawood, 29 November 1363. (ii) Institution of William, priest, to Morland; presented by the abbot and convent of St. Mary's, York. (iii) Mandate for his induction to the archdeacon of Carlisle. (iv) Institution of John Marrays to Welbury; presented by the prior and convent of Guisborough (*Gisburn*). [Fo.1v; p.142] (v) Certificate to the archbishop, returning the inquest. Rose, 13 December 1363.

**4** Note[5] that Thomas de Appelby was consecrated as bishop of Carlisle by Pope Urban V at Avignon. 18 June 1363.

**5** Licence, at the request of Thomas de Lucy, lord of Cockermouth (*Cokirmouth*), to Richard de Askby, rector of Uldale (*Ulnedale*), to be absent for one year while in that lord's service. Rose, 26 January 1364.

---

[1] John de Horncastle (see *Reg. Welton*, ix–x).
[2] The bishop's brother; see *BRUO*, I.41.
[3] Official of Carlisle, 1355–62 (*Reg. Welton*, 17, no.89; 88, no.467; 94, nos.509–10).
[4] The king released the temporalities on 10 Aug. (*CPR 1361–4*, 391).
[5] In lower margin of fo.1, in another hand using brown ink; not the same hand as the similar note in *Reg. Welton*, 4, no.15; and cf. **92** below.

**6**   Note of licence to John del Marche, rector of Kirkandrews (*Kirkandres*), to be absent until 11 November. Rose, 26 January 1364.

**7**   The like for John de Grete, rector of Ormside (*Ormesheved*), to be absent while in the service of Lord de Clifford. 12 April 1364.

**8**   Writ *cerciorari* of Edward III for the bishop to report to Chancery names of the rectors of [Great] Musgrave, and who presented them, since the death of M. John de Stokton, late rector. Westminster, 12 February 1364.
  [Return] The bishop has found by scrutiny of his register (*registro nostro*) that after Stokton's death, William de Sandford was collated by John de Kirkby, former bishop; next was William de Ellerton, but without record of his collation or presentation; and finally William [*sic*] de Soulby by the king's presentation. All had canonical possession; no others were found in the said register.[6]

**9**   Note of licence for Walter de Loutburgh, rector of Dacre, to be absent in a suitable place for two years from 12 May 1364, and excused from personal appearance at synods and chapters. n.d.

**10**   Licence to Brother [blank], abbot of Whitby, excusing him from personal appearance at synods in Carlisle as long as he is abbot. Rose, 31 May 1364.
  Note that he has a demise under the bishop's seal in respect of the appropriation of Crosby Ravensworth (*Crossebyravenswart'*) church; this demise was sent back to Rose, so that he only has the above licence.

**11**   Will[7] of M. William de Routhbury, archdeacon of Carlisle, dated 10 May 1364. Commends soul to God, Blessed Mary and all saints. Burial in [Great] Salkeld churchyard, with funeral expenses at his executors' discretion. 16 pounds of wax for burning round his body until it is buried, with a penny to every pauper then. 40s. for the roof of Salkeld chancel and repair of its windows, which should satisfy his successor as archdeacon for repairs, otherwise he is to have none of it. For his soul, 68s. 8d. to the Austin friars of Penrith. Equal portions of 60s. to the 3 other mendicant orders. £8 to 2 honest priests celebrating for one year; if this cannot be arranged, his executors are to distribute the sum among poor husbandmen. £4 to be disbursed among poor husbandmen of Salkeld named in a schedule below. £6 13s. 4d. to be divided among the most needy poor of the country[8] at his executors' discretion. Hugh de Salkeld, son of Ranulph Forestar, 66s. 8d. in coin or goods of his chamber of equal value, at Hugh's choice; also two big brass pots, a small brass pot, a

---

[6] Omitting Welton's collation of Peter de Morland, 18 July 1361, after John de Soulby's death (*Reg. Welton*, 68, no.386), and the king's presentation of Richard de Upton, *sede vacante*, 10 January 1363 (*CPR 1361–4*, 278). Robert Korrok (*alias* Kerrol), was also provided, 1357 (*CCP*, I.448; *Reg. Welton*, 53, no.289 and n.; **87, 89** below).
  [7] Printed in *Test. Karl.*, 74–6.
  [8] MS *patria* (for *parochia?*).

cooking pot bound with iron, an oven, a pitcher, a wine-cooler, a long bran-
dreth, a gridiron, and the best wagon, as well as small tools for husbandry and
all wooden dishes except those which, by custom, should be left in place. Hugh
Lowe, £20 in silver. John de Ormesby, 100s. in money or goods. William Bloxham, 26s. 8d. William Bowman, 20s. Alice Blaket, 13s. 4d. John Bloxham, 20s.
John son of Alice Blaket, 6s. 8d. John de Scales, 3s. 4d. John de Alenburgh, 5s.
Sir Robert [de Marton], rector of Newbiggin,[9] 100s. Christine wife of Stephen
Smerles, 20s. Idonea de Sandhowe, 5s. William de Stapleton, 17 spoons, a silver
cup. Sir Peter de Morland, vicar of Kirkby Stephen,[10] the best bed with its
fittings and the best hanging, viz. 'Docers Bankers'; also a cloak, surcoat [and]
furred hood; also £10 to employ for [the testator's] soul as he has charged
[Peter]. If his goods suffice, [Fo.2; p.143] a principal vestment, a little breviary
and a little journal to Salkeld church. Thomas de Wederhale, servant of
H[ugh] de Salkeld, 6s. 8d. Residue to executors to use for good works for his
soul as they would answer God on the day of judgment; appointing P[eter] de
Morland, William de Stapelton, H[ugh] Lowe and H[ugh] de Salkeld. Dated
under the official seal of the archdeaconry at Salkeld, as above. [Schedule]
Richard Batyson, 2 marks. John Batyson, 13s. 4d. Ellen del Bate, 6s. 8d.
Emmotte Milner and Denise, 10s. equally divided. Adam [or Ada] Lambe, 3s.
4d. Mariot Fart', 3s. 4d. Beatrice Baty 'doghtre', 3s. 4d. Hilda, 3s. 4d. Emma de
Irland, 3s. 4d. Idonea de Sandhowse, 3s. 4d. Emmotte Halt', 20d. Alexander
Blaket, 20d.

Sentence that the will was proved before the bishop, with grant of administration to the executors named, in the chapel of Rose manor, 18 May 1364.

**12** (i) Institution of Robert Bix, chaplain, to Thursby (*Thoresby*) church,
vacant by the death of Robert Boyvill; presented by Thomas de Ogle.[11] (ii)
Archdeacon to induct. Rose, 14 March 1364.

**13** (i) Collation of M. John de Appelby, official of Carlisle, to the archdeaconry of Carlisle, now vacant. (ii) Mandate for his installation to the prior
and dean of Carlisle. Rose, 18 March 1364.

**14** (i) Institution of William Beauchamp, rector of a mediety of Aikton (*Ayketon*)
church, to Kirkoswald church, vacant by the resignation of M. John de Appelby;
presented by Ranulph de Dacre, lord of Gilsland (*Gillesland*). (ii) Archdeacon to
induct. Rose, 22 June 1364.

**15** Note of licence to William de Pullowe, rector of Melmerby (*Melmorby*), to
be absent for five years, farming revenues etc. Rose, 19 June 1364.

---

[9] See *Reg. Welton*, 32, no.176; **50, 155, 442–3, 447–51, 475, 477, 490** below.
[10] Peter had been presented to Warkworth, 9 Aug. 1362, and John de Danby instituted
to Kirkby Stephen (*Reg. Welton*, 91, nos.490, 492).
[11] The king had already presented Thomas Hervy, chaplain, to this church in 1362,
and Richard Haukedon, chaplain, in 1364 (*CPR 1361–4*, 385, 473). See also **43–4**.

**16** (i) Institution of William Chaumbrelayn, chaplain, to a mediety of Aikton, vacant by the resignation of William Beauchamp; presented by Ranulph de Dacre, lord of Gilsland. (ii) Archdeacon to induct. Rose, 24 July 1364.

**17** Note of licence, at the request of Christopher de Moriceby,[12] to Thomas de Anand, rector of Asby, to be absent for two years. London, 29 September 1364.

**18** Note of similar licence to John de Grandon, rector of Scaleby. 15 August 1364.

**19** (i) Institution of William de Hayton, chaplain, to Dearham (*Derham*) vicarage, vacant by the resignation of John de Derham; presented by the prior and convent of Guisborough. (ii) Archdeacon to induct. Rose, 27 July 1365.

**20** (i) Collation of Nicholas de Stapelton, clerk (dioc. Carlisle), to Ousby (*Ulnesby*) church, now vacant. (ii) Archdeacon to induct. Rose, 27 July 1365.

**21** Note that William de Kirkby, chaplain, had a [letter of] collation to Gilcrux (*Gilcroux*) church under the bishop's seal. 21 October 1364.

**22** [Fo.2v; p.144] Memorandum that the prioress and convent of Rosedale (dioc. York) have a demise under the bishop's seal concerning their appropriation of Torpenhow church. This demise was the same word for word as another demise in the register of Gilbert', late bishop.[13] Rose, 1 August 1365.

**23** Oath of obedience by Brother Robert de Rawbankes, abbot of Holm Cultram (Cistercian order), to the bishop, his successors, the church of Carlisle and the Holy See, as ordered by the holy fathers in accordance with the rule of St. Benedict. n.d.

**24** Note of licence for an oratory with a chaplain at Blindcrake (*Blencrayk*), for two years, at the request of William de Tofte. 29 September 1364.[14]

**25** MANDATUM PRO PROCESSIONE FACIENDA PRO SERENITATE AERIS. Mandate to the prior and official of Carlisle to order, in haste, all clergy of cathedral and collegiate and non-collegiate churches in the diocese to hold processions with the seven penitential psalms, singing of the litany and suitable prayers for good weather, as is particularly needed at harvest-time. Priests celebrating singly are to include such prayers in their masses. Faithful [people] should also pray that God will command the rain-clouds to stop their inundant downpour; with an indulgence of 40 days for those taking part. Rose, 26 August 1365.

---

[12] Sheriff of Cumberland, 1360–5 (*CFR*, VII.121, 236, 268, 315).
[13] i.e. *Reg. Welton*, 23, no.122, dated 4 May 1356.
[14] Presumably in London, like **17**. Followed by a space 3 cm deep. See also **85**.

**26**   Letters patent. In a suit before the bishop, John Wethirhird of Threlkeld sought annulment of his contracted *de facto* marriage to Magota de Grysedall because they were related in the third and fourth degrees, as was well known. His libel (quoted) was delivered to Magota and a date set, when the parties and their witnesses were sworn and examined. At the term appointed for sentence, the bishop, with learned counsel, declared that John had proved his case [Fo.3; p.145] and the marriage was therefore null and void. Rose, 3 October 1365.

**27**   Mandate to the parish chaplains of St. Mary's and St. Cuthbert's, Carlisle. In the present autumn, unknown miscreants by their threats and deeds frightened [people] of the township of Rickerby (*de territorio et campo de Ricardby*) from separating tithes of peas and other corn due to the bishop as rector, incurring excommunication. They and their supporters are to be denounced on Sundays and feast-days, with enquiries for their names; to be certified by 18 October. Rose, 3 October 1365.
  Note of similar letters to the vicars of Stanwix (*Staynwyges*) and Crosby on Eden.

**28**   Note of probate of the will [not given] of Thomas Trewlove of Greystoke (*Craystok*), with grant of administration to John, his son, and John del Howe. Rose, 16 October 1365.

**29**   Will[15] of Thomas de Sourby, rector of Beaumont, dated 8 December 1365. Commends soul to God, Blessed Mary and all saints. Burial where God disposes. William de Bolton, his father, 10 marks. William, his kinsman, clerk, 10 marks and his books. Alice, William's sister, 10 marks. Three chaplains celebrating for his soul for one year, 21 marks. The light of Blessed Mary, Beaumont, 20s. Each executor, 20s. The friars preachers, Carlisle, 6s. 8d. The friars minor, 3s. 4d. Christine Morlay, 2 cows and 2 skeps of barley. William Sprote, 20s. Half the residue to be disbursed for his soul, and half to his kinsmen, William and Alice. Executors: William [del Hall], rector of Bowness, Robert de Kirkby, rector of a mediety of Aikton, and John de Midelton, chaplain. Sealed before [unnamed] witnesses under his seal of office.[16]
  Sentence of probate, with this change: after making the will, the testator bequeathed to his executors the portion assigned to the poor, so that they would administer all his goods. Rose (chapel), 24 December 1365.

**30**   Probate[17] of the nuncupative will of Richard de Hoton, rector of Greystoke.[18] He commended his soul to God, Blessed Mary and all saints. Burial in Greystoke churchyard, to the north of the church, with best beast for

---

[15]   Printed in *Test. Karl.*, 76–7.
[16]   As dean of Carlisle (?); see *Reg. Welton*, 87, no.478.
[17]   Printed in *Test. Karl.*, 77–8.
[18]   Instituted as Richard de Hoton Roef, clerk, 1357, later ordained (*Reg. Welton*, 36, no.196; 116–17, nos.614–16, 618); the following bequests to his children suggest he was a widower. He held in chief of the king, who ordered livery to his son and heir, John, in 1367 (*CCR 1364–8*, 359).

mortuary; his body is to be buried honourably with his ecclesiastical goods. He bequeathed to the choir of the church a surplice with a tapet and hanging of linen cloth, on condition that his successor was satisfied with these cloths for the repair of the church and buildings of the rectory and all other claims which his successor might make against him and his executors; if he is not satisfied, the cloths are given to his daus. Margaret and Isabel. All the goods of his chamber are given [Fo.3v; p.146] to Margaret and Isabel. His son John to have his share of all his beasts, on condition that he erects and repairs all his buildings at Hutton Roof and there, from his goods, supports his brother Richard, Margaret and Isabel; if he is unwilling to do this, they are to have all these beasts. Richard, Margaret and Isabel are to have the residue, after payment of above debts. Executors: Edmund de Hoton, John de Bencombe and Gilbert Bowet, chaplain.

 Administration granted to John and Gilbert; reserved for Edmund. Rose (chapel), 22 January 1366.

**31** Presentation to Thomas [Hatfield], bishop of Durham, or his vicar-general, of [the bishop of Carlisle's] 'dear clerk', Thomas Colerdowe, priest,[19] to Warkworth (*Werkworth*) vicarage (dioc. Durham), now vacant. Rose, 26 February 1366.

**32** (i) Institution (in the person of M. William de Raggenhill, rector of Caldbeck, his proctor) of John de Hermthorp, priest, to Greystoke church, vacant by the death of Richard de Hoton; presented by the king, having custody of the lands etc. of William, late baron of Greystoke.[20] (ii) Archdeacon to induct. Rose, 19 February 1366.

**33** (i) Institution of John de Merton, priest, to Brougham (*Burgham*) church, vacant by the resignation of Thomas de Derby; presented by Sir Roger de Clifford.[21] (ii) Archdeacon to induct. Rose, 26 February 1366.

**34** Memorandum of licence to Brother Richard, friar and sacrist of the house of friars at Penrith, to celebrate sacraments and other divine services to parishioners of Newton Reigny (*Neuton*) for four years from Christmas 1365. n.d.

**35** Memorandum of licence for one year to Brother Thomas de Thornton of the Austin friars, Penrith,[22] as confessor and penitentiary to the bishop's parishioners, even in reserved cases excepting violations of liberties of the bishop and his church, opposition of his jurisdiction, rape of nuns; perjury in assizes, indictments, matrimonial causes, disinheritance, homicide and mutilation; usury; and breaches of the bishop's parks at Rose and Bewley (*Beaulieu*).[23] Rose, 12 February 1366.

[19] Colerdone in margin. Previously instituted as 'Thomas de Cullerdoune, priest', to vicarage of Stanwix, 1359 (*Reg. Welton*, 50, no.271); see also **107**.
[20] See *CPR 1364–7*, 198, dated 24 Jan. 1366.
[21] The king presented John de Stayneburn, chaplain, 6 Feb. 1366, as having custody of lands of Isabel de Clifford, deceased (*CPR 1364–7*, 215). See also **42**.
[22] *BRUC*, 585.
[23] Except for the last category, as in *Reg. Welton*, 5–6, no.20*.

**36**  Citation of the prior and chapter of Carlisle to attend the bishop's visitation in their chapter house on Monday after Palm Sunday (30 March);[24] absentees are to be recalled, prejudicial acts forbidden, and a certificate listing present and absent canons delivered on that day. Rose, 5 March 1366.

**37**  [Fo.4; p.147] Commission to Adam [de Crosseby], rector of Bolton,[25] and the dean of Allerdale to hear accounts of their administration by executors of subjects in the deanery; with powers to take canonical proceedings against those disobedient and issue letters of acquittance. Rose, 5 March 1366.

**38**  Note of licence to M. William de Aykheved, rector of Uldale, to be absent for two years and excused from personal appearance in synods and chapters. 10 March 1366.

**39**  Note of licence for one year to Hugh de Yarum, chaplain, as questor for the hospital of Saint-Antoine[-de-Viennois]. 2 February 1366.

**40**  Mandate to the official of Carlisle quoting the king's writ of summons to a parliament at Westminster on Monday 4 May (dated Westminster, 20 January 1366), citing the prior and archdeacons [*sic*] in person, a proctor for the chapter and two for the clergy; asking the bishop to be in London on the preceding Sunday and thus present for the opening.[26] The bishop is to be certified by 19 April. Rose, 20 March 1366.

**41**  (i) Institution (in the person of Sir John de Etton, his proctor) of Thomas de Etton, chaplain, to Uldale church, vacant by the death of M. William de Aykheved; presented by the king, having custody of the lands etc., of Thomas de Lucy, kt., deceased.[27] (ii) Archdeacon to induct. Rose, 4 April 1366.

**42**  (i) Institution of Thomas de Derby, deacon, to Brougham church, vacant by the resignation of John de Merton;[28] presented by Roger de Clifford, lord of Westmorland. (ii) Archdeacon to induct. 8 April 1366.

**43**  [Fo.4v; p.148] Writ [of justices of assize] *admittatis non obstante reclamacione* ordering the bishop to admit the king's presentee to Thursby church because he has recovered his presentation against the bishop, Thomas de Ogle and Robert Byx[29] by judgment of the court before John de Moubray and Roger de

---

[24]  Cf. **106** below.

[25]  Instituted 1362 (*Reg. Welton*, 80, no.438).

[26]  See *CCR 1364–8*, 210.

[27]  See *CPR 1364–7*, 228, dated 25 Mar. 1366; and see **38** for William.

[28]  Cf. **33**. The king ratified Thomas's title as rector, 11 November 1366 (*CPR 1364–7*, 331). He was a clerk at his first institution to Brougham in 1362 (*Reg. Welton*, 91, no.496).

[29]  Instituted 1364 (see **12**).

Fulthorp, justices of assize in Cumberland at Carlisle. Tested by J[ohn] de Moubray, Carlisle, 7 August 1366.

**44**   (i) Institution of Robert Paye, priest, to Thursby church, presented by the king, having custody of the lands etc. of Robert de Ogle, kt., deceased.[30] (ii) Archdeacon to induct. Carlisle, 15 August 1366.

**45**   (i) Institution of Walter de Ormesheved, priest, to Beaumont (*Beaumond*) church, vacant by the resignation of M. Adam de Caldebek;[31] presented by William Beauchamp, rector of Kirkoswald, Thomas de Cowgate, vicar of Torpenhow,[32] and Robert Paye, chaplain.[33] (ii) Archdeacon to induct. Carlisle, 15 August 1366.

**46**   LITTERA DOMINI EBOR' ARCHIEPISCOPI PRO DOMINO JOHANNE DE WARTHEWYK MILITE. Informal letter (addressed *Reverende frater et amice carissimo.*) Sir John came to Archbishop [Thoresby] complaining that William de Tanfeld, prior of the cell of Wetheral (*Wedirhale*),[34] had failed to provide two chaplains to celebrate in Wetheral and Warwick churches, appropriated to the priory, and minister as parish chaplains, as his predecessors had done from time immemorial;[35] although often required, he had refused to do this without good cause. Sir John had also sought remedy from the bishop and his ministers, without effect. Believing that the bishop is disposed to do justice to complainants, [the archbishop] urges him to call the parties before him and settle the business impartially; otherwise he will intervene for this purpose. Bishop Burton (*Burton juxta Beverl'*), 1 August.
    Note that the bishop received this letter at Rose, 18 August 1366.

**47**   Note of licence to William de Corbrig', rector of Kirkby Thore, to be absent for three years in a suitable place in England; excused from synods and chapters. He has letters under the bishop's seal with the clause *Dum tamen etc.*[36] 11 November 1366.

**48**   Mandate of John de Cabrespino, canon of Narbonne, papal nuncio in England and Ireland. Benefices listed in a schedule owe payments to the papal chamber. The bishop is therefore ordered, by apostolic authority . . .[37]

---

[30]   See *CPR 1364–7*, 126, dated 24 May 1365.
[31]   Cf. **29** for previous known rector.
[32]   Peter de Morland, the previous known vicar, was collated to Musgrave in 1361 (*Reg. Welton*, nos.380, 386).
[33]   Probably feoffees of the patrons (see Nicolson & Burn, II.224–5).
[34]   See *Reg. Welton*, 8, no.35.
[35]   This was one of various misdeeds by the prior alleged in a commission of enquiry dated 5 Sept. 1366; Sir John was one of the commissioners (*CPR 1364–7*, 359–60).
[36]   i.e. to study (see *BRUO*, I.486; *Reg. Welton*, xvii, 94, no.508).
[37]   This incomplete entry occupies the last four lines of fo.4v (p.148), which is the last folio of the register's first quire. A mandate given fully in **88** could be an accidental repetition, but it is possible these are two examples of a common form.

**49** [Fo.5; p.149] (i) Collation of M. Richard de Kilvyngton, rector of Gateshead (*Gatesheved*), Durham diocese,[38] to the custody of the hospital of St. Edmund the King, Gateshead; quoting commission to the bishop from Thomas [Hatfield], bishop of Durham (dated Old Ford (*Oldforth*), 2 November 1366), to receive M. John de Appelby's resignation of the hospital, institute Richard, order his induction, and certify. (ii) Robert de Scolaclef', chaplain, to induct. Rose, 21 November 1366.

**50** Will[39] of William de Brampton, rector of Dufton, dated Sunday, 1 March 1366. Commends soul to God, Blessed Mary and all saints. Burial in St. Cuthbert's church, Dufton. Five pounds of wax for candles round his corpse on the day of burial; 5s. for an oblation then, and 20s. for the poor. Walter de Musgrave, a *grysell* beast of burden at Burthwaite (*Birthuayt*) and 20 sheep; his wife Alice, [the furniture of William's] chamber; his son William, a cow with calf. Robert de Wolselay, a beast at Burthwaite. Robert [de Marton], rector of Newbiggin, a beast there. Each godson, 12d. Each servant beside his wage, 2s. Mariota Crokebane, a cow with calf, and her dau. Maud, a cow with calf. Thomas Diker, a beast with calf. Andrew brother of Adam de Dufton, 4s. The friars of Appleby, 6s. 8d. Repair of St. Lawrence's bridge, Appleby, 3s. 4d. The high altar of Marton church, a beast of 2 years. St. Mary's light in Dufton church, 6s. 8d. St. Cuthbert's light there, 6s. 8d. Works at St. Mary's, Carlisle, 3s. 4d. Needy parishioners, 20s. William Dobson, a beast of 2 years. John Dobson, the same. John son of Thomas de Slegill, a beast of 3 years, and the same to his son William. The executors are to employ the residue for priests celebrating for his soul. Executors: Robert de Wolselay, rector of Marton, Robert, rector of Newbiggin, and Thomas de Slegill. Under his seal.

Grant of probate, Rose, 6 November 1366.

**51** [Fo.5v; p.150] CLAUSULA BULLE PAPALIS CONCERNENS REGNUM ANGLIE.[40] Pope Urban V has been informed that numerous clerks in England hold many benefices contrary to the canons, with scandalous results. All such pluralists, clerks and regulars who hold more than two priories, dignities, canonries and other benefices and ecclesiastical offices, and also expectations by papal authority, are to make written statements about them to the ordinaries of their places of residence; they may choose which two benefices (etc.) they wish to retain. This is to be done within six months, under penalty of deprivation; collation to benefices (etc.) thus vacated being reserved to the pope. Bishops are to send lists of the above priories (etc.) to their metropolitan, within another month; while metropolitans, after recording these lists in their

---

[38] See *BRUO*, II.1051.

[39] Printed in *Test. Karl.*, 78–9.

[40] The full text of this bull (*Consueta*) is printed in *Registrum Simonis Langham Cantuariensis Archiepiscopi*, ed. A.C. Wood (CYS, 1956), 1–5; this clause in Appleby's register is its second half from 'Cum autem ad aures nostras ..' (p.5), with occasional slight departures from the Canterbury text. See also *CPL*, IV.25; *Associated Architectural Societies' Reports and Papers*, XXXIII (1915), pp.69–72.

registers, are to send them to the pope within four months, under pain of excommunication and suspension. Avignon, 3 May 1366.

**52** [Fo.6; p.151] (i) Institution (in the person of Henry de Mallerstang, his proctor) of William son of Robert de Threlkeld to Dufton church, vacant by the death of William de Brampton; presented by the king, having custody of the heir of William, Baron Graystok.[41] (ii) Note of letter [to archdeacon?] to induct William or his proctor. Rose, 25 November 1366.

**53** Letters patent. Pope Urban V had granted the bishop a faculty to ordain as priests [22] secular clerks under 25 years of age, provided they were aged 22 or more, and there was no other obstacle.[42] Dispensation to John de Askby (dioc. Carlisle), as second in this number, after examination gave proof of his good life and his age as 22. Rose, 1 August 1366.

**54** Certificate to John [Thoresby] archbishop of York. The bishop has learnt from many [sources] that Pope Urban V has ordered, under heavy pains, that all clerks and ecclesiastical persons [summarising **51**]. He therefore reports that M. John de Appelby, archdeacon of Carlisle, and M. Thomas de Salkeld, rector of Clifton, have shown him written particulars of their benefices which have been recorded in this register (*nobis beneficia sua administraciones sive officia in scriptis exhibuerunt que in registro nostro ordinato*); these are sent to the archbishop under the bishop's seal. Rose, 6 November 1366.

**55** Letters patent appointing Richard de Appelby, chaplain, and William de Stirkland, clerk,[43] as his proctors to deliver the [following] written statements to the archbishop. Rose, 9 November 1366.

**56** [Fo.6v; p.152] Statement (*exhibita*) that M. John de Appelby, archdeacon, gave a written [list] of his benefices to the bishop on [blank] 1366, as follows:[44] the archdeaconry, with Great Salkeld (*Salkeld Regis*) church annexed, which is assessed at £12 by the old taxation and 40s. by the new, with *synodalia* and uncertain profits (*incerti proventus*) assessed at £10 (old) and 40s. (new);[45] also the archdeacon's portion in Dalston church, assessed at £15 which [M. John] never received, nor other archdeacons for 40 years;

---

[41] See *CPR 1364–7*, 330, dated 3 Nov. 1366, but revoked, 3 Feb. 1367 (ibid., 374); and see **155**. William son of Robert was dispensed for illegitimacy, 1342 (*Reg. Kirkby*, I.133, nos.658–9); and see his(?) will, **81**.

[42] In response to the bishop's petition reporting a lack of priests in the diocese as a result of the plague (*CPP*, I.437, which supplies the number of clerks - here left blank; and see *Reg. Welton*, xxiii).

[43] Bishop of Carlisle, 1400–19 (*BRUO*, III.1806).

[44] Expressed in the first person, after *In dei nomine amen*.

[45] For the two assessments, see *Reg. Kirkby*, I.83 (no.429); for the archdeacon's meagre endowments, see *Reg. Halton*, II.xxx–i, and II.188 for his 'uncertain profits' of 20s. in 1319; see also *Reg. Welton*, 58 (no.316*).

also a canonry and prebend in Norton collegiate church (dioc. Durham), assessed at 9 marks and worth £8 p.a.; also custody of the hospital of St. Edmund the King, Gateshead (dioc. Durham), not taxed and worth 40s. p.a. He has chosen to retain the archdeaconry and prebend at Norton, and to leave the hospital.[46]

**57** Similar statement to the bishop by M. Thomas de Salkeld, rector of Clifton. Pope Urban V had collated him to the vicarage of Crosthwaite (assessed at £20 by the old tax and £4 by the new) despite his having Clifton church,[47] and later to a benefice worth 25 marks in the gift of the bishop of Carlisle, despite his having Clifton and Crosthwaite.[48] 7 September 1366.

**58** Memorandum that William de Stirkland, clerk, delivered these statements under the bishop's seal to the archbishop, together with a certificate on the other side of this folio [i.e. **62**] at Cawood, 15 November 1366.

**59** Grant to John de Eskheved, clerk (dioc. Carlisle) with first tonsure, of letters dimissory to all orders. Rose, 6 November 1366.

**60** Mandate to the parish chaplain of the bishop's church of Penrith (*Penreht*). Many farmers of mills in Penrith have not paid tithes of multure to the bishop or his church there, to the peril of their souls (etc.). They are to be ordered to pay these tithes within 15 days of the publication of this monition, under pain of excommunication. n.d.

**61** [Fo.7; p.153] Commission to the dean of Cumberland, forwarding letters of William [Bragose], cardinal-priest of St. Laurence in Lucina, papal penitentiary, on behalf of William de Kirkbryd, clerk (dioc. Carlisle). He is to enquire by reliable clerks and laymen, sworn and secretly and singly examined, whether William is indeed the son of unmarried parents, not an imitator of his father's incontinence, of good conversation, and suitable to receive orders; certifying the bishop. Rose, 3 December 1366.

**62** Statement[49] by William de Kirkland, chaplain (dioc. Carlisle), proctor of John de Langholm, rector of Kirkland, who is well known to be staying far from

---

[46] Granted by the king, 1364 (*CPR 1364–7*, 61); for his resignation of the hospital, see **49** above.

[47] On 17 Jan. 1363, the vicarage was said to be vacant by the death of William de Esington (*CPP*, I.397; see also *Reg. Welton*, 58, no.318 and n.).

[48] On 17 Feb. 1363, when his petition to the pope alleged that he had received the vicarage in the vacancy of the see (*CPP*, I.402). The king, however, presented Thomas de Eskheved, chaplain, on 24 Jan. 1363, and on 10 Apr. 1363 ordered an enquiry into appeals by Thomas Salkeld and any others challenging his presentation of Eskheved, and their summons before the council (*CPR 1361–4*, 281, 362). Eskheved, a canon lawyer, was still vicar of Crosthwaite in 1374 and 1390 (*CPL*, IV.195, 377). See also **96**.

[49] Preceded by *In dei nomine amen* and expressed in first person.

the diocese; he wishes to obey a new constitution of Pope Urban V by showing Bishop Thomas that John holds the church of Kirkland (assessed by the new taxation at £8 and £40 by the old) with expectation of a canonry and prebend in the collegiate church of St. Wilfrid, Ripon (dioc. York) by the provision of Pope Urban in his first year [1362–3]. He took an oath on the Gospels in the presence of a notary on 11 November 1366, when he first received notice of the promulgation of this new constitution.

**63**    Certificate to the archbishop of York forwarding this statement, which was delivered to the bishop on 15 November[50] [repeating its details]. Rose, 8 December 1366.

**64**    Will[51] of Robert Ussher of Carlisle[52] dated 13 August 1366 (being sane of mind and memory). Commends soul to God, Blessed Mary and all saints. Burial in churchyard of St. Mary's, Carlisle, with best beast for mortuary; 3s. for wax burning on day of burial, and 10s. for bread for the poor. Each priest singing *Placebo* and *Dirige* for his soul, 12d. The parish priest, 3s. 4d. The parish clerk, 6d. Priests celebrating and praying for his soul and the souls of all his parents and forebears, 20 marks. John de [Sancto] Neoto, once subprior of Carlisle,[53] 13s. 4d. A pittance for the prior and convent, 20s. Margaret his wife and his two sons, all his buildings and tenements in Carlisle city, and also an annual rent from buildings which Christine, wife of John de Esshlyngton holds in Botcherby Street within the gate;[54] [Fo.7v; p.154] this tenement and rent shall wholly revert to his wife and two sons, and their children, in equal portions, viz. as much for the junior as the senior. If they leave or die without children, he leaves these tenements and rent to the prior and convent of St. Mary's, Carlisle, so that they pray and celebrate for his soul and the souls of all his parents, forebears and all the faithful departed. The fabric of St. Mary's, Carlisle, 20s. William de Corbryg, the clerk writing [this] will, 6s. 8d. Margaret and his children are to distribute the residue of his goods for his soul wherever it seems best to them. Executors: John de Malton, chaplain, and Margaret. Witnesses: Thomas de Stirkland and William de Corbryg.

Grant of probate, and of administration to Margaret; John de Midelton, clerk [*sic*], having refused to act. Carlisle cathedral, 4 December 1366.

**65**    Licence to collectors for the repair of Derwent bridge beside Cockermouth, granting an indulgence for 40 days to contributors; valid for one year. Rose, 14 December 1366.

**66**    Dispensation to William de Kirkbryde, clerk, in accordance with letters (dated Avignon, 19 November 1363) of William, cardinal-priest of St. Laurence

---

[50]  MS December.
[51]  Printed in *Test. Karl.*, 80–1.
[52]  In margin; *Hissher* in text.
[53]  Ordained priest, 1333 (*Reg. Kirkby*, I.18). Cf. **106**.
[54]  Now English Street.

in Lucina [quoted; i.e. **61**, adding that he may be dispensed to hold a benefice, provided that he resides, with penance for assuming the clerical order]. By an enquiry, the bishop has received testimony of his good character. Rose, 13 December 1366.

**67** Note of a licence (for one year) to William de Mulcastre to have a suitable chaplain celebrating in a decent oratory in his manor of Hayton. 1 January 1367.

**68** [Fo.8; p.155][55] Note of licence to Robert Paye, rector of Thursby, to be absent in a suitable place, for one year. 17 August 1366.

**69** Probate[56] of the nuncupative will of Christine, wife of William son of Gilbert de Briswode of Dalston, in these words. Commended her soul to God, Blessed Mary and all saints. Burial in Dalston churchyard, with her best beast for mortuary. The vicar [of Dalston], 6s. 8d. Her sister Agnes, a cow, half a skep of malt and half a skep of flour; also a short-sleeved gown. Residue to her husband William, to make disposal for her soul; appointing him executor. Administration granted to him. Rose (chapel), 21 January 1367.

**70** LITTERA PRIVATA DOMINO REGI SCOCIE DIRECTA (in French).[57] The bishop doubts if King [David II] is fully aware that the recent riot in the West March was on a greater scale than there had been for a long time. It was contrary to the truce between the kings of England and Scotland that breaches should lead to acts of war. The bishop believes that both kings will be displeased to learn about it. He asks [David] to take measures by good counsel to stop such disturbances, while he will urge restraint by the people of his country, so that there is peace in the march, in accordance with the truce. n.d.[58]

**71** Note of letter to King [Edward] about John del Halgh of Stapleton, senior, Christine wife of Adam Dykson of Lanercost, Thomas Milner, Isabel Milner *mayden* of Arthuret, Bertinus Walssh of Aikton and Thomas Yveson of Gilsland, who have been excommunicate for 40 days or more. 22 January 1367.

**72** Letters patent of Edward III appointing Bishop Thomas, Roger de Clifford, Anthony de Lucy and Ranulph de Dacre, clerk, wardens of the West March towards Scotland. [Fo.8v; p.156] Westminster, 27 May 1366.[59]

---

[55] On this folio the text has been written round a narrow hole in the centre of the 3rd to the 9th lines (30 cm deep, 5 cm at its widest).

[56] Printed in *Test. Karl.*, 81. Under marginal title is *R[eddidit] comp[otum]*.

[57] Partly printed in Hist. Man. Comm., *Ninth Report* (1883–4), I.192.

[58] The latest treaty was for a truce from 20 May 1365 to 2 Feb. 1369 (*Rot. Scot.*, I.894–5). The letter does not refer to the bishop being a warden, although it was probably written during his tenure of the office (see **72**).

[59] Printed in *Rot. Scot.*, I.903, where the commission is dated 18 May. Its terms are almost identical with those in the commission of 1359 (printed ibid., I.839, and sum-

**73**  Letters patent (in French)[60] of Bishop Thomas as warden of the West
March of England. Safe conduct for all men, women and children of Scotland,
with their horses and harness, to come to the next fair in Carlisle,[61] stay and
return freely, provided they do nothing against *la defense*; under the bishop's
seal and valid until 20 August. Rose, 8 August 1366.

**74**  Mandate to the parish chaplains of St. Mary's and St. Cuthbert's, Carlisle.
John de Galwida, perpetual chaplain of the chantry founded by John de
Capella, late burgess of Carlisle, in the chapel of St. Katherine in St. Mary's
[cathedral] church,[62] has complained that unknown evildoers have misappro-
priated many of the rents, possessions, buildings and burgages granted to the
chantry and its chaplains by its founder for celebration in perpetuity for his
soul and the souls of all faithful departed. [The chaplains] are to publicly warn
occupiers of the chantry's property to make restitution within 10 days, under
pain of excommunication; certifying the bishop in sealed letters any names
found by enquiry. Rose, 5 December 1366.

**75**  Note of probate before the bishop of the will [not given] of John
Pynknegh of Dalston and grant of administration to his wife Joan, named
executrix, and Thomas son of Thomas Hirde of Cumdivock (*Comdovok*).[63] 8
February 1367.

**76**  [Fo.9; p.157] Sentence. Agnes widow[64] of William Webster of Bromfield
related to the bishop that her marriage to John Bowman had been contracted
and solemnised in church and they had lived as man and wife for at least 3
years, but the marriage was never consummated as he was impotent; she therefore sought divorce. John swore on the Gospels before the bishop that this was
true. They were cited before the bishop, when witnesses and other evidence
were examined. The bishop enjoined a penance, and prayers and good works
so that God would allow this consummation. They returned to the bishop at
another term, when both said under oath, *consona voce*, that they could not consummate the marriage. The bishop then set a day when, with the sevenfold
hand of kinsmen and neighbours, they could swear to the truth. They came to
the chapel of Rose manor on 26 January and confirmed on oath that John
could not consummate with Agnes or any other woman. The bishop, with

marised in *Reg. Welton*, 75, no.416). It is repeated in **105**. The next commission for the
West March, dated 26 Oct. 1366, appointed only Clifford and Lucy as wardens. Next
followed a commission of 11 Feb. 1367, appointing the bishop, Clifford, Lucy and
William Windsor, kt. (*Rot. Scot.*, I.906–7, 910). For Lord Dacre, see *Reg. Welton*, 77,
no.423.

[60]  Printed in Hist. Man. Comm., *Ninth Report*, I.192.

[61]  15 August and 15 days following.

[62]  Founded in 1342: see R.L. Storey, 'The Chantries of Cumberland and Westmorland. Part I', *CWAAS*, 2nd ser. (1960), 71–3.

[63]  See *Reg. Kirkby*, II.12.

[64]  MS *nuper uxor*. Her former husband might have been a victim of the plague in 1362.

learned counsel, therefore divorced the marriage in this writing. [26 January] 1367.

**77** Note of letter asking the king to arrest the following, who have been excommunicate for 40 days and more: Robert servant of the vicar of Morland, Joan his handmaid, Agnes de Roughthwayt of Wharton (*Overton*), William Jonyson, Anota dau. of Adam of Appleby St. Michael's parish, Agnes Loksmyth, John Leeson of Kirkbyth[ore?], Adam Waryner, Alice Bell of Ravenstonedale, Isabel handmaid of John Hunter of Salkeld, Philip Lyster, Emanna Bauld of Penrith, William Bouche, Joan de Aspatrik', Ellen Shenayne of [Newton] Arlosh (*Arlosk*), Christine handmaid of Gilbert Couper of Crosby, Michael de Alaynby, Joan Cole of Bromfield, Simon Mason of Carlisle, Thomas de Bothell, Joan del Bryg' of Aspatria, William del Grene and William Davyson of Holm Cultram. 13 February 1367.

**78** (i) Collation to Richard Damysell, priest, of Wigton vicarage, vacant by the resignation of William de Cressopp in an exchange for a mediety of [Kirk] bampton church. (ii) Institution of William, priest, to the mediety resigned by Richard in this exchange; presented by Brian de Stapelton, kt. Rose, 30 April 1367.[65]

**79** Note of licence to Walter de Welle, rector of Lowther, to be absent and farm his church for 3 years from Easter [18 April]. 1367.

**80** Will[66] of Robert Tilliol [kt.] dated 5 April 1367 (being sane of mind and memory). Commends soul to God, Blessed Mary and all saints. Burial in church of friars preachers, Carlisle. All debts are to be paid fully and quickly, and his exequies performed honourably as suits his status, as he has arranged. Residue [Fo.9v; p.158] to Felicity his wife and his children. Executors: Felicity and Sir William, vicar of Arthuret. Witnesses: William de Artureth and John de Bredlyngton. Under his seal, at Ireby.
  Note of probate and administration. [Blank] April 1367.

**81** Will[67] of William de Threlkeld, vicar of Lazonby,[68] dated 14 May 1367 (being sane of mind and memory). Commends soul to God, Blessed Mary and all saints. Burial in [Lazonby] churchyard. Six pounds of wax to burn round his body. The high altar, Lazonby, 10s. to repair its ornaments. 2s. for the porch (*porticum*) at the church door. For the poor on the day of his burial, 6 stricks of oatmeal and a steer. John de Threlkeld, son of John de Threlkeld, 4 oxen of which 2 are in his keeping. Sir John Randolf, a bay horse. John son of John del

---

[65] Without notice of inductions.

[66] Printed in *Test. Karl.*, 82.

[67] Printed in *Test. Karl.*, 83. *Reddiderunt compotum* in margin.

[68] Previous known vicar (from 1316) was Adam de Otteley, 1341 (*Reg. Halton*, II.127; *Reg. Kirkby*, I.131, no.645). For the testator, see **52**. He may have been instituted after his disappointment at Dufton: the bishop had the collation to the vicarage of Lazonby (Nicolson & Burn, II.417).

Vikers, 2 cows. Joan dau. of John Ca[proun?], 3 cows. Thomas her brother, 2 cows. Priests to celebrate for his souls and the souls of his benefactors, 260[69] sheep. Half the residue to John [the testator's] son , and half to Christine dau. of his sister and Joan her mother. Executors: Henry de Threlkeld, junior, John son of John de Threlkeld and John Harpyne.

Note of probate and grant of administration to John de Threlkeld of Appleby; reserving to the bishop power to admit another administrator. Rose, 14 June 1367.

**82**   Note of probate of the will of M. Henry de Rosse, rector of Cliburn;[70] with grant of administration of goods in the diocese to Thomas de Barowe and William Bakester of Cliburn; reserving power to grant same to other named executors. Rose, 18 June 1367.

**83**   Letters patent appointing M. John de Karlo', clerk, as the bishop's proctor to make his obligatory visit to the apostolic court. 12 January 1368.

**84**   Licence to John del Thuaytes, chaplain, to celebrate in an oratory in Ewan-rigg (*Yvenryg*') manor for Lady Margaret de Malton and her family, in a humble voice without prejudice to the parish church, for one year, provided that he refrains from the sacraments and does not celebrate on the feasts of Christmas, Epiphany, Easter (and its vigil), Ascension, Pentecost, Trinity, Corpus Christi, Nativity of St. John and All Saints, the Assumption, Birth and Purification of the Virgin, the first Sunday in Advent, the fourth in Lent, Palm Sunday, the first before St. Peter *ad vincula* and Ash Wednesday; they shall then attend the parish church, unless [Margaret] is detained by infirmity, in which case he is licensed to celebrate. 31 March 1368.

**85**   Note of similar licence, for 2 years, for William de Isale, chaplain, to cele-brate in an oratory at Blindcrake (*Blencrayk*') for Lady del Legh, William de Tofte and their family, and even administer sacraments to her. Same date.

**86**   Note of similar licence, for one year, for Stephen de Hegheved', chaplain, to celebrate in the chapel of Highhead [castle] for Sir William Lenglys and his fam-ily, excepting sacraments at Christmas, Epiphany, Easter, Ascension, Pentecost, Trinity, Corpus Christi, Nativity of St. John, Michaelmas, All Saints, Assumption, Nativity and Purification of the Virgin and Ash Wednesday. Same date.

**87**   Mandate of John de Cabrespino, DCnL, canon of Narbonne, papal nuncio in England. Pope Innocent VI, on 28 February 1357, provided Robert Kerrot to [Great] Musgrave church, vacant by the death of John de Stoctoun.[71] Richard Upton, now rector, has told him that the provision [Fo.10; p.159] had no effect and thus no tax was due to the papal chamber. The bishop is ordered to

---

[69]   MS *pro quibus teneor, xiii* with superscript *xx*.
[70]   *Alias* Heynes (see *Reg. Welton*, 47, no.254).
[71]   See *Reg. Welton*, 53, nos.289–90 and n.; also **8** above.

confirm whether Robert did obtain the church and report the names of rectors since John de Sotton's death, by letters patent to [the nuncio's] office in London by 29 September[72] London, 20 February 1364.

**88**  Mandate of John de Cabrespino, canon of Narbonne, nuncio in England and Ireland. Benefices listed in a schedule owe payments to the papal chamber. Order, by apostolic authority,[73] to sequestrate all their revenues and collect them until these debts are paid, sending receipts and an account to the chamber in London; provided that these benefices are not defrauded of divine services. Objectors and violators of sequestrations are to be compelled by ecclesiastical censures. Anyone occupying these benefices is to appear before [the nuncio] in his hospice in London on the first lawful day after Hilary [13 January] to answer for their contempt of the sequestration, under pain of excommunication. Religious named on the dorse of the schedule are to be ordered to pay procurations due to [the nuncio], whom the bishop is to certify by letters patent by the said day. London, 12 October 1363.

**89**  Another mandate of the same. His sequestration of Musgrave church for the tax due for the provision of Robert Keirot is now removed and all processes suspended.
    Under his little seal, London, 16 February 1364.

**90**  Letters patent of Arnold, archbishop of Auch (*Auxitan'*), papal chamberlain, certifying that Thomas, bishop of Carlisle, who is bound to visit the Curia every 3 years, has performed this duty for the last triennium by his proctor, John Maresshall, rector of Rothbury (*Routhbury*); he paid nothing to the chamber on this account. Avignon, 10 July 1365.

**91**  [Fo.10v; p.160] Letters patent of the same. Bishop Thomas is obliged to pay the chamber 250 gold florins of the chamber for common services, 52 florins for part of 4 services to the pope's household and officers, and 17s. 7d. of money of Avignon to the clerks of the chamber, which he paid this day by the hands of Sir Nicholas of the Alberti (*Albertorum Antiquorum*) and so is quit. Avignon, 19 June 1365.

**92**  Letters patent of Nicholas [de Bessia], cardinal-deacon of S. Maria in Via Lata (*Violata*). By Pope Urban's oral command, Bishop Thomas was consecrated as bishop by Peter, bishop *Rinensis*, celebrant, in the presence of William [?], bishop *Apponnarum*, Thomas [le Reve], bishop of Lismore, and many others, in the chapel of [the cardinal's] house. Avignon, 18 June 1363.

**93**  Letters patent of William [de Aigrefeuille], cardinal-priest of S. Maria in Trastevere (*Transtiberim*), chamberlain of the college of cardinals, acknowledging

---

[72] The bishop replied that Robert's provision was not effected (*Accounts*, ed. Lunt, 302; also 206). See also **89** below.
[73] Repeating to here the last 4 lines of fo.4v (**48**).

payment by Bishop Thomas of 250 florins due to the college for common services and 13 florins 3s. 10d. to their households, by the hands of Nicholas de
Albertis, kt. Avignon, 14 June 1365.

**94** Letters patent of the same acknowledging receipts of 250 florins and 13
florins 3s. 9d., by the hands of Sir Nicholas de Albertis and his fellows. Avignon,
19 June 1364.

**95** Letters patent of Archbishop Arnold of Auch acknowledging receipts [as
in **91**] of 250 florins, 52 florins and 15s. 3d., by the hands of Thomas of the society of the Alberti. Avignon, 19 June 1364.

**96** [Fo.11; p.161][74] Mandate of John de Cabrespino, DCnL, papal nuncio in
England and Ireland. He lately ordered the bishop to sequestrate Crosthwaite
church and vicarage for its tax on account of the provision of the church
(assessed as £30 13s. 4d.) to John Henry, whose right was transferred to William
de Selario by Pope Innocent VI on 12 January 1357, as is shown in the chamber's registers; also for the tax of £20 from the vicarage because of Innocent's
provision to William de Esyngdon on 30 June 1360.[75] Thomas de Eskeheved,[76]
now vicar, came to [the nuncio] claiming that Esyngdon's provision was never
effected, but John Henry had possession of the church by papal authority
although it has for a long time been appropriated to the abbot and monastery
of Fountains; the vicarage is worth £4 by the new assessment. The bishop is
ordered to enquire into the truth of these provisions and the valuations
(including the reason for a new assessment, if there has been one); replying to
[the nuncio] or his lieutenants by Michaelmas, when Thomas is to be cited to
appear. [The bishop] is to end the sequestration and other processes.[77] London,
27 February 1364.

**97** Certificate [said to quote this mandate]. The bishop has enquired of rectors, vicars and others informed of this matter, and learned that John Henry's
provision came to nothing.[78] n.d.

**98** BREVE REGIUM CONCERNENS NOVAM TAXAM.[79] Mandate of Edward
III. [William Melton], archbishop of York, by order of Edward II [in 1318–19],
with the assent of his suffragans, chapters and clergy of his province, ordained
a new assessment for benefices in the dioceses of Carlisle and Durham and
archdeaconries of Richmond and Cleveland paying tenths and subsidies

---

[74] A new quire, preceded by three stubs.
[75] See *Reg. Welton*, 35, no.195; 58, no.318, n.
[76] See **57** above.
[77] This last sentence is written after the date.
[78] *Accounts*, ed. Lunt, 182, 206, refer to the bishop's certificates about Crosthwaite.
[79] Printed in *Foedera*, III (2), 780–1; also *CCR 1364–8*, 151–2. Copies of the writ were
also sent to the archbishop of York and the bishop of Durham.

granted to the king by popes and provincial clergy; also for first fruits to the papal chamber. These have been paid for 40 years, to the satisfaction of kings and popes, without any contradiction. However, William de Dalton, clerk,[80] with no consideration for the harm and prejudice of the clergy, has obtained two definitive sentences in favour of the old, higher rate, despite sentences in the Curia which have hitherto judged in the latter's favour. [Fo.9v; p.162] The king is anxious to protect the clergy from the threat of a heavier burden of taxation, with much treasure being exported from the realm. He therefore orders the bishop to summon in haste the abbots, priors, archdeacons, deans, rectors, vicars and other beneficed clergy of the diocese to discuss the likely consequences of annulling the new assessment and what remedy there might be, and empower two or three suitable [proctors] to come before to the king and his council at Westminster on 27 January to report their advice and deliberations, so that the king with the advice of learned counsel can ordain for the quiet of his subjects against these subtle inventions to the prejudice of the new assessment and the consequent losses and trouble. [King's] Langley, 17 December 1365.

**99** Letters patent of the abbots, priors, rectors, vicars and other beneficed clergy of Carlisle diocese. Bishop Thomas presided at their meeting held by his order, in the chapter house of the cathedral and showed and explained the king's letters, in these words [said to be fully quoted]. They discussed the above-mentioned perils and trouble, and appointed William del Hall, rector of Bowness, John [de Bowland], rector of Arthuret,[81] and Sir Robert de Derhame of Carlisle diocese, as proctors to appear before the king and council to report their discussion and advice with the bishop on the contents of the king's letters. Sealed under his seal of office by the official of Carlisle, at the clergy's request, in the above chapter house, Monday etc. [*sic*].

**100** Letter of Edward III under the privy seal (in French). By his writ under the great seal, he has ordered the bishop to hold an assembly of his clergy because they all believe themselves seriously threatened as a result of the suit by William de Dalton in the court of Rome for the approval (*laprobacion'*) of the old assessment and annulment of the new [repeating the contents of **98**]. The bishop is to set aside all other business, and any excuses, as he would avoid the king's indignation, bearing in mind the ease and quiet his subjects have for long enjoyed through the observation of the new assessment [Fo.12; p.163] and the intolerable harm its annulment would cause, a matter close to the king's heart. [King's] Langley, 20 December [1365].

---

[80] Possibly the former wardrobe clerk (from 1336), retired after 1361, and died 1371 (*BRUO*, II.538–1). He had already been charged before the council for his harmful suits at the Curia, and had replied in writing. He appeared in Chancery on 2 Dec. 1365, when the chancellor (Archbishop Simon Langham) ordered the two chief justices to terminate the proceedings. 8 Jan. 1366 was set for his next appearance before the council (*CCR 1364–8*, 205).

[81] A king's clerk: see *Reg. Welton*, 72, no.400; 91, no.494, n.

**101**   Letter under the privy seal (in French). The king's son, [John of Gaunt] duke of Lancaster has complained that the walls of his manor of the Savoy are being harmed by drainage from the bishop's inn next to it on the River Thames; its defects are to be repaired in haste. Westminster, 3 May [1366?].

**102**   Similar writ ordering the bishop's personal attendance of Parliament on 1 May, execution of other matters in the writ of summons, and his presence on the previous day [repeating the contents of **40**]. Windsor castle, 25 February [1366].

**103**   Similar writ ordering the bishop to come before the king and council in London on 13 October to take part in its business. Westminster, 23 September [1366].

**104**   BREVE DE SECRETO SIGILLO. [French version of Chancery letter of 17 December 1365 (**98**), [Fo.12v; p.164] to which it refers, as to privy seal letters (**100**), adding a shorter version of the latter's final sentence.] *Donne souz nostre secre seal,* Windsor, 25 December [1365].

**105**   Commission of Edward III appointing wardens of the West March [a duplicate of **72**. Fo.13; p.165]. 27 May 1366.

**106**   Certificate of the prior and chapter of Carlisle, fully quoting his citation for their visitation on Palm Sunday [29 March; cf. **36**]; they are ready to obey and send the following list of their names. Carlisle chapter house, 29 March 1366.
    John de Horncastell, prior; John de Sancto Neotho, subprior; Thomas de Warthole, Thomas de Colby, Richard Bully, William de Dalstoun, Thomas de Penreth, Adam del Gille, John de Overton, Thomas Orfeor, William Colt, Robert del Park and Robert de Edenhale.[82] Thomas de Penreth is absent, *causa studiorum,* and therefore not summoned.

**107**   Mandate of the official of the court of York. Robert de Bix, vicar of Stanwix, has petitoned that he gained the vicarage canonically and held it peacefully for a long time.[83] Thomas Culverdone, vicar of Warkworth (dioc. Durham), had likewise gained and held that vicarage for a month or months or a long time (*per mensem et menses et tempora non modica*).[84] He was favoured by his kinsman, Bishop Thomas, who despite his admission of Robert to Stanwix, deprived him without lawful process [Fo.13v; p.166] and admitted and instituted Thomas as vicar, expelling Robert and disturbing his possession; he therefore appealed to the court of York. The bishop and Thomas are therefore

---

   [82]   The first two were ordained priests in 1333, Warthole and Colby in 1342, and Dalston in 1354; the last six were ordained acolytes in 1361, Orfeor as Goldesmyth and Colt as de Karlo' (*Reg. Kirkby,* I.98, 133; *Reg. Welton,* 117).
   [83]   His institution is not recorded.
   [84]   He was presented by Bishop Appleby on 26 Feb. 1366, after being vicar of Stanwix since 1359 (**31** and n.).

inhibited from any measures against Robert pending his appeal, and Thomas is cited to York cathedral on 30 April to answer the appellant; the bishop may also appear then, and is to certify by letters patent. York, 3 April 1367.

**108** Letters patent appointing the bishop's clerks, Richard de Appilby, chaplain, and William de Stirkland his proctors to visit the church of York. Rose, 9 November 1366.

**109** Letter of Edward III under the privy seal (in French). His brother [the king] of Scotland has certified by letter that his envoys will come to the king in London by Michaelmas to treat for a final peace.[85] Order to the bishop to be there on the following Saturday [3 October] to advise on this business with other prelates and magnates of the council. Westminster, 13 September [1366].

**110** Certificate of the dean of Carlisle. He lately received the bishop's letters, as follow [repeating **61**]. John de Midelton, Richard Bleys, Robert Tailior, chaplains, [Fo.14; p.167] Robert de Sancta Trinitate, Adam de Bowetby and Robert Craistok declared under oath that William was thus born, does not imitate his father, of good repute and lettered, but whether sufficiently is left to the bishop's discretion, and there is no canonical obstacle to his ordination. Under the dean's seal of office, Carlisle, 12 December 1366.

**111** Mandate to the bishop or his vicar-general of [the same] papal penitentiary on behalf of John de Sutton, scholar (dioc. Carlisle), who has sued for dispensation as the son of unmarried parents. The bishop is to enquire about his suitability, continence, associates and letters, and if satisfied dispense John to be ordained and hold a benefice, provided that he resides, otherwise the dispensation will be void. Avignon, 2 April 1366.

**112** Will[86] of Robert de Leversdale dated 12 July 1367 (being sane of mind and memory). Commends soul to God, Blessed Mary and all saints. Burial in churchyard of St. Mary's, Carlisle, with best beast for mortuary. Elizabeth his sister, his burgage in Castle Street and £20 sterling. His sons, £20. The prior and convent of Carlisle, £20. Hugh his servant, £10. Rowland Carrok' his servant, 40s. Joan Cove, 20s. The wife of John Tinkler of Penrith, 20s. Margaret Walker, 20s. The friars preachers of Carlisle, 40s. The friars minor, 20s. The friars of Penrith, 20s. The friars of Appleby, 20s. The friars minor of York, 20s. John de Camera, 20s. The parish church of St. Mary's, Carlisle, 6s. 8d. for forgotten tithes. The vicar of Penrith, 6s. 8d. for forgotten tithes. The church of St. Peter the Little, York, 6s. 8d. for forgotten tithes. The 2 sons of William del Dikes, 40s. in equal portions. Thomas de Raughton, 20s. Agnes de Aikton, 20s. The parish priest of St. Mary's, Carlisle, 6s. 8d. William de Aiketon, 6s. 8d. Robert de Aikton, 6s. 8d. The residue to Sir T[homas] de W[arthole], canon [of

---

[85] A safe conduct for a large Scottish embassy coming to London was dated 18 Aug. 1366 (*Rot. Scot.*, I.904).
[86] Printed in *Test. Karl.*, 83–4.

Carlisle],[87] William del Hall, rector of Bowness, Richard de Redenes and John Barbeour, to be spent by the counsel of Sir Th. de W., as he deems best. Executors: the above William, Richard and John. Witnesses: Thomas de Kirkandres, chaplain, John de Middilton, and others.

[Fo.14v; p.168] Note of probate, and of administration to the rector of Bowness and John Barbeour. n.d.

**113** Will[88] of John Lovell, chaplain, fearing the approach of death. Commends soul to God, Blessed Mary and all saints. Burial at St. Mary's, Carlisle; a stone of wax for burning round his body then; 13s. 4d. for the poor; each secular priest attending his exequies and celebrating mass for him, 6d. The prior and convent of Carlisle, 10s. for a pittance. St. Mary's light in the choir, 3s. 4d. The friars preachers and minor, Carlisle, 6s. 8d. Eden and Caldew bridges, 6s. 8d. To celebrate for his soul, 100s. Stephen de Karlio', 13s. 4d. and a chest. Adam Taillor, a chest with a little chest inside it. Robert servant of M. Adam[89] de Caldebek', a second robe and a chest. John de Sourby, a chest. His kinswoman in Dalston barony, a copper pot and pan; her husband, a motley tabard. Sir John de Middeton, a water-jug and basin. Residue to M. Adam de Caldebek' and the other executors, to arrange for his soul as they would answer to God. Executors: M. Adam, John de Middilton, chaplain, Adam Taillor and Stephen de Karlio'. Under his seal.[90] n.d.

**114** Will[91] of Robert de Wolseley, rector of [Long] Marton,[92] dated 2 August 1367, being in good memory. Commends soul to God, Blessed Mary and all saints. Burial in Marton church. For ornaments at its high altar, 13s. 4d. Five pounds of wax for burning round his body and 2s. for oblations then; 20s. to the poor for his soul; and funeral expenses, 40s. Joan Wolseley his sister, £10 silver. Alice his maid, 66s. 8d., a cow and a bed. Thomas del Whall his groom, 66s. 8d. Margaret wife of John del Wall, 40s. Richard del Wall their son, 20s. John de Sourby, chaplain, 13s. 4d. and a robe. Adam his household-servant, a steer. Henry de Mallerstang', his best wagon, and Margaret Henry's [wife], his best belt, tabard and gown. The rector of Clifton, for the soul of [Robert's] father, an ox. Half the residue to Joan his sister, half for the poor and for a chaplain celebrating for his soul. Executors: John Soureby, chaplain, and Henry de Mallerstang'. 26s. 8d. to buy a breviary (*librum portatorum*) for St. Wilfrid's, Brougham.

**115** Licence addressed to abbots, priors, rectors, vicars, parish chaplains and others celebrating in churches and chapels of the diocese. Whenever Thomas de Cokirton, proctor of the hospital of St. Mary of Roncevalles (*Runcyvale*),

[87] See **106, 116**.

[88] Printed in *Test. Karl.*, 85.

[89] Correcting 'Robo' in *Test. Karl.* Adam was official of Carlisle, 1355–62 (*Reg. Welton*, 17, no.89; 85, no.467).

[90] Without date; note of probate etc. also omitted. Marginal note: *r.c.*

[91] Printed in *Test. Karl.*, 86–7. Marginal note: *r.c.* There is no note of probate etc.

[92] Supplied in margin. Instituted 1362 (*Reg. Welton*, 82, no.450).

comes to them seeking alms, they are to admit him with favour, allow him audience and to receive all offerings without any deduction, preferring him before any other quests except that for Carlisle cathedral; with grant of an indulgence [Fo.15; p.169] for 40 days; valid for one year.[93] Rose, 20 January 1368.

**116** Certificate of Thomas de Warthole, canon of Carlisle, the bishop's penitentiary. He has received the bishop's mandate, as follows:

Although administration of goods of intestates lawfully pertains to the bishop, many unknown subjects have taken goods of Robert de Musgrave who lately died intestate in the parish of Torpenhow, leaving goods in their care as well as sums of money under obligation. Order that in Carlisle cathedral, on this [Ash] Wednesday before the departure of penitents (*ante expulsionem penitentium*),[94] [Brother Thomas] is to admonish all subjects of the diocese, religious and secular, that all detaining Robert's goods or owing him money are to deliver them to the bishop or his administrator for this purpose within 12 days, under pain of excommunication. Rose, 22 February 1368.

Report of execution, under the seal of the archdeacon of Carlisle, with his approval [personally expressed]. Carlisle, 7 March [1368].

**117** (i) Collation to Robert Bix, chaplain, of Ormside church, now vacant.[95] (ii) Mandate for induction [fully quoted] to M. John de Appilby, archdeacon of Carlisle. [Fo.15v; p.170] Rose, 18 March 1368.

**118** Letters patent (in French) of the bishop as warden of the West March (*la Westmarche*). Safe conduct until Michaelmas (if the bishop is warden as long) for John Lambe of Eskdale (*Essedalle*), a companion, a groom, and their horses and harness, to enter Cumberland and the march of Carlisle, to stay at will and to return without harm by the king's subjects, provided they do nothing against *la defense*. Rose, 8 March 42 Edward III [1368].

**119** Writ of Edward III summoning the bishop to a parliament at Westminster on 1 May; also the prior of Carlisle and archdeacons (*sic*) in person, and the cathedral chapter and diocesan clergy by proctors. Westminster, 24 February 1368.[96]

**120** Letters patent of the archdeacon of Carlisle. Being prevented by physical infirmity from attending Parliament to consent to its common decisions for the welfare of the realm, as ordered in a writ to the bishop, he appoints William de Stirkland, clerk, his proctor. Under the seal of Bishop Thomas, with his assent [personally expressed]. Carlisle, 18 April 1368.

[93] The archbishop of Canterbury granted a similar licence (for 3 years) to this hospital, 6 Sept. 1368 (*Reg. Langham*, 193).
[94] For this custom, see *Reg. Welton*, 16, no.87*.
[95] John de Grete, instituted 1362 (*Reg. Welton*, 81, no.449), last occurs as rector in 1364 (**7**). See also **107** for Robert's previous benefice.
[96] As in *CCR 1364–8*, 467–8.

**121** Commission to the official of Carlisle to correct and punish excesses and crimes by Stephen de Cumquinton, rector of [Nether] Denton,[97] ordering suitable penance. Rose, 18 April 1368.

**122** Will[98] of Roger Beauchamp (Beuchammp). Commends soul to God, Blessed Mary and all saints. Burial in churchyard of St. Nicholas', Lazonby, with best beast for mortuary, 40s. for the poor, and 5 torches for light. A cow with calf [to each of the following]: Robert del Garth, John del Garth, James [Roger's] servant, William Coke, Adam Colier. John Whyteheved, a heifer. Katherine his wife, all his utensils and corn. [Fo.16; p.171] The fabric of St. Mary's, Carlisle, 40s. The friars preachers, Carlisle, 6s. 8d. The friars minor, 6s. 8d. The Austin friars, Penrith, 20s. The Carmelite friars, Appleby, 3s. 4d. Roger son of Adam del Garth, a cow. Sir William his brother,[99] his hawks (*ter[cell]ios*) which he has in the village of Croglin (*Kirketrogeline*). John Mauther, half his marriage-portion. Lord de Dacre, [Roger's] hauberk. Sir William his brother, 2 paltocks, with an iron cap and gloves and his silver belt. Thomas his brother, his [i.e. their] father's acton. John de Laysingby, his best horse (save for the mortuary). Chaplains celebrating for his soul and his father's in Lazonby church, £20 while they last. Residue to his executors to distribute among the poor. Executors: Sir William, Katherine [Roger's] wife and John Harpyne. Witnesses: John de Leysingby and Thomas del Garth. Under his seal, in his chamber at Lazonby, 20 December 1367.
Note of probate and administration to the executors named, 5 April 1368.

**123** Letter to the vicar-general or official of Thomas [Hatfield], bishop of Durham. The bishop [of Carlisle] has excommunicated Thomas de Cokirton, questor,[100] for contumacy, and published the excommunication in Carlisle diocese. As he lives in the diocese of Durham, the bishop requests *mutue vicissitudinis optentu* its publication in the parish churches of Durham [city], Brancepeth (*Brauncepeth*) and other churches in that diocese where he is known; asking to be certified by 6 June. Rose, 22 April 1367.

**124** Will[101] of Henry de Threlkeld. Commends soul to God and Blessed Mary. Burial wherever God pleases. The poor of Helton and Yanwath (*Yanewith*), 20 marks. Executors: William de Threlkeld, kt., Idonea [Henry's] wife, Henry de Threlkeld and John de Dent'. Under his seal.
Sentence of probate before the official of London, with administration of goods in London diocese granted to John de Dent'; reserved for the other executors. London, 20 May 1368.

---

[97] No named rector is known since 1317 (Nicolson & Burn, II.510). Stephen was ordained priest in 1344 (*Reg. Kirkby*, I.160).
[98] Printed in *Test. Karl.*, 87–8.
[99] Rector of Kirkoswald, presented by Lord Dacre, 1364 (**14**).
[100] See **115**.
[101] Printed in *Test. Karl.*, 88. This will and 2 following sentences were written by another scribe on ruled lines, of which the last was not used.

Sentence of approval and grant of administration of goods in [Carlisle] jurisdiction to William and Henry de Threlkeld and John de Dent'; reserved for
Idonea. Rose (chapel), 22 June 1368.

**125** [Fo.16v; p.172] Commission to M. John de Appelby, archdeacon of
Carlisle, M. Richard de Stayneweygs, rector of Hutton in the Forest,[102] and
M. Walter de Helton, vicar of Addingham.[103] John Pety, chaplain, defamed
of adultery with Katherine widow of Roger Beauchampp,[104] denied the crime
before the bishop, who ordered his purgation by the hands of 12 priests.
The commissaries, or two of them, are to expedite the purgation, reporting
[etc.]. n.d.

**126** Commission to Thomas [Hatfield], bishop of Durham, to effect an
exchange of benefices between William de Hayton, rector of St. Mary in the
North Bailey, Durham, and Richard Damysell, vicar of Wigton (dioc. Carlisle,
in the bishop's collation). Rose, 16 July 1368.

**127** Commission to the prior of Carlisle and M. Adam de Caldbek', skilled in
law. At the prosecution of John Pety, chaplain, the bishop cited Richard, vicar
of Lazonby,[105] to appear in Rose chapel before the bishop on 3 July [1368?],
when John presented his libel. This is sent, sealed, to the commissaries who
(or one of them) are to proceed with the case on 24 July in St. Cuthbert's,
Carlisle. n.d.

**128** [Extract from the roll of the court of Common Pleas, 1367.]
Pleas at Westminster before Robert de Thorpe and his fellow justices of the
Bench, Michaelmas 41 Edward III, rot. 621.
  Thomas, bishop of Carlisle, and John de Rouceby, clerk, were summoned to
answer the king in a plea to allow him to present a parson to the church of
Horncastle (Lincs.), now vacant and in his gift because of the vacancy of the see
of Carlisle. For the king, Michael Skillyng said that John de Kirkeby, once
bishop, had presented Simon [Fo.17; p.173][106] de Islipp', his clerk.[107] The
church fell vacant when he became archbishop of Canterbury and so remained

---

[102] The admission of Richard de Stayneweygs to the rectory of Hutton on the Forest
has not been found and it is just possible that the episcopal scribe miscopied his name,
because Henry de Staynwigges occurs as rector in 1356 (*Reg. Welton*, 42 (no. 231, n. 162))
and again in 1364 (no. 340 below, under subdeacons). Robert de Lowthre was instituted
in 1369, but no reason given for the vacancy (no. **144** below).
[103] Clerk skilled in law, 1354; ordained priest, 1356; instituted to Addingham, 1362
(*Reg. Welton*, 15, no.79; 86, no.470; 115).
[104] See **122**.
[105] Presumably Richard de Whitton, successor of the vicar who died in May
1367 (**81**).
[106] There are missing sections (ranging up to 115 × 85 mm in the top right-hand cor-
ners of folios 17–19.
[107] In 1338 (*Reg. Kirkby*, I.85, no.450).

when Bishop Kirkby died.[108] It was thus in the king's hand and he presented to it, but was opposed by Bishop Appleby and the said John, to the king's loss of £1,000. They answered in court, the bishop claiming the advowson as normal but admitting he was unsure of the king's right by reason of the vacancy [of Carlisle], while John claimed to be parson. [The record of pleading ends with quoting the king's writ] to John [Buckingham], bishop of Lincoln, presenting his clerk, John de Rouceby, to the vacant church of Horncastle, in his advowson because of the vacancy of Carlisle; dated [3][109] August, 1367.

The court observed that Michael had not shown that the king had recovered his presentation etc., and therefore considered that John might depart *sine die* and that the king should cease etc.

**129** [Informal letter to an archbishop.[110]] He had verbally proposed [to the bishop] while they were sitting together in the Exchequer during the last parliament that they should enquire in their localities what Sir James de Pikeryng, lately sheriff of Westmorland,[111] was doing on the king's business in the week after Michaelmas when he should have been accounting in the Exchequer. [The bishop] has learnt from knights and other reliable men in Westmorland that by order of Lord Clifford, warden of the march, James was then and in the 3 previous weeks continually engaged on the inspection and array of men at arms and archers for the defence of the march, and thus could not be at the Exchequer. Rose, 24 September [1368?].

**130** Note of dispensation to William de Dalton, clerk, as the third to be dispensed to be ordained as priest despite being under 25 years of age.[112] 1366.

**131** Exchequer writ. The king lately ordered William de Wyndesovere, sheriff of Cumberland, to survey the houses, walls, towers and other buildings in Carlisle castle, and to repair defects from issues of his bailiwick by view of the prior of Carlisle, to be allowed for in his account at the Exchequer.[113] The king is unwilling to proceed without the prior's testimony and counter-rolls, which the king trusts the bishop to obtain; he is to take the prior's oath about them and report to the treasurer and barons by 27 January. Tested by T[homas] de Lodelowe, Westminster, 15 November 1368.

[Return] The bishop ordered the prior to execute his writ. He replied that he had made no counter-rolls for costs in these works and had done nothing

---

[108] For (another) John Kirkby becoming rector of Horncastle after Simon's promotion in 1349, see ibid., 155, no.746, n. See also *BRUO*, II.1054.

[109] Lost by tear, but see *CPR 1367–70*, 4.

[110] MS *Reverendissimo pater et domine*. Probably John Thoresby of York.

[111] *Recte* under-sheriff for the hereditary sheriff, Lord Clifford. He was under-sheriff, Oct. 1365–7 and Oct. 1368–9, and thus not at the time of the parliament of 1–21 May 1368, which he attended as shire-knight for Cumberland (J.S. Roskell, 'Two medieval Westmorland Speakers, Part I', *CWAAS*, 2nd ser. 61 (1961), 85).

[112] See **53**.

[113] By letters dated 18 July 1367 (*CPR 1364–7*, 423).

about them, because (he says) that he had not been ordered to act. Thus the writ was not executed, and the bishop was unable to proceed.

**132** [Fo.17v; p.174] Commission to M. John de Appelby, archdeacon of Carlisle, to effect an exchange of benefices between William de Stirkland, rector of Stapleton, and Nicholas de Stapelton, rector of Ousby, making arrangements for inductions. Rose, 9 April 1368.

**133** Letter of the archdeacon collating William de Stirkeland, clerk, to Ousby in this exchange. Under the seal of the archdeaconry, Rose, 10 April 1368.

**134** Letters patent of the archdeacon certifying that he has put William in possession of Ousby. Under the same seal, Salkeld, 11 April 1368.

**135** Commission of John [Buckingham], bishop of Lincoln, for the bishop to effect an exchange of benefices between Walter de Lughteburgh, rector of Dacre, and Peter de Stapelton, rector of Wold Newton (*Waldeneuton*), enclosing a report by the archdeacon of Lincoln's official, showing that Walter was presented to Wold Newton by Thomas [Hatfield], bishop of Durham. Liddington, 6 May 1369.
   Note that the exchange was effected by Bishop Appleby. 16 May 1369.

**136** [Fo.18; p.175] Will[114] of William de Artureht', mayor of Carlisle,[115] dated 19 August 1369, being well in body and memory. Commends soul to God, Blessed Mary and all saints. Christian burial with best beast and cloth for mortuary; 5 stones of wax to burn in candles, viz. 'tapers' to burn round his body; 66s. 8d. for the poor; clerks and widows making vigil round his body, 10s. Sir John de Midelton, 6s. 8d. The parish clerk, 2s. Each parish chaplain celebrating in Carlisle at the time of his burial, 2s. The fabric of St. Mary's, Carlisle, 40s. Two chaplains to celebrate for his soul for 2 whole years, £10. The prior and convent of St. Mary's, Carlisle, 100s. Eden bridge, 20s. Caldewe bridge, 20s. The priors preachers, Carlisle, 20s. The friars minor, 20s. Richard . . . .[116] of his sister, 40s., a horse and armour basinet with a pa[ltock?]. John son of Thomas de Artureht, a bed with sheets, . . . . jug, basin and £10 in gold or silver. . . . .[117] Residue to his wife Mariota. Executors: Mariota, Alan de Blenerhayset and William, vicar of Arthuret. Under his seal. Witnesses: John de Midelton and Gilbert Groute, chaplains.
   Note of probate. 28 August 1369.

**137** Will[118] of William de Laton of Newbiggin, dated 31 August 1369. Commends soul to God. Burial in church of Austin friars, Penrith. His chief ox as

---

[114] Printed in *Test. Karl.*, 89–90.
[115] Supplied in margin.
[116] This is the first of 3 folios, which has lost the last 5 cm of 2 lines by tearing from the outer margin.
[117] This is a second, eye-shaped hole, near the inner margin, 5 cm wide. It recurs in ever-decreasing size up to fo.30.
[118] Printed in *Test. Karl.*, 90–1.

mortuary to Dacre church. An ox to the high altar for forgotten tithes. The fabric of Carlisle church, 6s. 8d. A cow each to John son of Thomas, John Lynbek, Matthew Wills, John de Lekyl. Margaret his wife and his unmarried children, all other cows and growing corn, with all other utensils in and outside the house. Thomas chaplain of Dacre, 20s. Three stones of wax for the day of his burial in the friars' church; oblations then, 3s. 4d., a wake for friends, 100s., and the poor, 20s. Margaret, all his other cattle. All his lambs in the custody of John son of William de Penrith are to be kept until they can best be sold profitably, except for a third of their wool to be given to Thomas Arnaldson for custody. His nine horses pastured in Greystoke park should be sold at the next fair in Brough, with their price to hire a chaplain to celebrate for the soul of John de Laton, his brother, and all the faithful departed. Residue to his executors to pay his debts and to spend for his soul and all the faithful departed in pious uses. Executors: Richard son of Elet, Thomas de Laton, Robert Abot, John Dewy and Adam Clerk of Ireby. Witnesses: John de Chambre and John son of Thomas; with Andrew de Laton, his brother, as coadjutor.

Note of probate. Rose, 22 September 1369.

**138**  Will[119] of Clement de Crofton, being well in memory and mind. Commends soul to God, Blessed Mary the glorious virgin and all saints. Burial in churchyard of Blessed Andrew, Thursby, with best horse [for mortuary]. [Fo.18v; p.176] Ten pounds of wax to make 5 candles round his body on burial day; the poor then, 13s. 4d.; a wake for friends and neighbours, 5 marks; and an oblation, 6s. 8d. The 4 orders of friars, 13s. 4d. equally divided. The master of the fabric of St. Mary, Carlisle, 6s. 8d. The fabric of St. Mary, Holm Cultram, 20s. The light of St. Mary in Thursby church, 3s. 4d. Its rector, to pray for his soul, 3s. 4d. Two chaplains celebrating there for the same cause, 2s. equally divided. The lord abbot of Holm Cultram, his hauberk valued 60s. in his inventory. His brother John, a pair of paunce and braces and a jack. Clement de Skelton, junior, one of his basinets with a movable visor. His lord, another [basinet?] with a better, heavier visor. His wife Joan, by custom of Holy Church and the country, to have half of all goods . . . . owed to him and of the residue of all goods. Executors: Robert de Byx[120] and Joan. Dated in his hall at Crofton. [Witnesses:] John de Crofton, his brother, Clement de Skelton . . . . . Walter Marshall, clerk, who wrote this will, 11 October 1369.

Note of probate. Rose, 19 October 1369.

**139**  Note that John de Bampton was instituted as vicar of Bampton; presented by the abbot and convent of Shap. 11 October 1369.

**140**  Will[121] of William Lenglys, kt. Commends soul to God and Blessed Mary. Burial in chapel (*porticus*) of Blessed Mary in St. Michael's, Appleby; 2 stones of

---

[119]  Printed in *Test. Karl.*, 91–2.

[120]  Rector of Thursby 1364–6 (**12, 43–4**).

[121]  Printed in *Test. Karl.*, 92–3. The will of William's brother Thomas, dated 14 Sept. 1362, is printed with a translation in F.W. Ragg, 'Lengleys', *CWAAS*, 2nd ser. 20 (1920), 91–3.

wax to make 5 tapers for light round his body; 20s. for oblations; a wake for friends, 20 marks; 100s. for the poor. Two priests celebrating for a year after his death at Appleby, where he is to be buried. Margaret Lenglys, widow of John de Hoton, 40s. Alice Lenglys, 40s. Roger de Fulthorp, his kinsman, 2 of his best horses. William Proppe, 40s. Isabel de Whytinghame, a mark. Residue of goods, his wife. Executors: his wife Margaret, Thomas de Warthecopp, senior, and Edmund Sandford. Under his seal, at Highhead, 1 August 43 Edward III [1369]. Note of probate and grant of administration to Margaret and John Sotherne of Ivegill; Thomas and Edmund refused to act. Rose, 20 August [1369].

**141** Note of collation of John de Midelton, chaplain, to Dalston vicarage, vacant; and of order for induction to John de Appelby, archdeacon of Carlisle. 6 October 1369.

**142** Will[122] of Margaret Lenglys, widow of William Lenglys, kt.,[123] dated 9 October 1369. Commends soul to God, Blessed Mary and all saints. Burial in St. Mary's church, Carlisle, with a horse. Her best horse to the bishop of Carlisle, as mortuary. Two chaplains celebrating for her soul for a year, 16 marks. Funeral expenses, [Fo.19; p.177] 40s., with 40s. for the poor. Anabel Bruyne, 13s. 4d. Bowet, 40s. Little Thomas Bowet, 40s. Isabel Bowet, 13s. 4d. Isabel de Whytingham, 40s. Little Robert Bowet, 20s. Little John Bowet, 20s. Cecily Swayneson, 20s. John Sothoroune, 13s. 4d. Isabel her dau., a ring with a diamond. Thomas Bowet, a jewel. Elizabeth her sister, a silver jewel. William Ros, 40s. John Spurlyng, 6s. 8d. John de Snawdon, 6s. 8d. John Coke, 6s. 8d. The vicar of Dalston, 20s. John Ellarle, 3s. 4d. William Bryde, 2s. Brice, 2s. William Petybone, 6s. 8d. . . . . Hyne, John Awkelour and Adam Hayward, 10s. Stephen de Meburn, . . . . . Agnes Amblour, a beast of burden. Ellota de Penreth, a cow with calf. . . . . Hobcrone, a cow. The 4 orders of friars, 20s. equally divided, and 2 . . . . . Residue of goods to priests [celebrating] for the soul of Sir William Lenglys and her soul. Executors: Thomas Bowet, Gilbert Bowet, chaplain, John de Midelton, chaplain, John Sothereyne. Dated at Highhead.

Note of probate and grant of administration to Thomas Bowet and John Sotheryn; reserved [for the others]. Rose, 12 October 1369.

**143** Will[124] of John de Dalston, dated 21 October 1369. Commends soul to God and Blessed Mary. Burial in Dalston church, with best beast for mortuary; for light round body and oblations, 13s. 4d. The lights in Dalston church of Blessed Mary, Holy Cross and St. Michael, 40d. each. Each pauper coming at his burial, 1d. The 4 orders of friars, 13s. 4d. equally divided. [A chaplain] celebrating for his soul in Dalston church for a year, 8 marks. Two oxen to be hired for his soul. The altar of St. Michael's, Dalston, 2s. for ornaments. The altar of Blessed Mary [in the same], 20s. for a missal. To repair the font [in the same], 12d. William his servant, 2 cows and a skep of oats. Joan del Feld his maid,

---

[122] Printed in *Test. Karl.*, 94–5.
[123] Supplied from margin.
[124] Printed in *Test. Karl.*, 95–6.

3 lambs. Thomas son of Adam Porter, 12 lambs. John de Midelton, vicar of Dalston, half a mark. Nicholas Lambe, chaplain, 40d. Thomas the clerk, 40s. Caldew bridge beside Carlisle, 12d. Caldew bridge beside Dalston, 12d. Residue to his wife Agnes and his children. Executors: John de Midelton, vicar of Dalston, Adam Porter and Robert de Briscawe. Under his seal.

Note of probate with grant of administration to these executors and his widow, with their consent. 24 October 1369.

**144** [Fo.19v; p.178] (i) Note of institution of Robert de Lowthre to Hutton [in the Forest] church; presented by the prior and convent of Carlisle. (ii) Archdeacon to induct. 5 November 1369.

**145** Note of probate at Rose, 3 November 1369, of the will of Richard de Aslacby, vicar of St. Michael's, Appleby, and grant of administration to William de Neuton, vicar of Barton,[125] and William de Stirkeland, executors named, as follows:[126]

Dated 26 October 1369, (*viva voce et sane . . . .*). Commends soul to God, Blessed Mary and all saints. Burial before the cross in St. Michael's, Appleby; 40s. for the poor; . . . . 40s. in a gathering of friends; 8 pounds of wax for light. Chaplains, viz. Richard de Brumlay and William de Aslacby, [celebrating] in that church, 16 marks; . . . . if William is unwilling to be employed, then Richard should celebrate for 2 [years]. John [the testator's] son, 100s. with a whole bed of . . . . and 4 silver spoons and a mazer. The bridge . . . ., 6s. 8d. Brough and Sowerby bridges, 13s. 4d. The Austin friars, Penrith, 20s. The friars of Appleby, 13s. 4d. The said Sir Richard, 6s. 8d. with a long gown of bluet. John Wynd', 3s. 4d. William son of Adam, 6s. 8d. with a steer, heifer and short green gown. His 2 handmaids, 4s. John his servant, 18d. Agnes Wryght, 3s. 4d. Christine Hyne, as much. Works at the churches of St. Peter, York, and St. Mary, Gisburn, his silver belt. Sir William de Neuton, 13s. 4d. M. William de Stirkeland, as much. John his son, his breviary of the use of York and a psalter. Sir William his kinsman, a black colt, a hanging, a [bench] covering and 6 cushions. Residue to his executors (William de Neuton, William de Stirkeland, Richard de Brumlay) to spend for his soul. Under his close seal.

**146** (i) Note of collation to John de Merton, chaplain, to the vicarage of St. Michael's, Appleby. (ii) Archdeacon to induct. 16 December 1369.

**147** (i) Note of collation of John Wartreward, chaplain, to Ousby church. (ii) Archdeacon to induct. 26 December 1369.

**148** Will[127] of John de Hothwayt', dated 18 November 1369. Commends soul to God, Blessed Mary and all saints. Burial in St. Cuthbert's, Plumbland, with best

---

[125] Instituted 1362 (*Reg. Welton*, 77, no.427). The king had presented John de Eskeheved to this church, 9 Jan. 1367, apparently without effect (*CPR 1364–7*, 348).

[126] Printed in *Test. Karl.*, 96–7.

[127] Printed in *Test. Karl.*, 97.

beast and cloth for mortuary. 5 pounds of wax for light. Thomas his brother, a silver knife, a vestment, a chalice, 4 books and a gold ring. G. his brother, a silver seal. Sir Thomas de Warthole, a silver knife. Residue to his brothers and sisters. Executors, John de Ireby, Thomas[128]

**149** [Fo.21; p.179] Notarial instrument.[129] On 30 August 1368, in the southern part of the churchyard of St. Nicholas, Newcastle upon Tyne (dioc. Durham), Thomas de Salkeld, rector of Clifton, as proctor of Bishop Thomas and the prior and convent of Carlisle, found Robert de Merlay, chaplain, cutting a stone, near new work on the church's choir. When he would not answer the proctor's request for the names of those responsible for this new work, the proctor showed the notary his letters of proxy, said that he had found Robert working and reputed to be in charge, and forbade any more building or demolition of the old choir. Witnesses: John de Perdysolke, literate (dioc. York), and John Sawer (dioc. Carlisle). Later that day, at the Sandhill in Newcastle, the proctor told Robert de Angirton and John del Chambre, burgesses of Newcastle, that he understood that Robert de Merlay had begun this work with their counsel and aid, and he repeated his prohibition of this building and demolition as prejudicial to his lords. Witnesses: Robert de Merlay and Richard de Stanhopp (both of Durham dioc.).

Letters patent of Bishop Thomas and the prior and convent of Carlisle as appropriators of the church of St. Nicholas, Newcastle. [Fo.21v; p.180] They have been informed that some of their parishioners of this church, and many others, have built a new work adjoining the church in its yard and intend to demolish its old [building],[130] against their will. M. Thomas de Clifton has therefore been appointed their proctor to forbid these works [with numerous powers to take legal actions]. Sealed by the bishop at Rose, 20 August, and by the prior and convent in Carlisle, 21 August 1369.

Subscription and sign of William de Stirkeland, clerk (dioc. York), notary.

**150** [Fo.22; p.181] Letters of the abbot and convent of St. Mary's, York, presenting John Pray,[131] vicar of Helmsley (*Helmeslay*; dioc. York), to Morland vicarage, in an exchange of benefices with William de Laysyngby; saving an annual pension of 4 marks to their prior. York, 30 July 1368.

**151** Certificate of the official of the archdeacon of Cleveland to John [Thoresby], archbishop of York, quoting his mandate (dated Bishopthorpe, 1 August) to enquire into the presentation by the prior and convent of Kirkham of William de Laysyngby to Helmsley vicarage [in the above exchange]. He reports that in full chapter at Overton (*Everton*), on 3 [Fo.22v; p.182] August 1368, Patrick vicar of Bossall, John vicar of Crambe (*Cramburn*),

[128] Incomplete, at end of line: the next original folio is lost.
[129] Partly printed in Hist. Man. Comm., *Ninth Report*, I.192–3.
[130] MS *Ebor'que antiquum ecclesie predicte destruere*: the word *Ebor'* has been struck through, and next restored by interlineation, as happens again later in the letter.
[131] See *Reg. Welton*, 18, no.96.

John vicar of Whenby (*Quenby*), Henry vicar of Easingwold (*Esyngwald*), Robert vicar of Overton (*Everton*), John rector of Dalby, and the parish chaplains of Newton (*Neuton*), Sutton, Easingwold, Brandsby (*Brandesby*), Brafferton (*Braferton*), and Sheriff Hutton (*Hoton Vicecomitis*) attested that Kirkham priory was patron of Helmsley; the church was not in dispute, charged with a pension or taxed, and worth 20 marks p.a., and the presentee was of free and legitimate birth, literate, of canonical age, a priest, vicar of Morland, and there is no obstacle. Under the official's seal and the seals of the witnesses. Everton, 3 August [1368].

**152**  Commission of the archbishop to Bishop Thomas to effect the exchange, enclosing the above certificate. Bishopthorpe, 3 August 1368.
 Note that the bishop effected the exchange and certified the archbishop. 16 [August 1368].

**153**  [Fo.23; p.183] Certificate of Thomas de Gretham, dean of Christianity of Durham and *locum tenens* of the archdeacon of Durham, to Thomas [Hatfield], bishop of Durham, quoting receipt of his mandate (dated Auckland, 7 September; received on the 8th.) to the archdeacon of Durham or his official, to enquire into the presentation by Richard de Castro Bernardi, archdeacon of Northumberland, of Richard Damysele to the church of St. Mary in the North Bailey, Durham, in an exchange of benefices with the vicar of Wigton (dioc. Carlisle); [causes of the exchange are added to the usual articles of enquiry in a presentation]. This was held in the church of St. Nicholas, Durham, on 9 September, when Reginald rector of St. Mary in the South Bailey, Durham, Hugh de Chilton, rector of Kimblesworth, and the following chaplains: William de Syreston, John Forester, Alan de Cotesford *perpetuar'*, Thomas de Neuton, Thomas Copp, John de Helpirby, Thomas parish chaplain of St. Oswald's [Durham], Peter parish chaplain of St. Margaret's [Durham], Adam Tabelar and William de Essh, attested that Richard, archdeacon of Northumberland is patron and last presented; the presentee is of good and honest repute, free [etc.], priest and vicar of Wigton. Under the seal of the dean of Christianity and the seals of the jurors. Durham, [9 September 1368].

**154**  Commission of the bishop of Durham to Thomas, bishop of Carlisle, to effect this exchange between William de Hayton, rector of St. Mary in the North Bailey, and Richard Damysele; [Fo.23v; p.184] enclosing the above certificate. Auckland, 10 September 1368.
 Note that the bishop of Carlisle effected the exchange. 30 September [1368].

**155**  Certificate of the dean of Westmorland quoting the bishop's mandate (dated Rose, 14 February 1367). Anthony de Lucy, lord of Cockermouth, who claims the advowson, has presented Thomas de Setrington, chaplain, to Dufton church, vacant by the death of William de Brampton,[132] although William de

---

[132] See *Reg. Welton*, xxii, n.73.

Therlkeld is in possession on presentation by King Edward.[133] Wishing to do justice, the bishop orders the citation of William de Therlkeld to the chapel of Rose manor on 13 March, to answer Thomas before the bishop, his commissary or commissaries, and that [the dean] enquires by rectors, vicars and others, in full chapter, into the right of the presenter, who last presented, [Fo.24; p.185] who should present, and also the ability and merits of the presentee; certifying the bishop or his commissary or commissaries by letters patent under his seal of office and the seals of the witnesses.

On 11 March 1367, in Clifton church, Thomas de Anand, rector of Asby, Robert [de Marton], rector of Newbiggin, William de Lesyngby, vicar of Morland, Robert de Feryby, vicar of Askham,[134] John de Wynder, . . . . .,[135] Nicholas de Preston, vicar of Warcop,[136] John de Regyll, vicar of Crosby Ravensworth, and Thomas Goldyll, Robert de Carleton and John Hyne, chaplains, said that Anthony de Lucy has the presentation by right of his wife's dower. William de Creystok, kt., deceased, as husband of the same wife, last presented effectively. Anthony should present now. The presentee is able, worthy, free, of legitimate birth, a priest and not beneficed, and there is no canonical obstacle. Under seals [as above], at Clifton, 11 March 1367.

[The dean] could not cite William de Therlkeld in Dufton church because he could not be found nor had he left a proctor. He has been cited publicly before known parishioners and friends.

**156** General letter to all deans and parish clergy. The prior and brethren of the hospital of St. John of Jerusalem have complained that unknown evildoers have taken and hidden their lands, revenues and goods without consent from them and their deputed keeper, in peril of their souls [Fo.24v; p.186] and the hospital's prejudice. Mandate to announce in churches on Sundays and feast-days, as required on the hospital's behalf, that if these goods [etc.] are not restored to the hospital or Thomas de Mothirby, its attorney, within a month, all those culpable will incur sentence of greater excommunication; the sentence is to be published on Sundays and feast-days, with candles lit etc. [unfinished].

**157** Notarial instrument dated 2 May 1369. As M. Peter de Stapilton, rector of All Saints, Wold Newton (dioc. Lincoln), and Walter de Louthburg', rector of Dacre (dioc. Carlisle), intend to exchange churches, Walter - in the notary's presence in Keelby church (dioc. Lincoln) - appointed Thomas de Thorgramby, parish chaplain of Dacre, and Thomas le Clerke of Goxhill (*Couxyll*) proctors to

---

[133] Cf. **52** for William's institution on the king's presentation, 25 Nov. 1366. The king revoked his presentation, 3 Feb. 1367, when it was found that the patronage was in the dower of Joan, widow of Baron Greystoke, now married to Anthony Lucy (*CPR 1364–7*, 241, 374).

[134] The previous known vicar was John de Wyntryngham, canon of Warter, instituted 1359 (*Reg. Welton*, 49, no.263).

[135] Lost by hole: as it is small (1 cm), perhaps Shap.

[136] Canon of Shap, occurs 1354, 1359 (*Reg. Welton*, 51, no.279; 101–2).

resign Dacre church to Thomas, bishop of Carlisle, obtain institution and investiture to Wold Newton, and receive its revenues. [Fo.25; p.187[137]] Dated in Keelby church as above. Witnesses: Robert de Kelby and William Wyncente of Waltham (dioc. Lincoln).

Subscription by Richard North of Wold Newton, clerk (dioc. Lincoln), notary, who confirms erasure in *Louthburg'* in the fifth line from the head, another at the begining of the third line from the end, and three more in the subscription.

**158**  Letter to the bishop of his 'devoted son', Ranulph de Daker, patron of Dacre church, assenting to [the above] exchange and presenting M. Peter to Dacre. Dacre, 23 April 1369.

**159**  Commission of John [Buckingham], bishop of Lincoln, for this exchange [repeating **135**. Fo.25v; p.189]. Liddington, 6 May 1369.

Note that the bishop of Carlisle effected the exchange; both those beneficed have his sealed letters and a certificate was sent to the bishop of Lincoln. Rose, 16 [May 1369].

**160**  Letters patent testifying that R. de Bolton of Carlisle diocese contracted marriage with Maud, dau. of Henry Loeson; it was solemnised in the parish church of St. Mary, Carlisle, and they have lived as man and wife for some time, as the bishop has learnt from many witnesses. n.d.

**161**  Letters patent of John de Appelby, priest. His brother (*germanus*), Bishop Thomas, has presented him to the church of Horncastle, now vacant.[138] In order to seek his institution and induction from John [Buckingham], bishop of Lincoln, and to receive its fruits and sue for its rights, he has appointed his clerk, William de Stirkland, [Fo.26; p.190] his proctor. Under the bishop's seal, with his consent (personally expressed), Rose, 1 August 1367.

**162**  Letters patent acknowledging that the bishop has received £40 from John etc. [*sic*] for the sheaves of Warkworth church last autumn, viz. £20 at Durham by the hands of John Bone, the bishop's receiver,[139] and £20 at Rose by T[homas] de Skelton. Rose, 15 April 42 [Edward III: 1368].

**163**  [Unaddressed letter.] The bishop has learnt from his ministers and other inhabitants of Penrith that many unknown parishioners have not paid tithes for corn and hay; indeed, some have been consumed by their beasts or hidden, without any fear for the sentences of excommunication promulgated by sacred constitutions for defrauding churches or ecclesiastics of tithes. To remedy these offences and obtain absolution, mandate, etc. [unfinished].

[137] There is no page numbered 188.
[138] Cf. **128**, **193**.
[139] Rector of Kirklinton, 1362 (*Reg. Welton*, 84, no.464).

**164** [Fo.26v; p.191] Mandate to the parish chaplain of Crosth[waite] to order parishioners who have taken or hidden tithes of lambs, wool, calves, hay and other tithes due to the vicarage since it came into the bishop's hands, to make restitution within ten days; and also of concealed mortuaries, oblations and other profits, to be made or revealed to the bishop or W. White, his deputy, under pain of excommunication. n.d.

**165** Constitution of Pope Urban V.[140] Many appropriations (*uniones*) of priories, dignities, parish churches and other benefices are being planned, threatening the cure of souls and performance of divine services. All pending processes for appropriations to cathedrals, monasteries, episcopal and abbatial *mense* and other offices are therefore declared void and forbidden for the next ten years. Avignon, 1 December 1366.

**166** [Fo.27; p.192] Letter (in French) of [John of Gaunt,] duke of Lancaster, asking the bishop to order the clergy of his diocese to sing masses and pray for the soul of his consort, Blanche, who has died, and the souls of all Christians, with a pardon for so doing.
Tutbury (*Tuttebury*) castle, 12 September [1368].[141]

**167** Commission of John [Thoresby], archbishop of York, for an exchange of benefices between William de Hayton, vicar of Wigton, and John de Welton, rector of Cowesby (*Couseby*), William having been presented by Hugh de Hastynges, kt.; enclosing the report of an inquest by the keeper of the spiritualities of Allerton and Allertonshire. Bishopthorpe, 28 June 1369.
Note of execution in the same month; both [parsons] have customary letters under the bishop's seal, and the archbishop certified.

**168** Letters dimisssory of Archbishop [Thoresby] for the further ordination of Robert de Hilton, acolyte (dioc. York). [Fo.27v; p.193] Bishopthorpe, 4 November 1365.

**169** Certificate of John, parish chaplain of St. Mary's, Carlisle, quoting the bishop's mandate (dated Rose, 8 September 1369) ordering him and the parish chaplain of Stanwix, to oversee penance by Joan Remywyf' of Carlisle for violence to Henry Moys, a canon regular, and Joan Rawlyndogtre of Stanwix for a carnal lapse with John Strako', chaplain, viz. both women are to be whipped round their parish churches on the next six Sundays, and round Carlisle market place on as many market days, penances which the bishop had imposed instead of suspension and excommunication. [John] had called Joan Remywyf' on two feast-days but she had refused to do penance; he had therefore suspended her from entering church and later excommunicated her in writing, denouncing her publicly. Sealed n.d.

---

[140] Printed (from this manuscript?) in Wilkins, *Concilia*, III.65; a fuller summary in *CPL*, IV.180.
[141] An order for prayers etc. for Blanche by the archbishop of Canterbury was dated at Otford, Kent, 11 Oct. 1368 (*Reg. Langham*, 214–15).

**170**   Letters patent of the prior and convent of Carlisle, as appropriators of the parish church of Edenhall, with the chapel of Langwathby, appointing Thomas de Warteholl their subprior as their proctor to consent to an ordinance by the bishop about a suitable portion for the vicar of Edenhall, and his duties and charges. 10 March 1369.

**171**   [Fo.28; p.194] Letters dimissory of Archbishop [Thoresby] for the ordination as priest of John Benson of Kirkby Lonsdale, deacon (dioc. York). Bishopthorpe, 11 March 1369.

**172**   Writ of Edward III summoning the bishop to a parliament at Westminster on 3 June; also the prior (and other clergy). Westminster, 6 April 1369.[142]

**173**   Letters patent of the archdeacon [of Carlisle]. Being prevented from attending Parliament (as in **120**), he appoints his dear [clerk], W[illiam] de S[tirkland] [incomplete].

**174**   [Fo.28v; p.195] Letter[143] (in French) of [Edward] prince of Aquitaine and Wales, thanking the bishop for arranging processions and prayers and asking for them to be continued so that, by God's grace, he may have greater success. Under his privy seal, Angoulême (*dengolesmo'*), 10 May [1368].

**175**   (i) Commission of Alan de Schutlyngton, vicar-general of Thomas [Hatfield], bishop of Durham, for an exchange of benefices between Richard de Whitton, vicar of Lazonby, and John de Castro Bernardy, vicar of Kirknewton (*Neuton in Glendale*); Richard has been presented to Kirknewton by the prior and convent of Kirkham. [Bishop] Middleham, 12 August 1368. (ii) [Fo.29; p.196] Letters of Bishop Appleby instituting Richard de Whitton, priest, to Kirknewton. (iii) The like of John, priest, to Lazonby (in the bishop's collation), in the person of M. John de Bernyngham, his proctor. Rose, 10 September 1368.

**176**   Letter of Edward III under the privy seal (in French). In case Scots enter the realm to rob and otherwise harm the king's subjects, the bishop is charged not to allow *chivauchées* or other injuries to provoke the Scots to seek revenge. He is to inform the king, in writing, about the manner of invasion by the Scots, what they did, and about their array and arms; the king will then send full orders of his will: he does not want any of his lieges to take revenge on Scots outwith the king's obedience without just cause. Westminster, 1 June [1368?].[144]

**177**   [Fo.29v; p.197] Citation of the prior and chapter of Lanercost to attend the bishop's visitation in their chapter house on 14 July; absent brethren and *conversi*, if any, are to be recalled, prejudicial acts forbidden, and a certificate listing canons delivered on that day. Rose, 3 July 1368.

---

[142] As in *CCR 1369–74*, 83–4.
[143] Mostly printed in Hist. Man. Comm., *Ninth Report*, I.193.
[144] Cf. **70**.

**178** Exchequer memoranda. The bishop of Carlisle, viz. John de Kyrkeby, owes £17 2s. 9d. for the first and second years of a biennial tenth granted by the clergy in 25 Edward III [1351];[145] also £18 12s. 1d. for various tenths: total, £35 14s. 10d.

The bishop [Appleby] accounted for this debt in the Treasury, by three tallies for £7 10s., and so owes £28 4s. 10d. for which he has the king's pardon by a writ of privy seal enrolled in the memoranda roll for Hilary 42 Edward III [1368] and thus is quit in the pipe roll for the 41st year under Cumberland.

**179** Letter of Edward III under the privy seal (in French). He has been advised by his council to go abroad with his army to defend the realm.[146] He therefore asks the bishop to give him two packhorses (*somers*) with saddles, harness and cloths, and two grooms to bring them to the king at Westminster by 24 June, to provide transport for his army; and certify by the bearer of this letter. Westminster, 16 May [1368].

**180** [Fo.30; p.198] Will[147] of M. Walter de Hilton, rector of Moorby,[148] being *compos mentis*, dated 30 July 1369. Commends soul to God, Blessed Mary and all saints. Burial in All Saints', Moorby. To the fabric of Moorby church, 2s. The fabric of the mother church, Lincoln, 12d. Residue to M. William de Hilton, appointing him executor, to dispose of goods as he thinks best for [Walter's] soul. Sealed at Moorby, as above.

Sentence of probate before the dean of Horncastle and Hill, in Horncastle church, 2 September 1369. As the only executor is dead, administration granted to Thomas de Whithill of Moorby, named as executor in William's will.

**181** (i) Letter of the abbot and convent of Holm Cultram presenting Eudo de Ravenstandale, chaplain, vicar of Edenhall,[149] to the vicarage of Burgh by Sands (*Burgh juxta Sablones*), vacant by the resignation of John de Kerby[150] in an exchange of benefices. 16 March 1369. (ii) Letter of the prior and convent of Carlisle presenting John to Edenhall, vacant by the resignation of Eudo, chaplain, in this exchange. 15 March 1369. (iii) Note that the exchange was effected. 20 March 1369.

**182** [Fo.30v; p.199] Letter of the prior and convent of Carlisle presenting Robert de Lowther, chaplain, to Hutton [in the Forest] church. 2 November 1369.[151]

---

[145] See *Reg. Welton*, 100, no.537.
[146] Thus far partly printed in Hist. Man. Comm., *Ninth Report*, I.193. The next three lines are blank.
[147] Printed in *Test. Karl.*, 98.
[148] Cf. **125**.
[149] Possibly instituted after the death of John Mareshall in 1362 (*Reg. Welton*, 90, no.486).
[150] Occurs as vicar in 1357 (*Reg. Welton*, 31, no.174).
[151] See **144** for his institution.

**183**  Will[152] of Robert Bruyne, dated 26 July 1369. Commends soul to God,
Blessed Mary and all saints. Burial in church of Bowness [on Solway], with mortuary as customary and like his ancestors.[153] All funeral expenses, £30. The light
of Blessed Mary in Bowness church and Drumburgh chapel, 13s. 4d. in equal
portions. The friars preachers and minor, Carlisle, 20s. equally divided; the
same to the friars of Appleby and Penrith. Caldew bridge, 10s. Maud Broyn,
40s. John Broyn, senior, 40s. Gilbert Rose, 20s. and a bed. William Petybon, 40s.
Geoffrey Story, 13s. 4d. Richard Rivyn and his wife, 13s. 4d. Adam de Brunskayth,
20s. Thomas Brun, 100s. Walter Dobson, 20s. All his debts to be fully paid. All
his servants to have wages unpaid. Restitution to be made for any unjust
receipts. Executors: William [del Hall], rector of Bowness, John Broyn, William
[Beauchamp], rector of Kirkoswald, Robert [Pay], rector of Thursby, Adam [de
Crosby], rector of Bolton. Sealed before witnesses at Bothel. Residue of goods
and money received for all lands sold to be spent in celebrations of masses and
other works of charity.
   Note of probate, 24 August 1369.

**184**  Letter (in French) of Queen [Philippa]. Her tenants at Langwathby
(*Langewatby*) are grievously oppressed by the bishop's subjects; some at Edenhall
have made a charge such as their ancestors never made from time immemorial.[154] They are also entangled by monitions of his officials (*ordinares*) to
appear before them in distant places, at heavy cost. [Fo.31; p.200] They have
entreated her for remedy, so that they are charged no more than in the time of
her ancestors, their lords, for which she now beseeches the bishop, asking him
to have the cause between them and his subjects brought before him, examine
their grievances and ordain that they enjoy their customary rights. Windsor
castle, 1 February.

**185**  Letter of Edward III under the privy seal (in French). He has written to the
bishop under the great seal about a payment of £700 due to Alice Perrers (*Per-
eres*) by Anthony, lord de Lucy, deceased, which he is asked to execute. Most of
the sum is due to the queen, whose interests the king cherishes.[155] Westminster,
4 March.

**186**  Letter under the privy seal ordering the bishop to be in London on the
morrow of next Trinity[156] to attend the king's council on the next day, together
with other prelates, nobles and great men, on business about the king's estate
and the safety of the realm, as will be shown. Westminster, 6 May [1369].

---

[152] Printed in *Test. Karl.*, 98–9.
[153] Patrons of the church (Nicolson & Burn, II.215).
[154] Langwathby was ancient demesne of the Crown and a chapelry in Edenhall parish,
at this time part of Queen Philippa's dower (Nicolson & Burn, II.447–8; *Reg. Welton*, 18,
no.97; 90, no.486). She died 15 Aug. 1369.
[155] Philippa was granted the wardship of Anthony's lands, 1 Feb. 1369 (*CPR 1367–70*,
210).
[156] Presumably 28 May, a week before the parliament already summoned (**172**).

**187** [Fo.31v; p.201] Mandate to the rectors of Marton and Dufton (*Dofton*) to warn all holding debts and goods of John Taillour of Marton (*Merton*) parish, who died intestate, to restore or reveal them within 15 days to William de Crakanthorp and Sir John Bone, the bishop's receiver, under pain of excommunication. [The rectors] are also to make enquiries and report names to William and John, and to sequestrate all the goods they find. n.d.

**188** Letter missive from [John Buckingham] bishop of Lincoln asking Bishop Thomas to show favour and make an amicable settlement with his subject, Thomas de Salkeld, [Bishop John's] familiar clerk; he has canonical possession of Caldbeck by a papal grace.[157] Liddington, 3 August [1369].

**189** Will[158] of Robert Marsshall of Tallentire dated 9 March 1371. Commends soul to God, Blessed Mary and all saints. Burial in church of St. Bridget [Bridekirk], with best beast with cloth for mortuary; 3s. 4d. for light and 6s. 8d. in oblations; the high altar, for forgotten tithes, a stott; and 40s. for a wake for neighbours on the burial day. The fabric of a belfry at Bridekirk church, 23 marks if the parishioners wish to build a new one. The friars preachers of Carlisle, a skep of barley. The friars minor there, a skep of barley. The friars of Penrith, half a skep of barley. The friars of Appleby, half a skep of barley. The vicar of Bridekirk, 13s. 4d. William son of John de Burgh, 40s. Mariota dau. of Robert Marsshall, 40s. Sir William, chaplain, 3s. 4d. The parish clerk, 12d. John son of John de Burgh, a stott worth 6s. 8d. Robert Hede, 7s. The abbot and convent of Holm [Cultram], 13s. 4d. The prior and convent of Carlisle, 13s. 4d. Robert Hede of Brigham, 5s. William Gryme, 6s. 8d. Enota Bell, 6s. 8d. The prior and convent of Guisborough, £10. Nicholas Saundreson, 26s. 8d. John son of John Marsshall, 20s. Priests celebrating for his soul, £22. Residue to his wife Agnes. Executors: Nicholas Saundreson, Agnes, John de Burgh and Robert Hede. Witnesses: William, chaplain of Bridekirk, John Dogson of Tallentire, and others.
    Note of probate and administration to executors named. Rose, 20 June 1371.

**190** [Fo.33; p.202] Certificate of the official of the bishop of Durham that he has executed the letter of the bishop of Carlisle (dated Rose, 24 April 1368) asking him to publish the excommunication of Thomas de Cokirton before 28 May [as in **123**]. Durham, 23 May 1368.

**191** Certificate of Adam [de Crosseby], rector of Bolton, quoting a mandate to himself and the dean of Allerdale (dated Rose, 4 March 1369). The bishop had dispensed William de Ragenhill, rector of Caldbeck, to be absent provided

---

[157] In 1371 Thomas, described as BCnL, received papal confirmation of his possession under provision to a benefice in the bishop of Carlisle's gift following its resignation by William de Ragenhill (*CPL*, IV.163). Thomas had obviously failed to obtain Crosthwaite vicarage by a papal grace (see **57**) and was still in Bishop Appleby's service in Aug. 1368 (**149**). For William's resignation of Caldbeck, 17 July 1369, see **195**.

[158] Printed in *Test. Karl.*, 99–100.

that he supported the duties of the church, which he has failed to do: many buildings of the manse, close, park and others in the rectory are reported to be threatened with ruin. The bishop has a special affection for the church, with good cause, and wishes to save the buildings and chancel from ruin; he orders an early enquiry by trustworthy and informed men into defects in the chancel, buildings, water mill and closes of the park and manse, and a report estimating costs for their repair and the names of jurors.

[Adam] went to Caldbeck on 17 March and enquired with John de Whynfell, Michael de Sourby, Richard del Bek' and Thomas de Wildyng', parishioners. There are notorious defects which cannot be repaired for less than the following sums: chancel, 53s. 4d.; hall, 40s.; principal chamber, 13s. 4d.; [Fo.33v; p.203] chamber for guests, £10; kitchen, 20s.; the old granary, ruined to its foundations, £10; kiln (*thorale*), 20s.; long grange, 20s.; big grange, £10; cow house, 6s. 8d.; wood house (*domus boscaris*), 13s. 4d.; guests' stable, 6s. 8d.; new granary, 6d.; dovecot, ruined to foundations, £10; gates of manse, 20s.; its close, 20s.; close of park, 40s. Under the dean's seal, with his consent. Aspatria, 21 March [1369].

**192**  [Incomplete] mandate for processions and prayers to turn aside God's wrath: there have been two pestilences in recent times, and now a third in various parts of the kingdom, causing many deaths; also drought and floods destroying crops.[159]

**193**  Notarial instrument dated 2 August 1367, in the chapel, Rose. M. John de Appelby, presented by letters patent of his brother, Bishop Thomas, to Horncastle church (said to be vacant), appointed Hugh de Bolton and John de Fuysedale his proctors to sue the bishop of Lincoln [as in **161**]. Witnesses: John de Appelby, Thomas de Stirkland, clerks, and Roger Baker.

[Fo.34; p.204] Subscription by William de Stirkeland, clerk (dioc. York), notary.

**194**  Letters patent of Edward III presenting his clerk, John Miles, to Skelton church, now vacant and in his gift because he has custody of the lands and heir of Richard Kirkebrid. Westminster, 5 November 1367.[160]

**195**  Notarial instrument dated 17 July 1369 in the cloister of the friars preachers, London. M. William de Ragenhill, claiming to be rector of Caldbeck, resigned the church to Bishop Thomas in order to have possession of the church of North Collingham (dioc. York).[161] Witnesses: Walter Power, canon of

---

[159] A different mandate in the same connection, with an indulgence, was issued by the archbishop of Canterbury, 23 July 1368 (*Reg. Langham*, 197–8).

[160] As in *CPR 1367–70*, 26. On 22 June 1368, however, the king ratified Adam Armstrong as rector of Skelton (ibid., 286); he last occurs as rector of Bewcastle, 1362, when John Parvyng was rector of Skelton (*Reg. Welton*, 77, no.426; 88, no.480).

[161] The king had presented him to North Collingham, 30 May 1366, but ratified Thomas de Clopton as rector there, 4 Feb. 1367. On 15 July 1369, however, he ratified William as its rector (*CPR 1364–7*, 247, 373; *CPR 1367–70*, 288). See also **188**.

Lincoln, Nicholas de Spayn, rector of Althorpe, Matthew de Bolton, vicar of
St. Nicholas', Newcastle upon Tyne, and Robert de Ragenhill, clerk, of the dioceses of Lincoln, Durham and York.

Subscription by Hugh son of John de Bolton, clerk (dioc. Carlisle), notary.

**196** Mandate to the official forwarding a mandate of John [Thoresby], archbishop of York, received on 30 December, which is to be obeyed fully and
returned with the [official's] certificate, [Fo.34v; p.205] which the bishop will
send to the archbishop. Rose, 6 January 1370.

**197** Mandate of the archbishop quoting the king's writ (dated Westminster,
11 October 1369). For the defence of the realm and other matters explained to
[the archbishop's] proctors, prelates and others in the last parliament, the king
needs a subsidy from the clergy as the king sought there; with order to call suffragans, deans and priors of cathedrals, abbots, priors, archdeacons, chapters,
convents, colleges and diocesan clergy to St. Peter's, York, or elsewhere, as soon
as possible, explaining the need and obtaining a subsidy.[162]

The bishop is therefore cited and by him the prior and chapter of Carlisle,
abbots, priors and archdeacons in person, convents, chapters and colleges by
single proctors, and diocesan clergy by two proctors, sufficiently informed and
empowered, to appear before the archbishop or his commissaries in St. Peter's,
York, on 4 February 1370, to give counsel and ordain further. Bishopthorpe,
10 December 1369.

**198** Letter missive (*excusatoria*) to the archbishop.[163] The bishop is unavoid-
ably (*inevitabiliter*) detained on difficult business of the march and his church
so that he cannot personally attend the provincial convocation [*sic*] of clergy
on 4 February and sends [William del Hall, rector of] Bowness, official of
Carlisle, as his proctor. n.d.

**199** [Fo.35; p.206] Institution of John Lukesson, chaplain, to the vicarage of
Burgh by Sands, vacant by the death of Eudo de Ravinstanedale; presented by
the abbot and convent of Holm Cultram. Rose, 4 November 1369.

**200** Letter of the bishop and Lambert [Morland],[164] abbot of Shap, to John,
archbishop of York, presenting Robert de Aynderby, priest, to Maltby church;
in their gift by grant of the noble lord, Roger de Clyfford. n.d.[165]

**201** Licence to Hugh de Jarum to seek alms for the hospital of Saint-Antoine-
de-Viennois; valid for one year. Rose, 22 December 1368.

---

[162] As in *CCR 1369–74*, 111; *Foedera*, II(1).880.
[163] Compressed into the bottom margin, with interlineations not entirely legible.
[164] *Reg. Welton*, 101, no.544, n.; **259** below.
[165] The institution to Maltby is recorded in Archbishop Thoresby's register and took
place on 30 Nov. 1369 (York, Borthwick Institute, Reg. 11, fo.156v).

**202**   Similar licence to Hugh de Jarum as proctor for the fabric of Carlisle cathedral, a cause which should be preferred to all others, with indulgence [Fo.35v; p.207] for 40 days; valid for one year. Rose, 22 December 1368.

**203**   Letters dimissory of John, archbishop of York, to Ralph son of Adam Bland of Lonsdale, clerk with first tonsure, for his ordination to all orders. Bishopthorpe, 16 September 1367.

**204**   Letter to the bishop of the abbot and convent of Coverham, Premonstratensian order (dioc. York), presenting Ralph son of Adam de Bland of Sedbergh (*Sadebergh in Lonesdale*), their clerk, for ordination on their title. 19 December 1369.

**205**   Certificate of the official of Carlisle quoting the bishop's mandate (dated Rose, 28 January 1370) to enquire into the presentation by the provost and scholars of Queen's College, Oxford, to Brough vicarage of John de Merton, chaplain. Thomas [de Anand], rector of Asby, John [Donkyn], rector of Marton,[166] Thomas [de Derby], rector of Brougham, John [Pray], vicar of Morland, Nicholas [de Preston], vicar of Warcop, and William [Colyn?], vicar of St. Lawrence's, Appleby,[167] said that the vicarage of Brough (*Burgh subtus Staynesmore*) was vacated 8 days ago by the resignation of John de Appelby in an exchange.[168] Queen's College is patron and last presented; there is no dispute or portion, but [Fo.36; p.208] there is an annual pension of 20s. to the bishop of Carlisle; the vicarage is worth 10 marks p.a. The presentee is free, legitimate, of lawful age and a priest; there is no canonical obstacle. Under their seals, Appleby, 1 February [1370].

**206**   Letter of the provost and scholars of Queen's College presenting John de Merton, vicar of St. Michael's, Appleby, to Brough vicarage, in an exchange with John Raynald. Oxford, 12 January 1370.

**207**   Writ of Edward III to William de Fyncheden and Roger de Fulthorp, justices of gaol delivery in Cumberland. Royal charters granted to bishops of Carlisle that no sheriff or other royal minister should enter their lands except to make attachments for pleas of the Crown.[169] The king has learnt that the sheriff has made inquests outside these lands into felonies committed in them, and indictments before coroners, and arrested and imprisoned [those

---

[166] Occurs 1369 and 1373 (Nicolson & Burn, I.360; *CPR 1367–70*, 206; *CPR 1370–4*, 288); presumably successor of Robert de Wolseley, who died 1367 (**114**).

[167] Occurs 1359 (*Reg. Welton*, 50, no.268).

[168] Cf. **206**, naming him John Raynald; but occurs as John de Appelby, 1369 (*CPR 1367–70*, 206). He could have been the John son of Simon, son of Reginald, ordained acolyte, 1332, and in further orders as John son of Simon de Appelby, with a title from Asby (*Reg. Kirkby*, I.15, 24, 39, 45). There is no record of his or other institutions to Brough.

[169] Apparently quoting a charter of Henry III to Bishop Walter Mauclerk, 1231 (Nicolson & Burn, II.545).

accused] so that the bishop and his bailiffs have lost his jurisdiction over these prisoners. Order to inspect the bishop's charters and allow him to enjoy his liberties without hindrance, as his predecessors have done. Westminster, 13 June 43 Edward III [1369].

**208** Commission to Peter de Morland, vicar of Kirkby Stephen (*Kyrke-bystephane*), to confer the vicarage of St. Michael's, Appleby, on John Raynald, priest, vacant by the death of Richard de Aslacby and in the bishop's collation; [Fo.36v; p.209] and to induct him. Rose, 12 December 1369.

**209** Writ of Edward III to the sheriff of Cumberland ordering him to allow the bishop of Carlisle to enjoy the various liberties granted by previous kings, without hindrance, as his predecessors have done. Westminster, 13 June 1369.

**210** Letter of Edward III under the privy seal (in French) asking that the bishop and his clergy will pay the triennial tenth they have granted for the defence of the realm (in equal portions on 2 February and 24 June in the three years following last Michaelmas), according to the grant of three tenths in the last parliament. The bishop is to appoint collectors, reporting their names to Chancery. Westminster, 26 October [1369].
[Margin] Note that 'nothing was raised by virtue of this writ'.[170]

**211** Writ of Edward III to the sheriff of Cumberland [almost identical to **207** save that Bishop Thomas was said to have informed the king that the present sheriff (*tu*) was violating his liberties, and omitting the order to examine his charters]. Westminster, 23 June 1369.

**212** [Fo.37; p.210] Writ to William de Fynchedene and Roger de Fulthorpp', justices of gaol delivery [as in **207**; date as in **211**?].

**213** Letter under the privy seal (in French). The king had recently appointed the bishop and other lords of Cumberland, by letters patent under the great seal, to guard the West March and exercise certain powers. He has, however, told the king that he cannot perform these duties in full without prejudice to his conscience and episcopal status. [The king] discharges him from these duties but asks that he fully assists the defence of the march against enemies and malefactors, for the comfort of the king's subjects. Westminster, 6 November.[171]

---

[170] Written in same hand as other marginal titles. The parliament mentioned was presumably that of June 1369, when the king reassumed the title of king of France and sought financial support, including a substantial clerical contribution (see *Rot. Parl.* II, 300). It is curious, however, that a fortnight earlier than this privy seal letter (unless it is misdated here), the king had ordered both archbishops to convoke their provincial clergy to grant him subsidies (**197** and note). These were held in Jan. and Feb. 1370 and granted triennial tenths payable at the dates quoted in the privy seal letter (*HBC*, 596; *CFR*, VIII.72–3).

[171] After 5 months as a warden in 1366 (**72**), the bishop was reappointed in commissions dated 11 Feb. 1367 and 16 Oct. 1369 (**223**, **235**). The appointment in 1369 would

**214**  Letter under the privy seal. [The king] has just received news from
Lombardy (*Lumbardie*) of the death of his son Lionel, duke of Clarence.[172] He
asks for prayers and masses to be celebrated for the souls of the king and his
said son in Carlisle [cathedral] and collegiate and conventual churches on
a day appointed by [the bishop] soon before 2 February, making necessary
orders to the prior and convent [of Carlisle], abbots and priors and their
convents, and deans and chapters of collegiate churches.[173] Westminster,
10 December [1368].

**215**  [Fo.37v; p.211] Will[174] of John de Burdon, master of Carlisle schools,[175]
being healthy in mind and memory, dated in the schoolhouse, 17 March 1371.
Commends soul to God and burial as He disposes. For the poor on his burial
day, 13s. 4d. A priest celebrating for his soul for a year, that of Christine his late
wife, and all those living and dead whose goods he has justly or unjustly kept, £5,
6 silver spoons and a mazer bowl. Appleby bridge, 40d. The four orders of friars,
40d. equally divided. John Wryghson, his kinsman, 40s. The children of Ralph
Neux, 40s. Buysefell, 40s. and all his books. Alice wife of Stephen Lange, 6s. 8d.
and a fur tunic with a hood. Mariota wife of John del Bakhous, a coffer in her
keeping with all the jewels in it. Residue, John del Bakhous. Executors: Thomas
del Slegill, canon [of Carlisle?][176], John de Bakhous and John de Buysfell.
   Note of probate, with administration to John del Bakhous and John de Buysfell; reserved [for Thomas]. Rose, 21 June 1371.

**216**  Note of licence to John de Midelton to hold the grammar schools in
Carlisle for his pleasure. Rose, 16 May 1371.

**217**  Commission to the prior of Carlisle and M. John de Appelby, archdeacon
of Carlisle, to act as the bishop's vicars-general whenever he is absent [as in **1**].
Rose, 18 September 1371.

**218**  Mandate to the dean of Cumberland and all rectors and vicars of the
deanery or their lieutenants. Man's ancient enemy ceaselessly strives to lead
simple and unwary people from the path of truth. In Penrith, people have
given money or promises to John del Rose, who claims to be a priest,[177] in order
to recover stolen goods by magic or consulting demons. [Fo.38; p.212] Order

---

seem to be referred to in the privy seal letter of 6 Nov. [only]. The commission of 1367,
however, was later recorded in the register (**223**), and the letter refers to 'other lords' as
being appointed then, whereas only one lord (Clifford) and 11 others were appointed in
1369.
   [172]  On 17 Oct. 1368.
   [173]  There were no such colleges in Carlisle diocese: no doubt identical letters were sent
to the archbishops and other bishops.
   [174]  Printed in *Test. Karl.*, 101.
   [175]  Supplied from margin. He was licensed 1362 (*Reg. Welton*, 95, no.513).
   [176]  Ordained priest 1363 (**338**), but missing from the list in 1366 (**106**).
   [177]  Probably John Rose of Dalston, ordained deacon and priest, 1354 (*Reg. Welton*,
112–13).

to prohibit all parishioners from resorting to John or his like for this purpose, under pain of excommunication. As he feigned to know how to recover stolen goods, he was cited to answer before the bishop *ex officio*, and excommunicated for not appearing. This sentence is to be published, with a further citation to the chapel of Rose manor, and the bishop certified before Christmas. Absolution of those culpable or giving credence to these wicked incantations is reserved to the bishop or his penitentiary. Rose, 1 December 1371.

**219** Mandate to all rectors, vicars and parish priests. The master[178] and brothers of the hospital of St. Nicholas by Carlisle have complained that many unknown subjects withhold rents, incomes and goods. All concerned are to be ordered to make restitution within ten days, particularly of corn commonly called 'thraves of St. Nicholas' due to the hospital by grants of kings in olden times, under pain of excommunication. Rose, 1 December 1371.

**220** Mandate to the dean of Cumberland. Ugly (*implacidus*) rumour has told the bishop that some sons [of iniquity] have attacked John Alaynesone, the bishop's apparitor in the deanery; as is well known, he was appointed to carry out orders by the bishop and his ministers relating to matters in the church court. They have threatened that if he exercised his office against them and their accomplices, [Fo.38v; p.213] they would do him atrocious harm, thus impeding the bishop's jurisdiction. They have consequently incurred excommunication, as is to be announced with bells and candles on Sundays and feast-days until they have made reparation and earned absolution. n.d.

**221** Writ *de supersedendo* to the bishop and diocesan collectors of the subsidy granted to the king by the clergy of York province at the petition of the prior and hospital of St. John of Jerusalem in England: in the past, they have paid subsidies with laymen, but the bishop is requiring them, by ecclesiastical censures, to pay the last clerical subsidy. Order to stay this demand, except in respect of their ecclesiastical benefices. Westminster, 3 February 1372.[179]

**222** Writ under the privy seal (in French). The king has planned (*tailliez*) to be with his army at Portsmouth on 1 May next for his passage overseas to recover his rights there and defend England. The bishop is therefore asked, on his fealty, to collect in his diocese the subsidy of £50,000 granted by the clergy of England, due at last Michaelmas and 2 February last;[180] [the money] is to be

---

[178] The king granted custody of the hospital to M. John Appleby, 1368 (*CPR 1367–70*, 115); see also W.G. Wiseman, 'The hospital of St. Nicholas, Carlisle; part 2', *CWAAS*, 2nd. ser. 96 (1996), 58–9.

[179] Similar to writ to all archbishops and bishops dated 8 Sept. 1371 (*CCR 1369–74*, 251–2).

[180] The king acknowledged that this grant had been made in orders for its collection dated 5 May 1371 (*CFR*, VIII.118). The convocation of Canterbury had met 24 Apr. to 3 May, but York's followed on 8 May (*HBC*, 596; and see below, **259**). The parliament of 24 Feb. 1371 also granted £50,000 (*CFR*, VIII.110).

brought to the treasurer in London so that it is delivered at the Exchequer of receipt by 7 March in order to repay nobles and magnates regards and wages for them and their men-at-arms and archers in the king's expedition, as has been ordained by the king and council. Westminster, 11 February [1372].

[Postscript] If the bishop is responsible for any delay in payment, the king will take measures through his temporalities according to law.[181]

**223**  [Fo.39; p.214] Letters patent of Edward III appointing Bishop Thomas, Roger de Clifford, Anthony de Lucy and William de Wyndesore wardens of the West March. Hopes for a peace-treaty with his Scottish enemies have been dashed by their envoys' latest reply. To provide for his kingdom's defence against their malice [continuing as in **72**[182]]. Westminster, 11 February 1367.[183]

**224**  Mandate to the dean of Cumberland. The bishop recently ordered all religious and other ecclesiastical persons to arm and array themselves before 8 September, as instructed by the king.[184] The bishop wishes to be assured these orders have been obeyed. The dean is therefore [Fo.39v; p.215] to order all these monks and parsons of his deanery, including chaplains, to appear before the bishop or his commissaries at Addingham on 5 October to show that they are duly armed and arrayed, warning that he will proceed against any default-ers and report their names to the king.[185] The dean is to certify, naming all those arrayed in the deanery and the values of their possessions and resources (*facultates*). Rose, 21 September 1369.

**225**  Mandate to the vicar of St. Lawrence's, Appleby. Richard de Aslakby, vicar of St. Michael's, Appleby, has complained that unknown wrongdoers broke into the close of his manse, attacked his servants and wounded his animals; they are to be ordered to make compensation within 15 days, under pain of excommunication. Rose, 30 November 1365.

**226**  Letter under the privy seal (in French) ordering the bishop to appoint collectors of the triennial tenth granted by prelates and clergy in convocation

---

[181]  Followed by 7 dots marking lines left blank; this is the last folio of a quire.

[182]  With these changes from the summary in *Reg. Welton*, p.75: omission of opening words to 'in France'; insertion after 'Westmorland' of 'and in the king's lordship in Scot-land'; insertion after 'Scottish enemies' of 'They are to hear complaints of injuries con-trary to truces and do justice promptly'; replacement of 'until the king shall order' with 'and punish them according to their faults'; correct 'punish' with 'punishment of'; replacement of sentence 'When dangers threaten . . . England invaded.' with 'They are to array all fencible men of the [two] counties aged between 16 and 60, and all men-at-arms, hobelars and archers, organising them in companies so that they are ready to oppose invasions.'; and replacement of 'rebels . . . ordered.' with 'They are to certify Chancery of the number of men-at-arms, hobelars and archers thus arrayed.' Described in the margin as LITTERA DOMINI REGIS AD PREMUNIENDUM OMNES HOMINES ARRAJANDOS.

[183]  Printed in *Rot. Scot.*, I.910.

[184]  See **230**.

[185]  Printed thus far in Hist. Man. Comm., *Ninth Report*, I. 193(ii).

in St. Peter's, York, for the defence of the realm and the king's expedition; certifying the treasurer and barons of the Exchequer by 16 June. Westminster, 20 April 44 Edward III [1370].

**227** Mandate to the dean of Cumberland. Penrith church has been polluted by bloodshed in the churchyard by John Tynkeler of Penrith. He was required to have it reconciled and promised to do so, by paying the bishop's procurations and fees of his clerks and ministers, as is customary. He has refused to pay the fees and is to be admonished to do so within ten days [Fo.40; p.216] under pain of excommunication. Rose, 26 July 1369.

**228** Exchequer writ asking the bishop to inform the treasurer and barons (by 22 April) how many secular aliens have benefices in the diocese, their values, counties and archdeaconries, and the names of these clergy. Tested by T[homas] de Brantingham, treasurer, at Westminster, 18 January 43 Edward III [1370].

**229** Note of licence to Robert Jardyne, junior, to seek alms for the fabric of St. John's, Beverley; valid for one year. Rose, 28 February 1370.

**230** Writ of Edward III.[186] It was agreed in the last parliament that all men in the kingdom, clerks as well as laymen, should be armed according to their rank and means and arrayed in readiness to defend the church and realm against invaders. Commissioners have been appointed in counties to array all fencible men aged between 16 and 60, and organise them in thousands, hundreds and twenties. The French, in breach of the peace made at Calais, have invaded the king's lands overseas and gathered a huge fleet to invade his realm. [Fo.40v; p.217] Order to array abbots, priors, religious and other ecclesiastical persons of the diocese of the same ages, organised as above for the same purpose. Westminster, 6 July 1369.

**231** Letter of Edward III under the privy seal (in French), thanking the bishop for his support in matters concerning the king's estate and the defence of the realm, and asking him to arrange prayers of clergy and people in the cathedral and other churches, with processions every Friday thanking God for his past favours and humbly praying for his estate, the safety of the church and realm and success on land and sea. Westminster, 12 July [1369?].

**232** Letter of Edward III under the privy seal (in French). The bishop knows how much the king has done for the defence of the realm, and particularly about a *viage* he is about to make in person with an army to restrain the malice of his enemies. For this, however, the profits and revenues of the kingdom are insufficient. He therefore pleads for the aid of his subjects with as much money as they can, to be delivered to his clerk, Thomas de Brantyngham, his treasurer,[187] at

---

[186] Printed in *Foedera*, III(2).876; partly in Hist. Man. Comm., *Ninth Report*, I. 193–4; *CCR 1369–74*, 38–9.

Westminster before 8 April. They may be assured of repayment from a tenth granted by the clergy,[188] or customs and subsidies, or other profits, at their choice. These letters will be brought by the king's clerk, John de Stokes, and his esquire, William de Risceby, who will report to the king. Westminster, 20 February [1370].

**233** Letter of Edward III under the privy seal (in French), asking the bishop to grant William Restwold a licence for his chaplain to sing divine service in his oratory in Highhead (*Hehed*) castle or in the chapel in its park, for a suitable term set by the bishop.[189] 14 November [1369?].

**234** [Fo.41; p.218] Letter of Edward III under the privy seal (in French). He plans to be in the port of *Orewell*[190] on 1 May and sail with his army to defend the kingdom of England. The bishop is ordered to stay with his household (*houstel*) in his lands in *nostre Westmarche descoce* and do what he considers best for its security, with diligent care; enforcing the commission to him and others under the great seal while the king is engaged on his campaign so that there should be no enemy invasion of the march. Westminster, 16 March [1370].

**235** Letters patent of Edward III appointing the bishop, Roger de Clifford, Thomas de Musgrave, Alan de Heton, Adam Hoghton, John atte Wode, William de Fyncheden, Adam Parvyng, Roger de Fulthorp, John de Thirlewall, senior, Thomas de Blenkansop, Richard de Vaux and John Brun wardens of the West March towards Scotland. Westminster, 16 October 1369.[191]

**236** [Fo.41v; p.219] Letter of Edward III under the privy seal (in French) [to the wardens of the West March]. His brother [the king] of Scotland has sent his clerk, John Lyonn, with letters mentioning, *inter alia*, that he had done his best to repair breaches of truces in the marches by both sides;[192] days had been appointed for the wardens of his marches and their deputies to meet [Edward's] wardens and deputies, who had failed to come. Lately a day had been held on the East March between Henry, Lord Percy, and Archibald de Douglas of Scotland, kt., when they had agreed on some points about these misprisions which are contained in an indenture made there. [Edward] would be displeased if the default was on his side, as [David's] letters suppose. In remedy he has made a commission under the great seal [to the recipients][193]

---

[187] Appointed 27 June 1369; he would have been shown as bishop (of Exeter) from May 1370 (*HBC*, 105).

[188] In Jan. and Feb. 1370 (ibid., 596; *CFR*, VIII.72, 73).

[189] Licence to Lengleys, 1359 (*Reg. Welton*, 46).

[190] Harwich?

[191] Printed in *Rot. Scot.*, I.935. Terms as in **223** but omitting the opening sentence about a peace-treaty, substituting *homines de Scocia* for *dictos adversarios nostros*, and adding (repetitively) that at least 5 of the wardens will collectively exercise these powers.

[192] Thus far printed in Hist. Man. Comm., *Ninth Report*, I. 194(ii).

[193] See **235** and *Rot. Scot.*, I.935 for the East March. The only novel feature of the two commissions issued a week before this letter was the unusually large number of

to defend the West March in Cumberland and Westmorland and the truces made with his brother;[194] they are to redress violations of the truces by [English] subjects and ensure that other points in the commission and the schedule sent with it are fully executed, in accordance with the said indenture, in Percy's absence, so that no default can be found on [Edward's] part. Westminster, 23 October [1369].

**237** CONCORDIA CONCERNENS MARCHAM. Indenture (in French) dated at Gretna in Annandale (*Gretenowe en Ananderdale*), 9 August 1369, between Lord de Percy and Sir Archibald de Douglas. They agreed redresses should be made for [violations of truces] in the West March by both sides since 2 February 1367[195] until the present day. The said lords shall appoint deputies to meet at Gretna on Monday [13 August] and other appointed days to make full redress of all trespasses and damages done in the march in that time, except for the damages done in Annandale (*la vaal danande*) on Friday after St. Peter's Chains [7 August], 1368, which the lords will redress on Tuesday, 5 September next at *More Honslawe* in the East March, if they can agree with their counsel how to bring this matter to a close. All prisoners, goods and chattels, and ransoms of prisoners levied and damaged on the same Friday on both sides in Annandale are to be put to pledges and repaid on surety in the 18th day after making these [letters] to remain until an end be made on the East March of the said trespasses. So that these conditions should be faithfully kept the said parties have put their seals to these interchangeable indentures on the said day and place.

**238** Letter under the privy seal (in French), ordering the bishop to attend his great council at Westminster on 10 January 1370 [Fo.42; p.220] without fail, to treat with other prelates, nobles, lords and other magnates, and give his advice. Westminster, 5 December [1369].
[Postscript] asking the bishop, with suitable array, to attend the interment of the queen in Westminster conventual church, from Windsor on 23 January and the six days following.

**239** Informal letter [of the archbishop of York[196]] reminding the bishop the official of Carlisle had made a definitive sentence against John Warthwyk', kt.,

---

wardens, and this must have been intended to meet King David's complaint: 13 were appointed for each march, including 3 appointed in both marches of whom 2 were professional justices of gaol delivery (Fyncheden, a justice of Common Pleas, and Fulthorp: see **207**), while the third, John atte Wode, may have been the recipient of 40 marks p.a. at the Exchequer (*CPR 1370–4*, 375). The sheriffs of Northumberland and Cumberland (Parving) were also appointed. Others - beside both bishops and local magnates - were knights and gentry of the kind often appointed to *ad hoc* commissions for local duties.

[194] The most recent, for 14 years, in June 1369 (*Rot. Scot.*, I.933–4; *Foedera*, III(2). 873).
[195] For the previous truce, see n. 58.
[196] In margin.

in a suit about tithes of pasture by the abbot and convent of St. Mary's, York, and their fellow-monk, William de Tanfeld;[197] following devolution to the court of York, he was excommunicated by the official of York for his disobedience. As the bishop was informed by his official, this sentence was published in the diocese. As he persisted in his contempt of the Church, the official [of York] cited him to appear and show cause why the secular arm should not be invoked, when he proposed nothing effectual. The archbishop therefore, on his official's certificate, wrote to the king to invoke the aid of the secular arm, as may be seen in his letters patent brought by the bearer of this letter; lest his insolence should be an example, the bishop is asked to send his letters patent to the king. Bishopthorpe, 24 October [1369?].

**240** Exchequer writ *venire faciatis sicut pluries* [to Bishop Thomas]. Further order to cause John Longe, chaplain, executor of William de Bergham of Bridgnorth (*Burgenorth*), [the bishop's] clerk, to come before the treasurer and barons on 30 September to answer for William's debt of £35 2s. 3½d. for the price of 2½ sacks, 11 stones, 4lbs. of wool he exported uncustomed in 11 Edward III [1337–8].[198] Tested by T[homas] de Lodelowe, Westminster, 21 February 1370 (as in the Memoranda rolls of 37 Edward III [1363–4], Hilary *recorda*, and 44 Edward III [1370–1], Michaelmas *brevia retornata*).

**241** Certificate of John [Buckingham], bishop of Lincoln, [Fo.42v; p.221] that he has executed the bishop of Carlisle's commission [quoted; dated Bewley, 11 May 1370] for an exchange of benefices between William de Pullawe, rector of Melmerby, and John Pety, rector of Moorby (dioc. Lincoln, in Carlisle's gift), enclosing the certificate of an inquest by the official of Carlisle, which is returned. Liddington, 24 May 1370.

**242** Letters patent of William del Orchard, rector of Dacre, testifying his appointment of Thomas de Ingelby, priest, as his proctor to resign the church to Bishop Thomas; as few know his seal, he has had these letters made under the sign and subscription of M. John de Hakthorp, notary, in Durham cathedral, 19 May 1370; witnessed by M. William de Farnham, official of the bishop of Durham, John de Skendelby, chaplain, and Richard de Doncastre, clerk, of York and Lincoln dioceses.
 [Fo.43; p.222] Subscription by John de Hakthorp, clerk (dioc. Carlisle), notary.

**243** Notarial instrument testifying that on 11 May 1370, in the third hour, in the Galilee [chapel], Durham [cathedral], William de Orchard, rector of Whitburn (*Qwhitbern*, dioc. Durham), appointed Thomas de Ingylby and Thomas de Thorgramby,[199] priests of Durham and Lincoln dioceses, as his

---

[197] Prior of Wetheral (**46**).

[198] The first writ of summons for this debt, dated 12 Dec. 1364, was addressed to the bishop of Lincoln, as was a second *sicut pluries* dated 12 July 1371 (*Royal Writs addressed to John Buckingham, Bishop of Lincoln*, ed. A.K. McHardy, CYS, 1997, nos.25, 139).

[199] Parish chaplain of Dacre, 1369 (**157**).

proctors to resign the church to the ordinary in an exchange of benefices with M. Peter de Stapilton, rector of Dacre, and to receive Dacre church and its revenues. Witnesses: Richard de Whitton, rector of Kirknewton, and William Welefeld, clerk (dioc. Durham).

Subscription by Richard Damysel, priest (dioc. York), notary.

**244** Letters of Ranulph de Dakre, lord of Gilsland, presenting William de Orchard, rector of Whitburn, to Dacre church, in [the above] exchange with Peter de Stapilton. Halton, 18 May 1370.

**245** [Fo.43v; p.222 *bis*] Commission of Thomas [Hatfield], bishop of Durham, for the above exchange. Auckland, 20 April 1370.

**246** Letters of Ranulph de Dakre, lord of Dacre, presenting John Ingelby, priest (dioc. Durham), to Dacre church, vacant by the resignation of William de Orchard. In his manor of Eccleston (*Heclyston in Laylandechyr'*), 22 May 1370.

**247** Statement (in first person) by Thomas de Ingylby, chaplain, as proctor of William de Orchard, resigning Dacre church to Bishop Appleby, in the chapel in Bewley manor, 21 May 1370. Witnesses: Thomas de Stirkland, clerk, and Simon de Franc', layman (*layico*), of the dioceses of Carlisle and Paris (*Parisien'*).

**248** Certificate of the dean of Cumberland quoting the bishop's mandate (received and dated, at Bewley, 22 May) to enquire into the presentation by Ranulph de Dakre, lord of Gilsland, of John de Ingelby, chaplain, to Dacre church. John Waterward, rector of Ousby, John, vicar of Penrith, John [de Castro Bernardi], vicar of Lazonby, Thomas, vicar of Addingham,[200] Thomas, vicar of Edenhall,[201] and John de Dokwra, Thomas de Thorgramby, Thomas de Penereth and Thomas de Barton, chaplains, [Fo.44; p.222 *ter*] said that Ranulph de Dakre was patron and last presented. The church was vacant from Tuesday after St. Dunstan's [21 May]; there is no pension or portion. The presentee is fit to hold a benefice. Under their seals, Penrith church, 22 May 1370.

**249** Privy seal letter (in French) to the bishop of Carlisle (*Kardoill*), Roger *sire* de Clifford and Adam Parvyng.[202] The king requires a great sum of money by 3 July to meet his costs in defending the Church and his kingdom and making war abroad to regain his rights, for which his revenues are insufficient. To spare the poor commons, it has therefore been ordained, with the advice of his council, that the king should hastily have loans from churchmen and wealthy laymen. [The bishop and others] are asked to call before them some of the wisest men of

---

[200] Walter Helton was vicar in (?) 1368, but died as rector of Moorby, 1369 (**125, 180**). His successor at Addingham is not known.

[201] John de Kerby was instituted 1369; the next known vicar was Thomas de Hayton, 1380 (**181**; *Test. Karl.*, 147).

[202] Sheriff of Cumberland (*CFR*, VIII.36). The letter is summarised in Hist. Man. Comm., *Ninth Report*, I.194(a).

Cumberland and Westmorland, who will know about the means (*lestate*) of everyone in these counties and help to choose the six richest churchmen in each county and six wealthiest laymen, with whom they are to treat for the king for loans totalling 1,200 marks, that is for an average of 50 marks from each one at their discretion, to be delivered at Westminster by 28 June. They are to report in the office of the privy seal within ten days, with the names of lenders; each will be sent a tally of assignment or letters patent under the great seal for repayment at a convenient day. Westminster, 17 June 44 Edward III [1370].

**250** [Fo.44v; p.223] Privy seal letter[203] (in French) asking that they levy all the money which they had been asked to borrow in the king's letters patent under the privy seal in Westmorland, appointing a clerk to collect it from the church-men and a layman from the laymen, to be brought to the [Exchequer of] Receipt at Westminster by 26 July at the latest. The collectors and their companions are to be given sufficient security; the king has written to the sheriff to arrange their safe conduct to Westminster. Westminster, 9 July 44 Edward III [1370].
Privy seal letter [in identical words, with 'Cumberland' replacing 'Westmorland']. Westminster, 9 July [1370].

**251** Letter (in French) of the treasurer[204] to the bishop and [unnamed] lords. The king has been informed that the king of Navarre intends to come to England to perform the treaty with King [Edward], who is most willing to meet his prom-ises but cannot do this soon unless the bishop diligently carries out the business about which he has written [to the bishop] and all the others charged with it; ordering that the moneys should be levied as agreed and sent to London in all haste, and that [the treasurer] should stay there until the whole sum has been paid by every county and reports [Fo.45; p.224] on the performance of all the per-sons concerned. [The bishop] and lords are to consider what pleasure they will give the king and the dishonour he would incur if he failed to keep his covenants with the king of Navarre, asking them to certify [the treasurer] who hopes to give the king good news about them. London, 16 July [1370].

**252** Privy seal letter (in French).[205] In previous letters, explaining his neces-sity, the king had charged them to borrow 12,000 marks from churchmen and laymen in Cumberland and Westmorland. He is displeased not to have received this loan: most other prelates and faithful subjects have done their duty, as was ordained with the consent of prelates, lords and great men of his council to make a payment to King [Charles] of Navarre according to a treaty between councillors [of both kings]. [Charles] has now come to [Edward] for this cause.[206] It would greatly dishonour and harm the king and his realm to

[203] Addressed to *Treschiers et bien amez foialx*: the same as **249**?
[204] From margin: *Littera domini Thesaurarii*, i. e. Thomas Brantingham (see **232**).
[205] Addressed as in **250**.
[206] Charles was with Edward at Clarendon in August 1370; a safe-conduct for his return to France was dated there on the 12th (*Foedera*, II(2).899–900; see also P.E. Russell, *The English Intervention in Spain and Portugal*, Oxford 1955, 209, 218, 443).

prejudice the treaty for want of this sum of 12,000 marks from the churchmen and wealthy laymen of the two counties. [The bishop] is charged to treat with those he knows to be able to aid the king, so that the sum is delivered to the Receipt at Westminster on 17 August, appointing two collectors; without fail or any excuse. Clarendon, 1 August [1370].

**253** [Fo.45v; p.225] Privy seal letter (in French).[207] They have written to the privy seal office about [the above] loan. The king understands that some people of the two counties rich enough, who ought to aid him, have lent nothing but made feeble excuses without any heed for his great necessity; he marvels, because the cause is not personal to himself but concerns the whole realm, the welfare of churchmen as well as laymen, and to be raised throughout the realm with the approval of the king's council. He will not accept excuses from anyone. The bishop is charged to arrange loans of 100s. by anyone found able by good testimony, to be paid to the Receipt at Westminster on 19 August. Clarendon, 8 August [1370].

**254** Privy seal letter (in French).[208] [Charles] of France and Henry *soi-disant* king of Spain are preparing to attack England, its navy and people; while the king's sons, nobles, knights, squires and others, are abroad, and others in transit, in defence of the realm and recovery of the king's right. The bishop is asked to arrange that all churchmen of the diocese should say a special collect in their masses for the Church, king, his realm, sons and others, and to pray for their safety and peace, with processions and special masses sung every Wednesday and Friday in the cathedral, conventual and parish churches. Clarendon, 10 August [1370].

**255** Privy seal letter (in French).[209] The king has often written to them about secured loans by certain churchmen and laymen in Westmorland and Cumberland in aid of great business. [Fo.46; p.226]. He now no longer wishes to charge them with this loan and asks [the bishop, Roger Clifford and Adam Parving] to summon these people and wholly restore the money levied for this loan, thanking them on the king's behalf for their support and good will, for which he will be gracious in all their future dealings with him. Clarendon, 12 August [1370].

**256** Privy seal letter to the bishop (in French).[210] The king had ordered him by writs under the great seal to appoint collectors in the diocese of the triennial tenth granted by clergy of the realm, certifying their names to the Exchequer by 16 June.[211] He orders that the tenth due from the diocese for the term of 24 June be levied in haste and delivered to the Exchequer on that day in its

---

[207] Addressed as in **250**. Mostly printed in Hist. Man. Comm., *Ninth Report*, I.251(b).
[208] Mostly printed in Hist. Man. Comm., *Ninth Report*, I.251(b).
[209] Addressed as in **250**. Partly printed in Hist. Man. Comm., *Ninth Report*, I.251(b).
[210] Extracts printed in Hist. Man. Comm., *Ninth Report*, I.194–5.
[211] As in letters under both seals dated 20 Apr. 1370 (**226**); see also **232**.

entirety, without any deduction by authority of any order, tally or assignment against the bishop or collectors. Westminster, 20 May [1370].

**257** Privy seal letter to the bishop (in French).[212] The king is seriously displeased that the bishop has not yet certified the names of collectors of the triennial tenth; he needed to have the money in his Treasury in the fortnight after 24 June. The certification should be sent to the treasurer and the entire tenth as soon as [the bishop] is able; and also, before 1 August, payment of the loan which the king had assigned the bishop and Roger lord de Clifford to make from certain churchmen and laymen of Cumberland according to other letters sent earlier, about which the king marvels that nothing has been reported. Westminster, 16 July [1370].

**258** [Fo.46v; p.227] Letters patent of Edward III presenting M. John de Wyke, rector of Denham (dioc. Lincoln) to Arthuret church, in an exchange with his clerk, John de Bouland. Westminster, 4 September 1370.[213]

**259** Certificate to John [Thoresby], archbishop of York, of the bishop's vicargeneral,[214] quoting his letters to the bishop or his vicar-general received on 21 April. These quote a writ of Edward III received on 2 April ordering him to call the bishops and clergy of the province at an early date to grant a subsidy for the defence of the realm and Church, as had been sought in the present parliament; dated Westminster, 27 March 1371.[215] The archbishop therefore summons a provincial council, [Fo.47; p.228], citing the bishop, prior and chapter of Carlisle, abbots and priors, deans and provosts of collegiate churches, and archdeacons, to appear in person, and chapters and diocesan clergy by proctors, in St. Peter's cathedral, York, on 8 May. Absentees will be prosecuted. Anyone with pertinent grievances should appear. The bishop should be cited if he is absent from the diocese. York, 8 April 1371.
[The vicar-general] has cited abbots, priors and others named in the diocese, and its clergy, to appear in the council, viz.:
John de Hornecastell, prior of Carlisle, and the chapter
Robert de Rabankes, abbot of Holm Cultram, Cistercian order
Lambert de Morland, abbot of Shap, Premonstratensian order, and the convent
John de Marton, prior of Lanercost,[216] and the convent
John de Appilby, archdeacon of Carlisle
M. Adam [de Crosby], rector of Bolton
Peter de Morland, vicar of Kirkby Stephen
Bishop Thomas could not be found in the diocese and thus was not cited. Under the seal of the vicariate, Carlisle, 2 May 1371.[217]

---

[212] Mostly printed in Hist. Man. Comm., *Ninth Report*, I.195(a).
[213] As in *CPR 1367–70*, 461.
[214] See **1** for the only commission to vicars before this date, and **217** for the next.
[215] Printed in *Foedera*, III(2).912; *CCR 1369–74*, 286–7. The parliament met 24 Feb.–29 Mar. 1371 (*HBC*, 563).
[216] Not otherwise known; cf. *VCH Cumberland*, II.161.
[217] The remainder of this page (7.5 cm) is cancelled with crosses.

**260** [Fo.47v; p.229] Exchequer writ. Christopher de Moriceby, late sheriff of Cumberland,[218] accounted for the year 1366–7; he claimed to have spent £25 6s. 10½d. repairing defects in the turrets, walls, houses and gates of Carlisle on the king's order, by view of the prior. Margaret de Moriceby and Isabel, his widow, executrixes of his will, delivered the Exchequer an indented schedule of particulars of these expenses and sought allowance for this sum. Before proceeding, the Exchequer requires a certificate that the money was spent on repairs. The bishop is therefore ordered to call the sheriff and examine him on oath, receiving particulars to be sent to the Exchequer in the week after 24 June, with this writ. Tested by T[homas] de Loudelowe, Westminster, 20 May 1371. From the Memoranda roll of 1367–8, Trinity, *precepta*, rot. 1.
[Return] The prior was called, the bishop received his oath, and the expenses confirmed.

**261** Memoranda of institutions of William de Kirkeby to the chantry of Hutton in the Forest and Richard de Irland to Gilcrux vicarage,[219] in an exchange of benefices; also of a letter for their induction. 21 July [1371].

**262** Certificate to Brother John de Cariloco, prior of Lewes (*Lowon'*), commissary and subcollector of John de Cabrespino, DCnL, canon of Narbonne, nuncio and collector of the papal chamber in England, quoting his letters (dated 1 August). Benefices listed in the following schedule owe money to the chamber for reasons as shown. The bishop is ordered to sequestrate them, keeping receipts for the pope until payments are made. Their occupiers and others interested are to be warned [Fo.48; p.230] not to infringe the sequestrations and cited to [the subcollector's] hospice in Southwark (*Sowthwerk*, dioc. Winchester) on the first law day after 1 November to show why these sums should not be paid, under pain of excommunication. Names of possessors found in person are to be reported in [the bishop's] certificate. Under the collector's seal, Southwark, 14 June 1371.
    [Schedule] (i) Crosthwaite church. £30 13s. 4d. tax owed for the provision of John Henry.[220]
(ii) Crosthwaite vicarage. £20 owed for the provision of William de Esyngden.[221]
(iii) Wigton church. Vacant by the death of Gilbert de Wiggeton; tax or fruits owed for the provision of Richard de Tirneby.[222]

---

[218] He died by 15 Jan. 1370 (*CFR*, VIII.60).
[219] William had been collated to Gilcrux, 1364 (**21**); for the chantry's foundation, see *Reg. Welton*, 69–71.
[220] In 1357 (*Accounts*, ed. Lunt, 103, 132, 182, 206, 323; see also *Reg. Welton*, 35, no.195; 58, no.318, n.; **57** and **96**).
[221] In 1360 (see **96**).
[222] Gilbert had resigned and a vicar collated when Holm Cultram appropriated the church, 1336 (*Reg. Kirkby*, I.59–60). Other vicars followed, the last being John de Welton, 1369 (**167**); he obtained royal ratification, 1373 (*CPR 1370–4*, 245). In 1364, Richard de Thirneby alleged that the church had been vacant since Gilbert's death and thus obtained papal provision; the collector subsequently sought payment until he learned of the appropriation (*CPP*, I.497; *Accounts*, ed. Lunt, 288, 340, 342–3, 383).

(iv) Bowness [on Solway] church. Tax or fruits for the provision of William del Hall.[223]

(v) Kirkland church. £40 owed for tax for the provision of John de Kirkeby.[224] The bishop certifies that he has duly sequestrated the revenues of all these benefices into the pope's hands, and cited their possessors in person, except for the rector of Bowness, who is absent. The possessors are the abbot of Fountains (dioc. York), of Crosthwaite church; M. Thomas de Eskheved, vicar of Crosthwaite;[225] the abbot of Holm Cultram, of Wigton church; M. William de Hall, rector of Bowness; and John de Langholm, rector of Kirkland. Rose, 10 [August 1371].[226]

**263** [Fo.48v; p.231] Memorandum of institutions of John del Marche, chaplain, to Dalston vicarage, and John de Midilton, presented by the prioress and nuns of Marrick (*Marrig*), to Kirkandrews church, in an exchange of benefices; and of mandate for their induction to the archdeacon. 17 September 1371.

**264** Dispensation to Robert de Lowthre, clerk (dioc. Carlisle), quoting letters of Francis,[227] cardinal-priest of St. Eusebius, papal penitentiary (dated St. Peter's, Rome, 29 January 1370). After making enquiries about his character etc., the bishop dispenses him as the son of unmarried parents to be ordained to all orders and hold a benefice, if he resides. Rose, 18 September 1371.[228]

**265** [Fo.49; p.232] Mandate of Simon [Langham] and John [de Dormans] cardinal-priests of St. Sixtus and *Sancti Quatuor Coronati*, to Bishop Thomas, his vicar-general, official, lieutenants, etc. Pope Gregory XI has sent them as legates *a latere* to negotiate peace between the kings of England and France;[229] they need aid with their expenses, which they should receive as customary procurations for cardinals (quoting papal letters to them, and others addressed to all archbishops, bishops, chapters, etc., dated Avignon, 9 March 1371). [Fo.49v; p.233]. They have incurred great expenses in the first year of their nunciature, beginning from 27 March last, which [the bishop and others addressed] should levy from prelates and clergy of Carlisle diocese, at the customary rates for Roman cardinals in England; books and other records of similar procurations are to be shown, also the names of all churches in the diocese

---

[223] Instituted following the lay patron's presentation, 1354, but incurred the collector's attention by obtaining papal confirmation of his title (*Reg. Welton*, 8, no.36; 111, n.).

[224] The church had been held by another provisor (John de Skelton), but John de Langholm was rector 1350–79; for Kirkby's unsuccessful provision, see *Reg. Welton*, 9, n.36.

[225] From 1363 (see n. to **57**).

[226] Followed by lower margin of 7.5 cm, cancelled by crossings.

[227] But 'Stephen' in quotation of his letter.

[228] Followed by a margin of 9.5 cm, cancelled by crossings. This is the last folio of the quire from fo.39; p.214. The next quire begins with two 'stumps', of fos.53 and 54.

[229] See Lunt, *Financial Relations*, 662–3.

and their old taxations, under penalties for default etc. [Fo.50; p.234] Receipts are to be sent to Lincoln city and delivered to Richard de Chesterfeld, canon of Lincoln, [the legates'] proctor and receiver,[230] with lists of payments and benefices under the bishop's seal. Benefices held by the cardinals are exempted from the two procurations, as are hospitals and poor nuns. [Fo.50v; p.235] These letters or instrument are to be published by notaries and registered. Dated at Paris in the house of the grand prior of St. John of Jerusalem in France; witnessed by Aymeric, bishop of Paris, M. Adam de Eston, DTh.,[231] Roger de Freton, auditor of causes in the papal palace, John of Paris, Ddec., William de Villemouteir, archdeacon of Chavignon [or Chaudun?] (*Tardano*) in the church of Soissons (*Suession*), and many more; 2 May 1371.[232]

Subscription by Richard de Croxton, clerk (dioc. Ely), notary by apostolic and imperial authority.

Subscription by Adam Wagneti of Villemoutoyr (dioc. Soissons), notary by papal authority.

**266**  Letter to a cardinal.[233] [The bishop] is sending his clerks M. Robert de Byx and William de Stirkeland, bearing these letters, extracts, evidences and copies from the registers of his predecessors showing what procurations and sums cardinal-legates were accustomed to receive in Carlisle diocese;[234] they are fully informed of this business and their oral testimony may be believed. With thanks for the numerous honours and benefices [the bishop] has received from the cardinal. n.d.[235]

**267**  [Fo.51; p.236] Letters patent of Cardinal Simon acknowledging receipt from Bishop Thomas (by the hands of M. Robert de Byx, BCnL, and M. William de Stirkeland, notary public) of 28 marks 12s. 8d. owed by the bishop and his clergy for the first year of the two cardinals' legation. London, 4 December 1371.

**268**  Another letter of the same to M. Robert de Bix, BCnL, and John de Dokwra, chaplain, empowering them to absolve from censures all persons, even a bishop, who had been negligent in paying procurations due to the two cardinals for the first year of their legation. London, 5 December 1371.

**269**  Letters patent of John Aldebrandini and Gianus Luchetti, merchants of the society of Clarenti, Pistoia (*Pistorien*), proctors of B[erard] and S[imon], cardinal-bishops of Albano and Palestrina,[236] acknowledging receipt from the

---

[230]  See *BRUO*, II.408.

[231]  *BRUO*, III.620–1.

[232]  After a space of 2–3 cm, the last 6 words of this text are spaced out over a full line. The first subscription follows a blank line, and others precede and follow the second subscription. Text and subscriptions appear to be in the same hand.

[233]  According to the margin.

[234]  See *Reg. Kirkby*, I.279–80, 429, 443–4, 593, 645; *Reg. Welton*, 184–94, 394–7, 603.

[235]  Followed by a space of 5.5 cm above a ruled lower margin.

[236]  For their legation in 1295, see *CPL*, I.562–3; *Reg. Halton*, I.47–8, 90–1; Lunt, *Financial Relations to 1327*, 553–7.

official and prior of Carlisle, collectors in Carlisle diocese of the procurations ordered by the legates of 37 marks, by the hands of M. Adam de Novo Castro who had explained that the collectors had expenses of 5 marks in sending that sum to [the proctors] in London. This total of 42 marks matches the seven procurations of 6 marks each paid by the bishop and prior of Carlisle, the abbots of Holm Cultram and Shap, the priors of Wetheral and Lanercost, and the nuns of Armathwaite. London, 10 January 1296.

M. Geoffrey de Vezano, papal nuncio, added his seal.


**270**  Letters patent of Richard [Bintworth], bishop of London, proctor of Peter, cardinal-priest of St. Praxed's, papal nuncio (with Bertrand, cardinal-deacon of St. Mary's in Aquiro),[237] acknowledging payment to his and the cardinals' deputies Nicholas Housbond, rector of Chelsea (*Chelchicch*; dioc. London), and John de Claketton, rector of All Hallows, Honey Lane (*Honelane*; in London city) by the official of Carlisle, collector in Carlisle diocese, of £14 9s. 6½d. as the portion due from the bishop and spiritualities of the clergy. London, 9 May 1339.


**271**  Mandate[238] of Berard and Simon, cardinal-bishops of Albano and Palestrina, nuncios of Pope Boniface VIII in England, to archbishops and bishops and their collectors. Reliable men have informed them that Ottobuono [Fieschi], cardinal-deacon of St. Adrian's, while he was legate in England,[239] received 6 marks each for his procurations from all archbishops, bishops, abbots, priors, deans, archdeacons and religious houses. They intend their own procurations to be 6 marks from each of the same persons, under pains by apostolic authority (including suspension of prelates). [Fo.52; p.238] These and other letters are to be obeyed. London, 25 July 1295.


**272**  Mandate of Cardinals Berard and Simon to the official and prior of Carlisle, appointing them collectors of these procurations in Carlisle diocese within the following month, with powers to swear deputies to render accounts, impose canonical pains, invoke the secular arm, and act as proctors; quoting [three] letters from the pope [Fo.52v; p.239] dated at the Lateran, 18 and 20 February 1295.[240] London, 8 July 1295.


**273**  [Fo.53; p.240] Certificate of the bishop to John [Thoresby], archbishop of York, quoting his letters received on 23 June. As the bishop will know, clerks [of the archbishop], at the urgent request of the clergy of the province were recently sent to the king. The king ordered [the archbishop] to convoke his prelates and clergy in haste to be told about dangers to the realm. He has

---

[237]  See Lunt, *Financial Relations*, 626–8; *Reg. Kirkby*, I.82, no.429.
[238]  A marginal note in another, possibly contemporary hand, observes 'Multum valet pro solucione nunciorum curie Romane cum venerint in Anglia'.
[239]  In 1265–8.
[240]  Printed in *Reg. Halton*, I.91–4.

therefore called a convocation to meet at York on 10 July, and cites the bishop [etc., as in **259**]. Absentees will be prosecuted. Bishopthorpe, 19 June 1371.

[The bishop] has cited the prior and chapter of Carlisle, the abbots and convents of Holm Cultram and Shap, the prior and convent of Lanercost, John de Appilby, archdeacon of Carlisle, M. Adam [de Crosby], rector of Bolton, and Peter de Morland, vicar of Kirkby Stephen. 1 July [1371].

**274** [Schedule to the following mandate.] The king in his last parliament at Westminster asked the English clergy for a subsidy of £50,000, and sent letters to the archbishops of Canterbury and York to hold convocations about this.[241] The clergy of York province, in a provincial council [Fo.53v; p.241] at York on 10 July last, granted the king their appropriate portion of this sum according to the new assessment, viz. 8,800 marks [£5,866 13s. 4d.]. The prelates and proctors, after full discussion, agreed that the clergy of York diocese should pay 6,700 marks, of Durham 1,700 marks, and of Carlisle 400 marks, in equal portions on 30 November and 28 March [1372].

Item. It was ordered that all untaxed possessions and benefices, hospitals, chantries, free chapels and stipends of stipendiary priests should contribute. After deduction of a third of their value, tenths are to be paid of the two other portions, the same rate as for the benefices.

It was also ordered that full payment of the sum should be made at York [on the above dates], to be levied by ecclesiastical censures in the same way and process as is usual against defaulters at the papal chamber.

**275** Mandate to the rectors and vicar of Kirkland, Kirkoswald and Penrith, and dean of Cumberland. In the provincial council held at York on 10 July at the king's request, Archbishop John, Bishop Thomas of Durham, [Bishop Appleby] and other prelates and clergy of the province, for the defence of the church, realm and people against invading enemies, granted the king as a voluntary (*gratuitum*) subsidy a portion of £50,000 due from possessions, temporalities annexed to spiritualities, hospitals, chantries, free chapels and vicars in cathedral and collegiate churches, to be paid on 11 November and 12 March [1372]. On 11 November, the fourth part of the tax according to the new assessment is due from benefices and taxed possessions in Carlisle diocese, and from hospitals, chantries and other benefices not previously taxed, being part of the whole portion imposed on them in [the bishop's] last convocation of his clergy held in Carlisle diocese, as [the commissaries] know (and as shown in the attached schedule).[242] A tenth of one year's salary is also due from stipendiary chaplains, without delay. The prior of Carlisle was deputed as collector for the diocese and untaxed benefices beyond the River Eden, and the deans for hospitals etc. in their deaneries, (as had been agreed in the said convocation). Order by the bishop's authority and the king's (committed to him) to collect the tenths due from stipendiary chaplains in the deanery [of Cumberland] and

---

[241] Dated 27 Mar. Canterbury's convocation met 24 Apr.–3 May (*HBC*, 596).
[242] Interlined, possibly by the same hand.

to make enquiries regarding receipts from hospitals, [Fo.54; p.242] chantries and other benefices. Stipendaries are to pay by 11 November or within the next ten days; if they can be found, defaulting chaplains are to be arrested. All defaulters are to be excommunicated, sentences being published according to the ordinance of the council [at York] and the king's command. The bishop is to be certified by 1 November. Rose, 12 September 1371.

**276**   Letters of Edward III to Bishop Thomas.[243] The clergy of Canterbury and York have granted the king £50,000 for the defence of the realm.[244] So that the burden may be more easily borne by all clergy, it is also to be paid by hitherto exempt houses and benefices and stipendiary priests. All bishops are to hold meetings of their clergy and charge them to make proportionate payments, appointing collectors to levy them in equal portions to be delivered to the king on 29 September and 2 February [1372]. [Fo.54v; p.243] Exempt clergy failing to attend the diocesan meetings, or refusing to pay, are to be cited to Chancery on 13 October, under pain of forfeiture. Henley, 5 May 1371.

**277**   Letters patent of Peter [d'Estaing], archbishop of Bourges (*Bituricen'*), regent of the papal chamberlain. Bishop Thomas is bound to visit the Roman Curia every three years. Certificate that he has so done for the next triennium through his proctor, Thomas Monis.[245] Avignon, 8 June 1371.

**278**   Privy seal letter of Edward III (in French) ordering the bishop to attend the great council at Westminster on 18 September to take part in its business about the king and realm. Westminster, 28 July [1371].[246]

**279**   [Fo.55; p.244] TAXACIONES EPISCOPATUUM REGNI ANGLIE

|              | £      | s. | d.     |
|--------------|--------|----|--------|
| Canterbury   | 8,868  | 16 | 2¼     |
| Rochester    | 2,304  | 10 | 2      |
| London       | 10,857 | 2  | 9¼     |
| Norwich      | 23,559 | 2  | 8½     |
| Ely          | 7,864  | 9  | 4¾     |
| Chichester   | 6,877  | 6  | 6¾     |
| Winchester   | 9,258  | 5  | 10¾    |
| Salisbury    | 14,225 | 11 | 10¾    |
| Wells        | 6,489  | 8  | 0½     |
| Exeter       | 4,883  | 14 | 10½    |

[243]  As in *CFR*, VIII.118, which shows that these letters were sent to all archbishops and bishops.

[244]  Canterbury's grant had been made in a convocation in session from 24 Apr. – 3 May 1371, but the session and grant by York were to follow on 10 July (D.B. Weske, *Convocation of the Clergy*, London, 1937, 164–5, 257, 286).

[245]  Merchant of Florence, a proctor at the Curia (*CPL*, IV.100, 104).

[246]  The remainder of the folio is blank. It is the last of the quire from fo.49; p.232 (**265**), which is preceded by 'stubs' of fos.53 and 54; pp.240–3.

| | | | |
|---|---|---|---|
| Worcester | 7,363 | 3 | 6½ |
| Hereford | 6,531 | 8 | 5 |
| Lichfield | 8,549 | 9 | 10¾ |
| Lincoln | 39,915 | 5 | 5¼ |
| St. David's | 2,735 | – | 5 |
| Llandaff | 2,073 | 4 | 10 |
| Bangor | 861 | 5 | 9½ |
| St. Asaph | 1,272 | 6 | 10 |
| York | 27,515 | 6 | 6½ |
| Durham | 10,848 | 9 | 10¼ |
| Carlisle | 3,171 | 5 | 7½ *id est* 4,356 marks, |
| | 12s. 3½[247] | | |

Total £204,043 19s. 2½; of which a tenth is £24,014 7s. 11d.[248]

**280** [Fo.55v; p.245] Certificate of John [Buckingham], bishop of Lincoln, that he has executed the bishop of Carlisle's commission (dated Rose, 14 November), to arrange an exchange of benefices between Thomas de Tughale, vicar of Torpenhow, and Robert de Byx, rector of Wardley (*Wardeley*, dioc. Lincoln).[249] Robert was admitted to Torpenhow (in the bishop's gift) in the person of John Harold, clerk, his proctor, who swore that he would reside. Stow, 29 November 1371.

**281** Privy seal letter of Edward III (in French). He had learnt that in the last parliament the prelates had agreed to grant him £50,000 to defend the realm. The bishop, however, has done nothing to obtain a grant from his clergy. [Fo.56; p.246] He sternly orders compliance, so that payments are made into the Exchequer on 29 September and 2 February [1372]. Westminster, 30 June 1371.[250]

**282** Mandate of Cardinal Simon [Langham], papal nuncio, ordering the official of Carlisle, under pain of excommunication, to cite M. Robert de Byx, BCnL, to come before him or his auditors on the first law day after 13 January in the cardinal's hospice in London to answer for his impediments to the cardinal and his mission, in contempt of the Holy See. London, 10 December 1371.

**283** Reply of the official to this mandate (received at Carlisle, 12 January). He has cited Robert in full chapter. Carlisle, 14 January 1372.

---

[247] *Recte* 4,756 marks. This was Carlisle's assessment in the *Taxatio* of 1291; it was reduced to £489 19s. in 1318 (*Reg. Halton*, II.xxvii–viii; *Reg. Kirkby*, I.128, no.638. See also **98**, **100**).

[248] The remainder of the page (7 cm) was left blank, as was the right-hand margin of 12 cm, which was later used for a list of the names (only) of 11 Scottish dioceses, omitting Dunblane and Moray. This was written in a 'bastard' hand, probably in the fifteenth century.

[249] Admitted there 4 July 1369 (*BRUO*, I.336); previously rector of Ormside, 1368 (**117**).

[250] See **276** for an earlier mandate, and **275** for the bishop's tardy compliance.

**284**  Letters patent of Cardinal Simon. Robert de Byx [Fo.56v; p.247], priest (dioc. Carlisle), was charged with impeding the cardinal's mission, which he denied and purged himself. The bishop and clergy are to declare his innocence. London, 26 January 1372.

**285**  Commission to John [Buckingham], bishop of Lincoln, to effect an exchange of benefices between M. John Wyk, rector of Denham (dioc. Lincoln), and John de Bouland, rector of Arthuret; M. John has been presented by the king.[251] Rose, 28 March 1372.

**286**  Commission to William [Russell], bishop of Sodor,[252] requesting that he deputise for the bishop, who is unwell, in blessing the chrism in Dalston church on next Ember Thursday [20 May]. Rose, 21 March 1372.

**287**  Letters of Edward III ordering him, with the advice of the council, to stay with his family and retinue in his lands near the marches of Scotland; he must hasten there to be ready, with other magnates likewise ordered, to oppose enemies. [Fo.57; p.248]. Arrayers of men-at-arms, hobelars and archers in the bishopric of Durham, Northumberland, Westmorland and Yorkshire are to obey orders from them and other wardens. Westminster, 26 February 1372.[253]

**288**  Privy seal letter of the same (in French) ordering the bishop to leave all other business and attend the council at Westminster on 4 April.[254] Westminster, 27 February [1372?].

**289**  Certificate to M. Arnold Garnerii, licenciate in laws, canon of Châlons (*Cathalann*), papal nuncio and collector, quoting his mandate (received 28 March) ordering the bishop to sequestrate benefices in debt to the chamber and citing their occupiers to the collector's house in London on 11 April to show [etc., as in **262**. Fo.57v; p.249]; dated London, 20 February 1372.
[Schedule] Kirkland church, £40 [as in **262**]; and Carlisle priory, £6 13s. 4d. for the annual census of 13s. 4d. [Peter's Pence] since 1360.
The bishop certifies that he has sequestrated the benefices since 29 March and has cited John de Horncastell, prior of Carlisle, and John de Langholm, rector of Kirkland, to appear in person on the above day. n.d.

**290**  Will[255] of Robert de Kirkeby, rector of a mediety of Aikton, dated 26 April 1371, being compos mentis. Commends soul to God, Blessed Mary and all saints. Burial wherever God disposes, with 10s. for wax and oblations. For

---

[251] Part 1 of the patent roll for 46 Edward III is missing (*CPR 1370–4*, 183).
[252] *HBC*, 314.
[253] Similar letters were sent to Bishop Hatfield of Durham, Henry Percy, Gilbert Umfraville, earl of Angus, Roger Clifford and Ranulph Dacre; printed in *Foedera*, III(2).936; *CCR 1369–74*, 361.
[254] MS *les dytanes de Pasche*.
[255] Printed in *Test. Karl.*, 101–3.

the poor at Aikton, 50s., and at Halton,[256] 10s. The friars preachers, Carlisle, 13s. 4d. The friars minor, Carlisle, 6s. 8d. The friars of Penrith, 6s. 8d. The friars of Appleby, 6s. 8d. The prior and convent of St. Mary, Carlisle, 20s. The prior and convent of Lanercost, 20s. His sister Alice, 20s. Brother Thomas Marschall, 13s. 4d., and his English book. John Awen, 6s. 8d. Thomas [Marschall], £4 in silver to celebrate for his soul for a year. William de Beaumont, chaplain, 10s. and a murrey money-belt decorated with silver. Each priest celebrating for his soul for a year, 100s. Each executor, 20s. The said Alice and William de Beaumont, all cloths for his bed and body. William Layalton, chaplain, 3s. 4d. Each secular chaplain celebrating in Carlisle, 12d. Each godchild coming [to his burial?] whom he had received at the font, 2s. Aikton church, his breviary. Andrew de Laton, all the residue. Executors: Andrew de Laton, and William de Arthuret and John de Midelton, then vicars of Arthuret and Dalston. As his seal is not well known, he has applied the seal of the deanery of Carlisle, as the dean confirms.

Probate, with grant of administration within the bishop's jurisdiction to Andrew de Laton; reserved to the other executors. Rose (chapel), 26 April 1372.

**291** [Fo.58; p.250] Mandate to the bishop or his official from M. Arnold Garnerii, papal collector. He had recently asked the bishop to sequestrate Kirkland church on account of the non-payment of tax for the provision of John de Kirkby by Pope Innocent VI on 25 October 1360 (see **289**). John de Langholm claims to be rector; he alleged before [the collector] that he does not owe tax nor was he provided, but has been in canonical possession for 20 years by authority of the ordinary. Order for an enquiry, to be reported by 24 June. London, 6 April 1372.

**292** Mandate of the bishop to the official of Carlisle, following complaint by the prior and sacrist of Carlisle. It is customary for all rectors and vicars of the diocese to visit the cathedral annually, in person or by suitable deputies, on set days in the week of Pentecost, processing in surplices after raised crosses, in reverence to the cathedral church. Many of them, however, are unwilling to make this visit, nor have done so in this or other dioceses in England. Order to make enquiries and cite all culpable rectors and vicars to the chapel of Bolton in Westmorland to answer for their contumacy to the bishop or his commissaries. Bewley, 24 May 1372.

**293** [Fo.58v; p.251] Certificate to M. Arnold Garnerii, quoting his mandate (**291**). The bishop has enquired with the sworn testimony of William [de Beauchamp], rector of Kirkoswald, John [Waterward], rector of Ousby, John [Pety], rector of Melmerby, William [de Wyllerdby], rector of Croglin,[257]

---

[256] Probably Halton, Lancs., because of his Dacre connection (*Reg. Welton*, 24, no.127; 77, no.423; and see date of **244** above).

[257] Previous known institution was of Patrick de Edenham, 1362, but William died as rector, 1376 (*Reg. Welton*, 81, no.447; *Test. Karl.*, 113–14).

Thomas [de Hayton?], vicar of Edenhall,[258] John [de Castro Bernardi], vicar of
Lazonby, Eudes, vicar of Ainstable, Thomas, vicar of Addingham,[259] and Gilbert
Bowet, Richard de Langwathby, Thomas de Barton and William de Wyggeton,
chaplains. They said that John de Langholm was instituted as rector of Kirkland
on 14 September 1350 and inducted on that day by M. William de Rotheburi,
then archdeacon of Carlisle; since then his possession has been peaceful and
unquestioned. Bewley, 4 June 1372.

**294**  Mandate of Edward III. He has learnt that his French enemies and their
adherents have assembled a huge fleet, with many armed men, threatening to
invade and destroy the realm and English church. He therefore orders the
bishop, other prelates and all the clergy and other true subjects to prepare for
resistance [incomplete].[260]

**295**  [Fo.60;[261] p.252] Commission to M. John de Appleby, archdeacon of
Carlisle, to correct etc. the excesses of certain chaplains and others of the
diocese. Rose, 10 August 1372.

**296**  Order of Edward III to the bishop. He is about to go abroad to defend
England from enemies. The bishop is to go to one of his castles near the march
with his entourage until the king returns in order to defend it against the Scots,
should they presume to invade. The men arrayed in the bishopric of Durham,
Northumberland, Cumberland and Westmorland are to be made ready, under
his and other wardens' orders. It is not the king's intention that the truce with
the Scots should be violated on this account. Westminster, 6 August 1372.[262]

**297**  Further order of the king to the bishop, earl of Angus, Henry Percy,
Roger Clifford and Thomas Musgrave, wardens of the marches in Cumberland
and Westmorland, appointing them to compel all fencible men in the two
counties (excepting the men-at-arms and archers retained for the king's voyage
and those going abroad with John, Lord Nevill), to stay in their homes so that
they will be ready to resist invasion. Rebels are to be arrested and imprisoned
until they give surety to be arrayed, and the sheriffs and other officers ordered
to obey the wardens. Westminster, 6 August 1372.[263]

**298**  (i) Institution of William de Kirkeby, chaplain, to the vicarage of Brampton
in Gilsland, vacant by the resignation of John de Hayton; presented by the prior
and convent of Lanercost. (ii) Archdeacon to induct. Rose, 4 September 1372.

---

[258] Previous known institution was of John de Kerby, 1369, but Thomas occurs 1380
(**181**; *Test. Karl.*, 146–7).

[259] See **248**.

[260] The text ends with a full line at the foot of the folio, the next obviously lost. This
order for the array of clergy, issued to all bishops, dated 16 June 1372. It is printed (from
the French roll of 46 Edward III) in *Foedera*, III(2).947.

[261] MS lx.

[262] Printed in *Rot. Scot.*, I.952

[263] Printed ibid., I.951–2.

**299** [Fo.60v; p.253] Commission to M. John de Appelby, archdeacon of Carlisle, to deputise for the bishop in the convocation of his clergy called to Carlisle on 7 August, as the bishop is too busy to attend. Rose, 6 August 1372.

**300** (i) Note of institution of Gilbert Groute, chaplain, to the chantry at the altar of the Blessed Virgin Mary in Hutton church; presented by William de Hoton. (ii) Archdeacon to induct. 6 September 1372.

**301** Letter (in French) [of Edward, prince of Wales]. His father, the king, the realm of England, and he himself know from experience that prosperity can only come with the grace of God. He intends to accompany the king to Sand-wich on his expedition overseas, and therefore asks that the bishop and his clergy will continue their prayers; he has written to other bishops, abbots, [etc.] to the same effect. Under his privy seal, Kennington, 9 August [1372].[264]

**302** Letters of Edward III [requesting prayers and processions for the success of his expedition; dated Westminster, 11 August 1372].[265]

**303** [Fo.59; p.254][266] Citation of the prior and chapter of Carlisle to attend the bishop's visitation on 3 October [as in **36**]. Rose, 6 September 1373.

**304** Mandate to the dean of Carlisle. The bishop intends to visit the clergy and people of the city and deanery. Order to cite all rectors, vicars, parish priests, chaplains and other clerks; religious and others claiming appropriated churches or partial tithes and pensions; keepers of perpetual chantries; and from every vill, depending on its size, four or six trustworthy men, on days and at places listed in a schedule. Rectors and vicars are to show their letters of institution and titles to benefices, and letters of ordination; likewise letters of appropriation or for par-tial tithes and pensions, or deeds of foundation for chantries, oratories and per-petual chapels. The laymen called are to be of good repute and well-informed, ready to answer truly to the articles of visitation. The bishop or his commissaries are to be certified by the first days listed in the schedule. Rose, 6 September 1373.

**305** Memorandum of written notice to the prior and convent of Lanercost for their visitation on 16 October. 16 September 1373.[267]

**306** [Fo.59v; p.255] Letters patent of John de Appelby, John de Penreth and Robert de Bix[268] announcing their appointment of M. Hugh de Burton, Henry de Haxholme and Nicholas de Esyngwald as their proctors in a cause appealed

---

[264] For the abortive naval operation, see R. Barber, *Edward, Prince of Wales and Aquitaine*, London, 1978, 228.

[265] Incomplete. Printed in *Foedera*, III(2).980; *CCR 1369–74*, 460.

[266] *Sic.* Note loss of folios for Aug. 1372 to Sept. 1373.

[267] Followed by space 3 cm deep, cancelled by crosses, and lower margin of 5 cm.

[268] Described in the margin as a proxy for M. John de Appelby, archdeacon of Carlisle, and M. Robert de Bix.

to the papal see, court of York or delegates.[269] Under their seals, Carlisle, 23 October [13]73.

**307**    Writ of Edward III summoning the bishop to a parliament at Westminster on 21 November; with *premunientes* clause for the clergy. Westminster, 4 October 1373.[270]

**308**    Will[271] of Robert de Tibbay of Carlisle,[272] being sound in memory and mind, dated 15 July 1373. Commends soul to God, Blessed Mary and all saints. Burial in choir of St. Cuthbert's, Carlisle, with best beast and cloth as mortuary; every pauper coming to the church at the hour for matins on that day, 1d.; and ten pounds of wax to make five candles burning then. The keepers of the light of the BVM in that church, an annual rent of 6s. from the houses of Nicholas son of Alan son of Walter which lies opposite the house or manse of the minorite friars, Carlisle. Joan de Derle, dau. of Roger de Derle, 20s. for her marriage-portion. His wife Beatrice, the tenement he lives in, for her life; and thereafter to Sir Robert Taillour, his heirs and assigns. Every chaplain coming to his exequies, 12d. The friars preachers and minor, a mark in equal portions. Two chaplains celebrating for his soul, £10, and to one chaplain, 100s.; and if none can be engaged, this [sum] shall be left to the disposition of his executors. Residue to John Bone and Robert Taillour, chaplains, his executors, to be spent for his soul and execution of the will. Witnesses: Adam Stafful, Patrick Bacastre and Thomas Strang.
    [Fo.70; p.256] Sentence of probate and grant of administration. Carlisle cathedral, [ . . . . . ] 1373.

**309**    Will[273] of John de Yarome,[274] compos mentis, dated 8 November 1373. Commends soul to God, Blessed Mary and all saints. Burial in the churchyard of the canons of St. Mary's, Carlisle, with best beast and cloth for mortuary. Priests ministering at his exequies, and friars attending, 6d. each. Two sheep, a heifer and 11s. 8d. in bread and drink for a wake of neighbours. The fabric of St. Mary's church [Carlisle] and light in the parish church, 4s. equally divided. For candles burning round his body, 6s. 8d. The friars minor and preachers, 2s. each. Sir John de Midelton, 40d. The bridges of Eden and Caldew, 2s. each. Sir William de Yarome, his son, a tenement lying between lands of the prior and convent, Carlisle, and John Frere, another in Caldewgate bought from John Dobson, and an acre on Caldecotes Bank[275] bought from Henry Kirkbalf, so that William should celebrate for his soul. John, his son, two tenements built

---

[269] Continuing with a comprehensive list of possible actions, but without direct reference to a particular cause.
[270] As in *CCR 1369–74*, 586.
[271] Printed in *Test. Karl.*, 103–4.
[272] Mayor in 1357 (Summerson, 333).
[273] Printed in *Test. Karl.*, 104–5.
[274] Margin: John Yarom of Carlisle.
[275] MS *Caldecotbank*.

between Butchers' Row and the highway, to be held by him, his heirs and assigns from the chief lord of the fee. The fabric of St. Mary's, an iron-shod wagon. All his goods after payment of debts to be divided into three equal parts, one for performance of his will, the second to be the portion of his wife Christine, and the third to his sons William and John. Any residue to be given to William so that he celebrates for his soul as long as it lasts. Executors: Sir William de Yarone and Robert Goldsmith. Under his seal before [unnamed] witnesses.

Note of grant of probate and administration to the executors. Rose, 5 December 1373.

**310** Mandate of the chapter of York, in the absence of the dean and the see of York vacant, to the bishop or his vicar-general, quoting the king's writ (dated Westminster, 10 November 1373). With the advice of John [Thoresby], late archbishop of York,[276] and other prelates and magnates of his council, he proposes to invade France, ordering that the bishops, [etc.,] of the province be called to St. Peter's, York, as soon as possible to grant a subsidy.[277]

For the pressing reasons declared in the writ, and others concerning the estate and liberty of the Church and province, and by their authority *sede vacante*, they will celebrate a council on 6 February, citing the bishop [as in **197**]. Absentees will be prosecuted. York, 10 December 1373.

**311** (i) Institution of Thomas Bell, canon of Conishead (Augustinian order), to Wharton vicarage, vacant by the death of Robert de Berdeslay; presented by the prior and convent of Conishead. (ii) Archdeacon to induct. Rose, 12 February 1374.

**312** (i) Institution of Thomas Roke, chaplain, to a mediety of Aikton, vacant by the resignation of Thomas de Hiton; presented by Ranulph de Dacre, lord of Gilsland. (ii) Archdeacon to induct. Rose, 26 February 1374.

**313** (i) Institution of Robert de Hayton, chaplain, to Farlam vicarage, vacant by the resignation of Thomas Roke; presented by the prior and convent of Lanercost. (ii) Archdeacon to induct. Rose, 'as above' 1374.

**314** [Fo.72; p.258] Admission of William de Bradford, monk of St. Mary's, York, STP, presented by St. Mary's to Wetheral priory, rule of its churches and cure of its parishioners; reserving rights of the bishop and his church in any current litigation.[278] Carlisle, [. . .] August 1374.

**315** Will[279] of Adam Broun of Scotby, dated 31 January 1374. Commended soul to God, Blessed Mary and all saints. Burial in churchyard of St. Cuthbert's,

---

[276] 6 Nov. 1373 (*Fasti*, VI.3).

[277] Printed in *Foedera*, III(2).993; *CCR 1369–74*, 595.

[278] In same form as in admission of previous prior, 1354 (*Reg. Welton*, 8, no.35, and printed in its appendix, p.124).

[279] Printed in *Test. Karl.*, 105–6. It is expressed in the third person, as for a nuncupative will.

Kirklinton, with best beast for mortuary, and 2s. for light. St. Mary's light in that church. Henry, his illegitimate son, a cow, a heifer, 18 skeps of barley and oats. The children of Adam del Banks of Carlisle, 12 skeps of barley and oats. William Fletcher of Scotby, 4 ells of russet cloth. Margaret dau. of John Broun, a sheep, a lamb and a russet tunic. Gilbert de Brunstath, a white tunic, a skep of oatmeal and a skep of malt. Joan dau. of Ellen de Brunstath, a white tunic. Mariota de Brunstath, 10s. John Smalham, his wagon; also the residue, for disposing for his soul, paying his debts; appointing John his executor. Witnesses: John Benson and John Wylkynson.

Sentence of probate. Rose (chapel), 6 October 1374.

**316**   To Alexander [Neville], archbishop of York, complimenting him on his accession.[280] The bishop asks him to excuse his failure to visit him: his absence from the diocese could have harmful consequences for himself and his subjects and tenants, as his clerk, M. Robert de Bix, the bearer of this letter, could reliably explain. [Fo.72v; p.259] Rose, 5 December [1374].

**317**   Will[281] of Thomas de Anandale, rector of Asby, being sound in mind and memory, dated 18 November 1374. Commends soul to God, Blessed Mary and all saints. Burial in the parish church or its choir; wax round his body, 6 pounds of wax; 6s. 8d. for oblations; £3 for the poor; £10 for wake for friends. 100 marks to celebrate for his soul at Newcastle upon Tyne, and 50 marks in Asby church. Bridges [over] the Eden by Carlisle, Kirkoswald, Salkeld, Temple Sowerby, Appleby, Eamont and Lowther, 8 marks equally divided. Patrick's bridge, Asby, a mark. The nuns of Armathwaite, 20s.

The four orders of friars, 4 marks equally divided. Each parish chaplain in Westmorland, 12d. St. Mary's church, Carlisle, 20s. Sir Thomas Gerrard, rector of Castle Carrock, 40s. William de Anandale, clerk, his kinsman, 10 marks. John de Askeby, chaplain, 40s. Agid, his sister, a mark. John Gerrard of *Carleton*,[282] his kinsman, 40s. Juliana his niece, of Annandale, a mark. John Raynaldson, 5 marks. John Prestonson and Maud his wife, 40s. Joan wife of Robert Prestonson, half a mark. John de Anandale, his servant, 5 marks. Sir John de Bampton, a mark and his better tunic. St. Mary's light, Asby, 20s. William de Hill, chaplain, 40s. Residue to executors, viz. Robert de Ormesheved, William de Hill, chaplain, and John de Anandale, his kinsman. Witnesses: Sir John de Bampton and John de Raynalson. Dated at Asby, as above.

Sentence of probate. Rose (chapel), 11 December 1374.

**318**   Sentence[283] of probate of the nuncupative will of John de Penreth of Carlisle, as follows: on 12 November 1374 he commended his soul to God, Blessed Mary and all saints. Burial in the churchyard of St. Mary's, Carlisle. He left all his goods to his wife Magota and son Robert, having paid his funeral

---

[280]   He was consecrated as archbishop on 4 June 1374 (*Fasti*, VI.4).
[281]   Printed in *Test. Karl.*, 106–8.
[282]   In Annandale?
[283]   Printed in *Test. Karl.*, 108.

expenses and debts. Executors: Robert de Musgrave, chaplain, and his wife Magota. 12 November 1374.

**319** [Fo.73; p.260] (i) Institution of Stephen de Meburn, priest, to Asby church, vacant by the death of Thomas de Anand; presented by the king, having custody of the lands and heirs of Christopher de Moriceby, deceased.[284] (ii) Archdeacon to induct. Rose, 11 January 1375.

**320** Writ *dedimus potestatem* ordering the bishop to receive the oath of John de Denton as sheriff of Cumberland; he was appointed by letters patent, which are enclosed. Westminster, 13 December 1374.[285]
    Form of oath (in French).[286] He will faithfully serve the king as sheriff of Cumberland, guard his and the Crown's rights nor allow their concealment, telling the king or his councillors if he cannot; nor respite for gifts or favour any debts which can be levied without harm to the king's debtors. He will treat the people of his bailiwick, rich and poor, faithfully and lawfully, nor harm any for gift, promise, favour or hatred. He will serve writs faithfully, and replace the under-sheriff of the previous year. He will appoint only loyal bailiffs, under oath, for whom he is prepared to answer.
    Return. The bishop received John's oath on 20 January 1375 and delivered him the above-mentioned letters patent.

**321** [Fo.73v; p.261] Letters patent. While visiting the diocese, the bishop learned that the prior and convent of Watton (order of Sempringham, dioc. York) hold the church of Ravenstonedale as appropriated to their use. Cited before the bishop, they were represented by a proctor, proved their title and were dismissed from further impeachment. Rose, 20 February 1375.

**322** Commission to M. John de Appylby, archdeacon of Carlisle, and John de Penreth, vicar of [Castle] Sowerby,[287] to correct and punish the offences of any rectors, vicars and chaplains, regular or secular subjects, enjoining suitable penances and proceeding, etc. in all causes, appointing them (jointly and singly) the bishop's deputies. Rose, 11 August 1374.[288]

**323** Mandate to the vicar of Crosthwaite. The bishop has read in the book of the Venerable Bede on the history of the English people that Herbert, a priest, was a disciple of St. Cuthbert. He lived as a hermit on an island in Derwentwater, but visited Cuthbert annually to receive his guidance. When Cuthbert happened to come to Carlisle, Herbert went to Cuthbert who told him he expected

---

[284] Cf. *CPR 1370–4*, 139.
[285] See *CFR*, VIII.272.
[286] Margin: *Littere de privato sigillo* in early-modern court hand. For a full example of this customary oath, for sheriff of Rutland, 1388, see *Royal Writs addressed to John Buckingham* (cited under **240**), 114.
[287] Canon of Carlisle when instituted, 1360 (*Reg. Welton*, 58, no.314).
[288] In the bishop's twelfth year, from 10 Aug. 1363; and see **329**.

to die soon. Herbert tearfully begged that Cuthbert would pray that he might die first. After a pause, Cuthbert replied that this prayer was granted. On 13 April following [687], Cuthbert died on Farne Island and Herbert on [his] island.[289] The bishop believes that few know about this miracle, and orders [the vicar] to go to Herbert's island on the said thirteenth day and celebrate the mass for St. Cuthbert *cum nota*; with grant of an indulgence for 40 days to those who attend.[290] Dated at Rose.

**324**  [Fo.75; p.262] Dispensation to Robert, son of Robert Blenkarne, clerk, quoting letters of Stephen, cardinal-priest of St. Eusebius, papal penitentiary, describing him as a scholar of Carlisle, dioc. (dated Avignon, 12 July 1371). After making enquiries about his character etc., the bishop dispenses him as the son of a priest and unmarried woman to be ordained to all orders and hold a benefice, if he resides. Rose, 15 November 1374.

**325**  Mandate to [unnamed] 'dear sons, etc.' Unknown evildoers have broken into the bishop's park at Rose, by both day and night, hunting his wild beasts enclosed there with dogs, nets and other devices, and taking many bodies so that the park has been stripped of wild beasts, to the peril of their souls etc. They are to announce in churches (with bell, book and candle) that all offenders and their accomplices have incurred excommunication, on Sundays and feast-days until otherwise ordered by the bishop, who reserves their absolution to himself; enquiring for their names. [Fo.75v; p.263]. Rose, 23 March 1375.[291]

**326**  Mandate to the dean of Carlisle, following complaint by the prior of Carlisle, subcollector of a biennial tenth granted to the king. Many rectors, vicars and other ecclesiastical persons named in a schedule have refused to make the payments due from them in Carlisle at past dates under pains of excommunication and interdict. The prior consequently ordered the deans to warn them under pain of interdict of their benefices. Order to cite all those listed to appear before the bishop on 16 April to answer why he should not proceed against them as rebels; inhibiting them from celebrating services during the interdict. Rose, 12 March 1375.

**327**  Mandate to the parish chaplain of Penrith. The bishop previously ordered by letter that parishioners there should repair the nave and belfry of their church, under pain of excommunication; this they have failed to do. Order to announce on three days when many will be in church that the bishop's mandate must be obeyed; anyone preventing willing parishioners

---

[289] Cf. Bede's *Ecclesiastical History of the English People*, ed. B. Colgrave and R.A.B. Mynors, Oxford 1969, 440–3; *Two Lives of Saint Cuthbert*, ed. B. Colgrave, Cambridge 1985, 124–5, 248–51.

[290] See also *EPNS Cumberland*, II.371. The mass is still celebrated there on the first Saturday after Easter.

[291] This entry in 22 lines is compressed into 11 cm; the date was inserted into the dorse of the folio.

from paying their portions is to be cited before the bishop in Dalston church. Rose, 18 April 1375.

**328**  Letters patent appointing Masters Hugh de Burton, Henry de Haxholme and Nicholas de Esyngwalde, clerks, as proctors for the bishop and his church in all causes and disputes.[292] [Fo.76; p.264] Rose, 10 April 1375.

**329**  Commission to M. John de Appelby, archdeacon of Carlisle, and John de Penreth, vicar of [Castle] Sowerby, to enquire about crimes and excesses by rectors, vicars and chaplains, correcting and punishing them, enjoining penances [etc., as in **322**]. Rose, 11 August 1374.

**330**  Certificate of Humphrey de Cherlton, archdeacon of Richmond, that he has executed the bishop's commission (dated Rose, 20 May 1375) for an exchange of benefices between Richard de Upton, rector of Musgrave (dioc. Carlisle), and Thomas de Maltby, vicar of Gilling (in the archdeacon's jurisdiction). Thornton Steward (*Thornetonseward*), 29 May 1375.

**331**  Note of licence to M. Robert Marrays, rector of Uldale,[293] to be absent for one year from 1 September 1375 and farm the church.

**332**  Note of licence to William [de Cressop], rector of a mediety of Kirkbampton, to be absent for three years from Whitsun 1375.

**333**  [Fo.76v; p.265] Mandate to the archdeacon of Carlisle to induct Thomas de Malteby or his proctor to Musgrave church (in the bishop's gift) in an exchange with Richard de Upton [**330**]. Rose, 7 June 1375.

**334**  Letters patent of John de Appelby, archdeacon of Carlisle. When he was acting as the bishop's commissary, in the cathedral on 10 February 1375, Richard de Upton, rector of Musgrave, was sentenced as suspended from celebrating for his contumacy in not appearing in the chapel of Rose manor on the previous day. He has sought absolution, as was granted after he swore to obey the bishop's orders. Under the archdeacon's seal, Rose, 6 June 1375.

**335**  Commission to John de Midelton, rector of Kirkandrews, and Richard Blese, chaplain, to claim and receive clerks indicted before the king's justices of gaol delivery in Carlisle, and keep them securely etc. 10 August 1375.
    Note of similar commission to the vicars of St. Michael's and St. Lawrence's, Appleby, for gaol delivery at Appleby. Same date.

**336**  Nuncupative will[294] of William de Hothwayt made in his chamber in Oxford,[295] 3 February 1375. He gave and bequeathed 100s. to a priest celebrating

[292] With an exhaustive list of powers; cf. **306**.
[293] See **337**.
[294] Printed in *Test. Karl.*, 108–9.
[295] He was admitted to Queen's College as a poor boy, 1371 (*BRUO*, II.991).

for the soul of Robert de Musgrave and the souls of all the faithful departed. Ellen de Hothwayt, his sister, 40s. Brother Robert Dencorte,[296] 3s. 4d. M. Thomas de Karlele,[297] 6s. 8d. M. John de Stokesleye,[298] 6s. 8d. John de Corkby, 6s. 8d. Thomas de Fawside, 2s. William de Artureth, 12d. Hugh Haynyng, 12d. The Austin friars, Oxford, 40d. Residue for disposal by of executors, viz. M. William de Bownese,[299] M. Thomas de Karlele and William de Stirkland. Witnesses: Sir Robert de Routhbury, canon regular, Thomas de Mulkastre, William Alnewyke, Hugh Haynyng.

Note of probate before William de Wilton, DTh., chancellor of Oxford University,[300] 27 February 1375.

Sentence of approval by the bishop in respect of goods in the diocese. Rose (chapel), 22 August 1375.

**337** Report of enquiry before the bishop. John de Penreth, vicar of [Castle] Sowerby, William [Chaumbrelayn], rector of a mediety of Aikton, M. Thomas de Karlo', John de Kerby, John Mason, chaplains, and Robert de Thorby, clerk, said that Joan de Lucy had the right to present to Uldale church in this turn because of her dower in the lands of Anthony de Lucy, her late husband; the king last presented in right of having custody of the lands of Thomas de Lucy;[301] the church is not in dispute and assessed at, and worth, £18 p.a., the presentee [Robert] is of good repute etc., a subdeacon, and there is no obstacle to his preferment.

Notes of resignations of their churches (quoted) to the bishop by Thomas de Etton, rector of Uldale, and of Robert Marrays, rector of Huggate (Hugate; dioc. York), in an exchange of benefices. Witnesses: John de Penreth, John de Kerby, John Mason, chaplains. Rose (chapel), 1 September 1375.

[ORDINATIONS BY BISHOP THOMAS]

**338**   [Fo.78; p.266][302] Carlisle cathedral, 16 December 1363.

*Acolytes*

| | | |
|---|---|---|
| Walter de Dyghton | ) monks | Alan de Warthole |
| Stephen de Pynchebek' | ) of Holm | William de Gilcrouce |
| John Bryane | ) [Cultram] | William de Isale |

---

[296]  OP (see *BRUO*, III.2170).

[297]  Fellow of Queen's; provost 1377–1404 (*BRUO*, I.357–8).

[298]  Also of Queen's, and died 1375 (*BRUO*, III.1784–5).

[299]  Only this notice given for him in *BRUO*, II.236: possibly an incomplete reference to William del Hall, rector of Bowness, official of Carlisle in 1370 (**198**).

[300]  *BRUO*, III.2055.

[301]  Anthony's father (see **41**). They died in 1365 and 1367 respectively (*Complete Peerage*, VIII.252–3).

[302]  There is no fo.77 now; the chronological order continues after **426**. The ordination lists are in two columns. They are on 9 single folios, stitched together, after 6 'stumps'. The lists of acolytes in the manuscript are here arranged in 2 lists, where the right-hand column is the second half of the MS list.

William de Morland ) monks
Henry de Sandford ) of Holm
John de Weston ) [Cultram]
Thomas de Tweng' )
John de Neuby )
Stephen de Kirkland
Peter de Irreby
John Laverok'
Robert de Appelwra

Richard Haliwell, OP
Alan de Irreby
Thomas de Overton
William the clerk of Brough (*Burgo*)
John Taillour
William de Isale
John Taillour
Peter de Rotham, OFM

*Subdeacons*
John Bell, title of Sir Thomas de Lumlee[303]
Walter de Dighton [and the seven other monks of Holm Cultram]
Robert de Derham, title of John Bruyne
Thomas de Sundreland, title of Robert de Tybay
John Suan, title of Christopher de Moriceby
Patrick de Edenham, rector of Kirkborthwick (*Kirkbewhok'*, dioc. Glasgow), by
letters dimissory, with his benefice as title
Peter de Rotham, OFM

*Deacons*
Thomas Orefeuer )
William de Karlo' ) canons of Carlisle
Robert de Parco )
Robert de Edenhall )
John Bell, title of Thomas de Lumlee [cancelled]
William de Merton, OP

*Priests*
Sir Thomas de Slegill, canon of Carlisle
John de Galway of Glasgow dioc., by letters dimissory, title of William de Artureht
Stephen de Haklonne, OP

**339**   Dalston church, 17 February 1364.

*Acolytes*
John de Brampton
William de Raghton
Robert de Lonesdall, OFM

John de Bampton
Matthew de Clifton

*Subdeacons*
Thomas de Overton, title of Sir William de Threlkeld
Stephen son of John Huetson, title of Robert Bruyn
John Laverok', rector of Penersax (dioc. Glasgow), by letters dimissory
William de Isale, title of Thomas de Irreby

---

[303]   Interlined in another hand; and see below under Subdeacons.

Robert de Appilwra, title of Sir Alexander de Moubray, lord of Bolton
Robert de Thorneton, OP
Richard de Haliwell, 'same order'
Thomas de Lonesdall, OFM
William de Karlo', 'same order'
William de Gilcrouce, title of John de Overton

*Deacons*
Sunderland, Derham, Edenham, Rothun, Suan; and the monks Dighton,
Pynchebek, Bryan and Morland [as in **338**]
Richard de Brighton, OFM
William Beauchampp, rector of a mediety of Aikton
John Bell, title of Sir Thomas de Lumlee [cancelled][304]

**340**   Dalston church, 10 March 1364.

*Subdeacons*
John de Bampton, title of Sir Gilbert de Culwen
John Whiteheved, title of Thomas de Neuton
William de Raghton, title of M. Henry de Staynwygs, rector of Hutton in the
Forest[305]

*Deacons*
Appilwra, Isale, Laverok, Overton, Gilcrouce [as in **339**]
Stephen de Kirkland [cf. 'son of John Huetson' in **339**]; title of Robert Bruyn
Thomas de Maltby of York dioc., by letters dimissory, title of papal grace to
[a benefice] in the gift of St. Mary's, York
John Bell 'etc. as above'

*Priests*
Sunderland, Derham, Merton, Suan, Edenham [as in **338**]

**341**   [Fo.78v; p.267] Carlisle cathedral, 23 March 1364.

*Deacons*
Bampton, Whiteheved [as in **340**]

*Priests*
Isall, Kirkland [see also **340**], Overton, Appelwra, Gilcrouce, Beauchamp,
Laverok' [as in **339**]
Thomas de Maltby, title of a papal grace [cf. **340**]
Karlo',[306] Parco [as in **338**]

---

[304]  This line was added in another hand to Deacons in **338**; and see **340**.
[305]  Occurs 1356 (*Reg. Welton*, 42, n.162).
[306]  As Orefeuer under Deacons, **338**; and see *Reg. Welton*, 117, *bis*, and n.442.

**342**   Carlisle cathedral, 13 September 1365.

*Acolytes*
William de Wygton
John de Kirkhalgth [OP; see **366**]
Roger de Beticombe
Ranulph Basset', monk of Holm [Cultram]
Nicholas de Whitryg'

*Deacons*
Alan de Irby, title of M. John de Appelby
John de Irby, title of the same
Sandford, Weston, Twenge and Newby, all monks [as in **338**]

*Priests*
Robert de Hayton, title of John del More
Dyghton, Pynchebek', Bryane and Morland, monks [as in **338**]
Edenhall and Colt', canons of Carlisle

**343**   Rose chapel, 20 December 1365.

*Acolytes*
John de Askby
Thomas de Ribton

*Subdeacons*
Nicholas de Whitryg', title of Sir Thomas de Whitryg'
Thomas de Hextildesham, canon of Lanercost
William de Wygton, title of William de Crakanthorpp
Ralph Basset', monk of Holm [Cultram]

*Deacons*
Nicholas de Gresmere, OFM
William de Watton, Ocarm.

*Priest*
Alan de Irby, title of M. John de Appelby

**344**   Rose chapel, 28 February 1366.

*Acolytes*
Robert de Holand of York dioc., by letters dimissory
Norman de Redmane
Thomas de Derwent

*Subdeacons*
John son of Luke Taillour of Carlisle, title of M. John de Appelby
John de Askby, title of Christopher de Moriceby

*Deacons*
Wygton, Whitryg' [as in **343**]

*Priests*
Robert de Irby, title of M. John de Appelby
William de Watton, Ocarm.

**345**   Rose chapel, 21 March 1366.

*Acolytes*
William de Dalston
Alexander de Burgh

*Subdeacon*
Robert de Holand of York dioc., by letters dimissory

*Deacons*
Taillour, Askby [as in **344**]

*Priests*
Whitryg', Wygton [as in **343**]

**346**   [Fo.79; p.268][307] Dalston church, 4 April 1366.

*Subdeacons*
Alexander de Burgh, title of John de Burgh
Thomas de Derwent', title of John de Edenham

[*Deacons*]
Robert de Holand of York dioc., by letters dimissory, title of M. John de Appelby
Thomas de Derby, title of John de Edenham

[*Priest*]
John son of Luke Taillour of Carlisle, title of M. John de Appelby

**347**   Rose chapel, 19 September 1366.

[*Acolytes*]

| | |
|---|---|
| John de Bethunne ) | John Lovell, OP |
| John de Esyngwald ) canons of Shap | Simon de Whityngjame ) |
| Richard de Kirkby ) | William de Hoton        ) OFM |
| Peter Bedyk', OP | Richard de Burgh        ) |

---

[307] The left-hand margin is so bound in that names of orders are hidden.

[*Subdeacons*]
Richard de Dunolm, OP
Thomas Ippeswell, OFM
William de Yarum of Carlisle, title of Michael del Sandes

[*Deacons*]
Hextildeshame, Basset [as in **343**]
John de Louthre, OSA
Robert de Blakburn, Ocarm.
Derwent, Burgh [as in **344**]

[*Priest*]
John de Askby of [Carlisle] dioc., title of Christopher de Moriceby

**348** Rose chapel, 19 December 1366.

[*Acolyte*]
William de Kirkbryde

[*Subdeacons*]
Whityngiame, Lovell, friars; Bethunne, Esyngwald', Kirkby, canons [as in **347**]

[*Deacons*]
John de Willesthorp )
William de Hoghton ) OP[308]
William de Kellowe )

[*Priests*]
Sandford, Tweng, Weston, Newby, monks [as in **338**]
Thomas de Hextildesham, canon of Lanercost
Derwent', Burgh [as in **343**]
Thomas de Derby, rector of Brougham, title of his benefice
William de Helmeslay ) OP
Richard de Durisme )
William de Yarum of Carlisle, title of Michael del Sandes[309]

**349** Rose chapel, 13 March 1367.

*Acolyte*
Robert de Hale

*Subdeacons*
John Wolsthorpp, OP
William de Dalton of Durham dioc., by letters dimissory, title of Robert Bruyne

[308] This trio (with Willesthorp as Wolsthorpp) reappear as subdeacons in **349** and deacons in **350**.
[309] *Recte* deacon in this list: subdeacon in **347** and priest in **351**.

Norman de Redmane
William de Kellowe   ) OP
William de Hoghton )

*Deacon*
John Lovell, OP

*Priest*
Robert de Blakburn, Ocarm.

**350**   Rose chapel, 3 April 1367.

*Subdeacon*
Robert de Hale, title of Richard de Hale, his father

*Deacons*
Wolsthorpp, Kellowe, Hoghton, OP [see **348**]
William de Dalton of Durham dioc., by letters dimissory, title of Robert Bruyne

**351**   Rose chapel, 12 June 1367.

*Acolyte*
Gilbert son of Robert Groute of Carlisle

*Subdeacon*
William Lyster, title of John de Derwentwatre

*Deacons*
Norman de Redemane, title of John de Bampton
Simon de Whityngiame, OFM

*Priests*
William de Yarum, title of Michael del Sandes
Robert de Hale, title of Richard de Hale

**352**   Rose chapel, 18 September 1367.

*Acolytes*
Richard de Hemerghanne, OFM          Adam de Ulnedall
John de Welhow, OCarm (*ordinis Karmel'*)   Thomas de Barton

*Subdeacon*
William de Hoton, OFM

*Deacon*
William Lyster, title of John de Derwentwatre

*Priest*
Norman de Redemane, title of John de Bampton

**353** [Fo.79v; p.269] St. Lawrence's church, Appleby, 18 December 1367.

*Subdeacon*
Richard de Kirkby, canon of Shap

*Priest*
William Lyster, title of John de Derwentwatre

**354** Rose chapel, 4 March 1368.

*Acolytes*

| | |
|---|---|
| Thomas de Wygton | William de Hextildeshame ) canons of |
| John de Midelton, OFM | Robert de Braken        ) Lanercost |

*Subdeacons*
Richard de Everyngham, OFM
Adam de Ulnedale, title of Sir Gilbert de Culwen
Robert de Hilton of York dioc., by letters dimissory, title of nuns of Yedingham
Roger de Boticonne, title of William de Arturet'

*Deacon*
William de Scoter, OP

**355** Rose chapel, 25 March 1368.

*Subdeacons*
William de Kirkbryde, title of John de Dalston
Hextildesham, Braken, canons [as in **354**]

*Deacons*
Hilton, Botycombe [as in **354**]

**356** Dalston church, 8 April 1368.

*Deacons*
Ulnedale, Hextildesham, Braken [as in **354**]

*Priests*
Botycombe, Hilton [as in **354**]

**357** Carlisle cathedral, 16 September 1368.

*Acolytes*
William Beaumond
William de Stirkeland, rector of Ousby[310]

---

[310] From April 1368 (**132**).

Thomas de Oxendene ) OP
John de Langton        )

*Subdeacons*
John de Hoton, Ocarm.
Richard de Burgh ) OFM
John de Midelton )
William del More, title of John de Dalston
William Esyngwad ('who is elsewhere called Harper'),[311] title of Adam Parvyng

*Deacons*
William de Hoton        ) OFM
Richard Everyngham )
William de Kirkbride, title of John de Dalston

*Priests*
John de Morpeth, monk of Calder
Adam de Ulnedale, title of Sir Gilbert de Culwen
Richard de Kirkby, canon of Shap

**358**   Rose chapel, 16 December 1368.

*Acolytes*
| John de Bampton | Thomas Marchall |
| John de Weston | John Hogg' |
| John de Ebor' | John Ussher |

*Subdeacons*
Thomas de Barton, title of Sir Thomas de Clifford
Thomas de Rybton, title of John de Ireby
William Beaumond, title of Clement de Crofton
Thomas Oxendene ) OP
John de Langton     )
John de Wellowe, OCarm.
Gilbert Groute of Carlisle, title of his patrimony

*Deacons*
Harper, More [as in **357**]

*Priest*
Robert de Braken, canon of Lanercost

**359**   [Fo.80; p.270] Rose chapel, 24 February 1369.

*Acolytes*
| William del Peke of Penrith | William Freman of Carlisle |
| Henry de Melmorby | William de Kirkby, OP |

---

[311] Added in another hand.

*Subdeacons*
John Hogg', title of Robert de Tybay
John de Weston, OP

*Deacons*
Barton, Beaumond, Rybton, Groute [as in **358**]

*Priests*
William Harper of Carlisle, title of Sir Adam Parvyng
William de More, title of John de Dalston

**360**   Rose chapel,[312] 31 March 1369.

*Subdeacons*
William Freman, title of John de Dalston
John de York, monk of Holm [Cultram]
John de Derwent, title of Christopher de Moriceby
Henry de Melmorby, title of Adam Parvyng
Thomas de Wygton, title of William de Artureht'

*Deacons*
John de Wenlowe, OCarm.
John Hogg', title of Robert de Tybay

*Priests*
Barton, Groute, Beaumond, Rybton [as in **358**]
John Benson of York diocese, by letters dimissory, title of Egglestone [abbey]

**361**   Rose chapel, 15 September 1369.

*Acolytes*

| | |
|---|---|
| M. Thomas de Karlo', MA | Ralph de Bland ) of York dioc., |
| M. Robert de Musgrave of Carlisle | Thomas de Graysothen ) by letters |
| Henry Clerc of Crosthwaite | Richard Swayne ) dimissory |
| Thomas Englys | |

*Subdeacons*
Ralph de Betherune ) OFM
Robert de Karlo'      )
William del Pray

*Deacons*
John de Aldburgh, monk of Holm [Cultram]
Melmorby, Wygton, Freman [as in **360**]

---

[312] Interlined.

*Priests*
William de Kirkebryde, title of John de Dalston
William de Hextildesham, canon of Lanercost
John Hogg' of Carlisle, title of Robert de Tybay

**362**   Rose chapel, 15 December 1369.

*Subdeacons*
Ralph de Bethunne, OFM
Ralph de Bland
Henry Clerc[313] of Crosthwaite, title of Christopher de Moriceby
William del Pray, title of William de Crakanthorp

*Deacon*
John de Hoton, OCarm.

*Priests*
Simon de Merton of York dioc., title of Shap [abbey]
John de Wellowe, OCarm.
Freman, Wygton, Melmorby [as in **360**]

**363**   [Fo.80v., p.271] Rose chapel, 9 March 1370.

*Acolytes*

| | | |
|---|---|---|
| John de Burgh        ) of York dioc. | Thomas de Fysshbothe | |
| John de Hextildesham ) by letters | Robert de Clifton ) canons of | |
| John Irengray        ) dimissory | John Cole          ) Carlisle | |
| John de Brampton | John de Arkelby | |

*Subdeacons*
Thomas de Graysothen
M. Robert de Musgrave, title of M. John de Appelby
Thomas Englys, title of his patrimony
William de Hanlawby   ) monks of Holm [Cultram]
William de Colyngham )
Richard Swan of York dioc., title of Sir Richard Flemyng'

*Deacons*
Ralph de Bland of York dioc., by letters dimissory, title of Coverham [abbey]
William de Loweswatre of York dioc., title of William Boyvill
Clerc, Pray [as in **362**]

*Priest*
John de Tunstall, monk of cell [of St. Mary's, York], Wetheral, by letters dimissory
of archbishop of York

---

[313] Preceded by *de*, underdotted to cancel.

**364**   Rose chapel, 30 March 1370.

*Acolytes*
Richard de Ebor'     )
John de Askebrygg ) canons of Carlisle
Richard Donkyn     )

*Subdeacons*
John de Santon          )
John de Feriby           ) monks of Holm [Cultram]
John Nonyngton        )
William de Hepworth )
Richard de Berwys      )
Robert de Clyfton       ) canons of Carlisle
John Cole                  )
John de Burgh of York dioc., by letters dimissory, title of Hexham [priory]
John Irengray of York dioc., by letters dimissory, title of Blanchland [abbey]
Robert de Karlo', OFM
John de Brampton, title of Thomas de Whiteryg

*Deacons*
Musgrave, Hanlawby, Colyngham, Englys, Swan [as in **363**]
Thomas de Graysothen, title of his benefice
Elias de Nethisdale of Glasgow dioc, title of John Stewa[rd][314]
Robert de Overton, canon of Conishead, by letters dimissory [of archbishop]
of York

*Priests*
Clerc', Pray, Bland [as in **362**]
William Lowsetwater of York dioc., title of William Boyvill
Thomas Donne of Glasgow dioc., by letters dimissory, title of his benefice

**365**   Dalston church, 13 April 1370.

*Deacons*
Burgh, Irengray, Brampton [as in **364**]

*Priests*
Swan, Musgrave, Lenglise, Nedesdale [as in **363**]
Thomas de Graysuch, title of his benefice

**366**   [p.272[315]] Rose chapel, 21 September 1370.

*Acolytes*
William Cobbe of York dioc., by letters dimissory

---

[314] Hidden by binding; cf. **365**.
[315] There is no folio number, nor later; the right-hand column of this page was left
blank; later cancelled by crossings.

William de Egelton        ) canons   John Spycer of Carlisle
William de Notyngham ) of Shap   Ralph de Derham

*Subdeacons*
Robert de Cokirmouth of York dioc., by letters dimissory, title of Lanercost
William de Kirkhalgth ) OP
William de Preston     )
John de Selby, OCarm
John de Patryngton ) canons of Shap
Robert Marshall      )
John de Eland of York dioc., by letters dimissory, title of Hexham [priory]
Thomas de Grysedale, title of Carlisle [priory]
Richard de Ebor' ) canons of Carlisle
John de Askebryg )

*Deacons*
John Frysell of Glasgow dioc., by letters dimissory, title of John de Ferylawe
Robert de Clifton ) canons of Carlisle
John de Oxon'[316] )

*Priests*
Burgh, Irengray [as in **364**]
William Goldyng of York dioc., by letters dimissory, title of Conishead [priory]
John Dune, rector of *Hollow*,[317] York dioc.


**367**   Rose chapel, 21 December 1370.


*Acolytes*
John Spycer of Carlisle [repeating **366**]
Robert de Dyssington
Thomas de Fisshbothe [repeating **363**]


*Subdeacons*
William Cobbe of York dioc., title of Hexham [priory]
John Marshall of York dioc., title of Robert de Hoddespeth


*Deacons*
John Lambe of Durham dioc., by letters dimissory, title of M. John de Appelby
Robert de Cokirmouth, title of Lanercost
John de Eland, title of William de Redeslawe [cf. **366**]
Thomas de Grysedale, title of Sir Adam Parvyng [cf. **366**]


[316] Same as Cole in **363** and **364**?
[317] Possibly to be identified with Healaugh. A John Doune was rector of Kirk Bramwith, York dioc. at this date (*Fasti Parochiales*, I, 44).

*Priests*
John Frysell of Glasgow dioc., title of John de Ferylaw
William Pate of York dioc., title of Sir Adam Parvyng


**368** [p.273] Rose chapel, 31 May 1371.[318]


*Acolytes*
Ralph Sandreson of Brigham, York dioc., by letters dimissory
Thomas de Chollerton of Durham dioc., by letters dimissory
Thomas de Wederhale
William Leisingby ) OFM
John Sourlay        )


*Subdeacons*
John de Notyngham ) canons of Shap
William de Egleston )
William de Langwathby, title of his patrimony
Thomas de Fysshbothe of Carlisle dioc., title of Holm [Cultram] abbey
John de Leventhorpp of Durham dioc., title of prior and convent of Lanercost
John Spycer, title of M. John de Appelby
Robert de Dissington, title of prior and convent of Hexham


*Deacons*
Cobbe, John Marsshale [as in **367**]
Santon, Feriby, Nonyngton, Epworth, Robert Brix (cf. Richard Berwys), monks
[as in **364**]
John de Patryngton, OFM[319]


*Priests*
Nicholas de Gresmer, OFM
John Eland of York dioc., title of Hexham [cf. **367**]
Robert de Cokirmuth of York dioc., title of Lanercost
Thomas de Grysedale, title of Sir Adam Parvyng


**369** Penrith church, 20 September 1371.


*Acolytes*

| | |
|---|---|
| John de Corkeby | William de Sotheby, OP |
| Walter de Langlee, OSA | William de Snaythe, OP |
| Henry Sissor' | Robert del Kirkbythore |
| Robert de Lowther | Richard de Graysothen of York dioc. |
| John Marsshall | Thomas Bakester |

---

[318] The bishop may have attended the parliament of 24 Feb.–28 Mar.1371 (*HBC*, 563).
[319] *Recte* canon of Shap?; cf. **366**, **369**.

*Subdeacons*
Laurence Lyster, title of William de Stapelton
Robert son of Alexander de Brigham of York dioc., title of Sir Robert de
Bampton, kt.
Richard de Karlio, title of Sir Ughtred, subprior of Durham
Robert de Seton of Durham dioc., by letters dimisssory, title of Brinkburn
[priory]
William de Kirkebrid of Glasgow dioc., by letters dimissory, title of Sweetheart
(*de dulci corde*) abbey

*Deacons*
William Framlyngton of Durham dioc, title of Brinkburn [priory]
Fisboth, Spyser [as in **368**]
Richard de Ebor'  ) canons of Carlisle
John de Ashebrige )
John de Notyngham ) canons of Shap
William de Egleston )
William Faldereley, title of subprior of Durham
John Leventhorpe of Durham dioc., title of Lanercost
William de Langwathby, title of William de Crakanthorp [cf. **368**]

*Priests*
William Cob of York dioc., title of Hexham [priory]
John Marsshall of York dioc., title of Robert de Hodesperth
Robert de Clifton  ) canons of Carlisle
John de Oxonia[320] )
William de Kirkehall, OP
John de Patri[n]gton, canon of Shap

**370**   Rose chapel, 20 December 1371.

*Acolytes*
John Mason          Robert Rossegill
John de Appelby

*Subdeacons*
Adam de Appelby, title of M. John de Appelby
William de Leysyngby, OFM
Robert de Lowther, title of Robert de Ormesheved
Robert de Kirkeby, title of abbot of Shap
William Sotheby, OP
William de Korkeby, title of William son of Christopher
Richard Greysothen, title of M. John de Appelby

---

[320] *Alias* Cole? See **369**.

*Deacons*
Wyardus de Canontroa, OFM
Lytster, Brigham, Seton, Kirkebride [as in **369**]
Robert de Dissyngton, title of Hexham priory

*Priests*
Framlyngton, Langwathby, Leventhorpp', Fisseboth [as in **369**]
John Spisor, title of M. John de Appelby

**371**   [p.274] Rose chapel, 20 February 1372.

*Acolytes*
John de Hautwysell          John de Artureth

*Subdeacons*
John Mason of [Carlisle] dioc., title of M. John de Appelby
Robert de Ketillwell of York dioc., title of Hexham [priory]
Thomas de Schallerton of Durham dioc., title of William de Cave
Walter de Langle, OSA
Richard Donkyn of [Carlisle] dioc., title of Edmund de Sandford
Henry Tailyour of Carlisle dioc., title of John de Levyngton
Robert de Rossegill of [Carlisle] dioc., title of William Bysette

*Deacons*
John de Korkeby of [Carlisle] dioc., title of William Kittison [cf. **370**]
Appelby, Louther [as in **370**]

*Priests*
Robert de Dissyngton of Durham dioc., title of Hexham
Littester, Brigham, Seton [as in **369**]
William de Egilston   ) canons of Shap
John de Notyngham   )
Richard de York ) canons of Carlisle
John de Asbrig    )

**372**   Rose chapel, 13 March 1372.

*Acolytes*
Thomas de Aram          Thomas de Karliole

*Subdeacons*
Thomas Bakester of Carlisle dioc., title of John de Karleton
John de Arthureth of Carlisle dioc. title of John de Irby
John de Hautwysell of Durham dioc., title of John de Thrilwall
Richard de Staynesdrope of Durham dioc., title of subprior of Durham cathedral
Adam de Karliole of Carlisle dioc., title of William Byset
William de Northcave of York dioc., title of William de Redshawe

*Deacons*
Mason, Donkyn, Rosegill, Schallerton, Ketillwell, Taillour [as in **371**]
Robert de Kirkeby of Carlisle dioc., title of the abbot of Shap
Thomas de Hextildesham of York dioc., title of the subprior of Durham cathedral

*Priests*
John de Corkeby of Carlisle dioc., title of William Kittison
Appelby, Lowther [as in **370**]
Richard de Karliel of Carlisle dioc., title of subprior of Durham cathedral
John de Feryby        ) monks of Holm [Cultram]
Thomas de Sandton )

**373**   Commission to William [Russell], bishop of Sodor,[321] to ordain on Easter
Saturday, in Dalston church or Rose chapel, religious and secular clerks,
beneficed or not, of Carlisle and other dioceses, presented by the bishop's commissaries who had examined them. Rose, 26 March 1372.

**374**   Ordinations by the bishop of Sodor in Rose chapel, 27 March 1372.

*Acolytes*
Michael de Mane        Gilbert Roynson[322]
Henry de Ruffyn

*Subdeacon*
Thomas de Aram of York dioc., title of Thomas Whitrig

*Deacons*
Bakester, Artureth, Hautwisell, [North] Cave [as in **372**]

*Priests*
Mason, Ketilwell, Rossegill, Donkyn [as in **371**]
Thomas de Hextildesham of York dioc., title of subprior of Durham cathedral[323]

**375**   [p.275] Ordinations by Bishop [Appleby] in Bolton chapel, 22 May
1372.[324]

*Deacons*
Walter de Langlee, OSA
Karlo', Staynedropp [as in **372**]
Thomas de Arame of York dioc., title of Sir Thomas de Whitryg', kt.
Richard de Graysothen of York dioc., title of M. John de Appelby
Robert Marshall, canon of Shap

---

[321] See **286**.
[322] Probably Manxmen: they do not reappear.
[323] Followed by space 3.5 cm deep cancelled by crossing.
[324] See **292**.

*Priests*
Hautwysell, Bakester, Artureth, [North] Cave [as in **372**]
Thomas de Choll[er]ton of Durham dioc., title of William de Cave
William de Kirkebrid of Glasgow dioc., title of Sweetheart abbey

**376** Rose chapel, 18 September 1372.

*Acolytes*
John de Culwen of York dioc., by letters dimissory
William de Hertilpole, OFM

*Subdeacon*
John Sourley, OFM

*Priests*
Richard de Graysothen, title of M. John de Appelby
Robert de Kirkeby, title of abbot of Shap
William de Hexhume, canon of Hexham
Robert Mareschale, canon of Shap
Richard de Staynedrope of Durham dioc., title of subprior of Durham cathedral

**377** Rose chapel, 12 March 1373.[325]

*Acolytes*

| | |
|---|---|
| John de Merton | John de Grisdale |
| Robert de Sourby | Nicholas de Lydell |
| William de Sourby, OFM | John de Roughcroft |

*Subdeacons*
John de Culwen of York dioc., title of Hexham [priory]
Robert de Overton, OFM
Ralph de Derham, title of Robert de Ba[mpton][326]

*Priests*
Walter de Langlee, OSA
Thomas de Arame of York dioc., title of Sir Thomas de Whitrig

**378** Rose chapel, 2 April 1373.

*Subdeacons*
William de Hardred, OFM
William de Egremond of York dioc. title of Robert de [Bampton]
John de Merton of Carlisle dioc., title of William de Crakanthorp

---

[325] A parliament at Westminster, 2–24 Nov. 1372 (*HBC*, 563) probably explains the lack of record of ordinations in December.
[326] Words lost in the inner margin have been supplied from other ordinations.

John de Risdale of Carlisle dioc., title of Thomas de Lucy of [Carlisle]
Robert de Lonesdale of Carlisle dioc., title of William de Crak[anthorp]

*Deacons*
Robert de Overton, OFM
John de Culwen of York dioc., title of Shap [abbey]
Ralph de Derham of Carlisle dioc., title of Robert de [Bampton]

**379**   Rose chapel, 16 April 1373.

*Deacons*
Grisdale, Lonesdale, Merton [as in **378**]

*Priests*
Robert de Overton, OFM
Ralph de Derham of Carlisle dioc., title of Robert de [Bampton]

**380**   Rose chapel, 11 June 1373.

*Acolyte*
John de Appelby, Cistercian monk of Calder, York dioc.

*Priests*
John de Culwen of York dioc., title of Shap [abbey]
John de Merton of Carlisle dioc., title of William de Crakanthorpp
John de Grisdale, title of Thomas Lucy of Carlisle
Adam de Karlio', title of William Biset

**381**   Rose chapel, 17 September 1373.

*Subdeacon*
Adam de Lancastre, OP
John de Appelby, monk of Calder (*Caldre*)

*Deacon*
William de Egremond of York dioc., title of Sir Robert [de Bampton]

[p.276] *Priests*
Simon Spenser, monk of Wetheral
Robert de Lonesdale, title of William Crakanthorp
Henry Taillour, title of John de Levyngton

**382**   Rose chapel, 17 December 1373.

*Acolytes*
John de Brampton          William de Carleton
William de Tuxford        John de Skelton

*Subdeacons*
John de Crosseby of Carlisle dioc., title of Robert de Ormesheved
William del Peke of Carlisle dioc., title of Adam de Blencowe
William de Helbek of Carlisle dioc., title of Thomas de Blenkansopp

*Deacon*
John de Appelby, monk of Calder

*Priests*
William de Egremond of York dioc., title of Sir Robert de Bampton, kt.
Nunyngton, Hepworth, . . . ras, monks of Holm [as in **364**, **368**]

**383**   Rose chapel, 25 February 1374.

*Acolytes*
[John] Haddon, OSA
[Richard] Smerles

*Subdeacons*
John de Hibernia, OFM
[John] de Brampton of Carlisle dioc., title of William Kittison

*Deacon*
[William] de Helbek of Carlisle dioc., title of Thomas de Blenkansopp

*Priests*
[John] de Appelby, monk of Calder
John Massam, OFM

**384**   Rose chapel, 18 March 1374.

*Subdeacons*
John de Haddon, OSA
Richard Smerles of Carlisle dioc., title of M. John de Appelby

*Deacon*
John de Hibernia, OFM

*Priest*
William de Helbek of Carlisle dioc., title of Thomas de Blenkansop

**385**   Rose chapel, 8 April 1374.

*Subdeacons* [deleted]

*Deacon*
Richard Smerles, title of M. John de Appelby, archdeacon of Carlisle

**386**   Bewley chapel, 27 May 1374.

*Acolytes*
John de Merton      John M[or]le
John Jacson         William de Hoton

*Deacons*
John de Brampton of Carlisle dioc., title of William Kittison
John de Crosseby, title of Robert de Ormesheved

*Priests*
Richard Smerles of Carlisle dioc., title of M. John de Appelby, archdeacon of
Carlisle
Robert de Castell, OSA

**387**   Rose chapel, 23 September 1374.

*Acolyte*
John de Morlay

*Subdeacon*
William de Hoton of Carlisle dioc., title of William de Hoton

*Priest*
John de Brampton, title of William Kittyson

**388**   Rose chapel, 16 December 1374.

*Acolytes*
Robert de Blenkerne
Nicholas de Wessyngtoun

*Subdeacons*
Alan Davidson of Mosser (Moser), York dioc., title [of Calder abbey]
John Marshall of [Carlisle] dioc., title of Thomas de Lucy
John de Morley, title of William de B[ur]ton

*Deacons*
William Bek' of [Carlisle] dioc., title of Thomas de Blenkan[sop]
William de Hoton of Carlisle dioc., title of William [de Hoton]
Thomas de Crobrig' of Durham dioc., title of Ingram church [Durham
dioc.]

**389** [p.277] Rose chapel, 17 March 1375.

*Subdeacons*
Henry de Mallirstang, title of his benefice as rector of Severn Stoke, Worcester dioc.[327]
Robert de Blenkern, title of Thomas de Lucy
John de Marton, title of Thomas Scayff'

*Deacons*
Nicholas de Derlyngton, OSA[328]
Alan Davyson of York dioc., title of Calder [abbey]
John de Morlaye, title of William de Burton
John de Sourlaye, OFM
John Marschall, title of Thomas de Lucy

*Priests*
John de Crosseby, title of Robert de Ormeshevyd
William de Hoton, title of William de Hoton

**390** Rose chapel, 7 April 1375.

*Deacons*
Robert de Blenkern, title of Thomas de Lucy
Henry de Mallerstang, title of his benefice as rector of Severn Stoke
John de Morton, title of Thomas Scayffe

*Priests*
Alan Davidson of York dioc., title of Calder [abbey]
John de Morland, title of William de Burton

**391** Dalston church, 21 April 1375.

*Subdeacon*
Nicholas de Ledell, title of John de Dalston

*Priests*
Henry de Mallerstang, title of his benefice as rector of Severn Stoke
Robert de Blenkarn, title of Thomas de Lucy

---

[327] In the patronage of the Lords Clifford of Westmorland (*A Calendar of the Register of Henry Wakefield, Bishop of Worcester 1375–96*, ed. W.P. Marett, Worcestershire Historical Society, n.s. 7 (1972), 43).
[328] Possibly the same as Nicholas de Wessyngtoun (**388**): Washington and Darlington were adjacent parishes, in Co. Durham.

**392**   Rose chapel, 9 June 1375.

[*Deacon*]
Nicholas de Ledale, title of John de Dal[ston][329]

**393**   Rose chapel, 22 September 1375.[330]

*Acolytes*
William de Lanercost, canon of Lanercost
William de Askpatrik
William Burhend

*Subdeacons*
John de Appelby, OP
William Preston, OCarm

*Deacons*
John del Bank' of York dioc., by letters dimissory, title of Holy Trinity [priory, York]
William Tydiman, OP

*Priests*
William[331] Marschale, title of Thomas de Lucy
John de Marton, title of Thomas Scayff
Nicholas de Ledale, title of John de Dalston

**394**   Rose chapel, 22 December 1375.

*Subdeacon*
William Burhend, title of William de Cracan[thorp]

*Priests*
John del Bank' of York dioc., title of Holy Trinity [priory,] York
William de Wygton, monk of Holm [Cultram][332]

**395**   [p.278] Rose chapel, 20 September 1376.[333]

*Acolytes*
Robert de Arkilby

[329] Gaps of 1 cm above and 2 below his name.
[330] Dated from St. Matthew's (like **387**).
[331] *Recte* John? (cf. **388–9**).
[332] The last 9 cm of the column are blank. On p.278, a hand is drawn beside the heading for each service to **399**.
[333] The bishop's attendance of the 'Good Parliament' of 1376 probably explains the lack of record since **394**.

John Tinctor, canon of Carlisle
John de Dufton

*Subdeacons*
Simon de Overton, rector of Ousby (Ullasby), title of his benefice[334]
Thomas Karduill, title of Thomas Lucy

*Deacon*
William Burhend, title of William de Crakanthorp

*Priest*
William del Peke, title of Adam de Blencowe

**396**   Carlisle cathedral, 20 December 1376.

*Acolytes*
John Mayson of Glasgow dioc., by letters dimissory
Roger de Morland
Thomas Forester
John de Brathley

*Subdeacons*
William de Lanercost, canon 'there'
John Tinctor, canon of Carlisle
John de Bery, canon of Carlisle
Robert de Arkilby, title of John de Cambreton
John de Dufton, title of William de Stapelton

*Deacon*
Thomas Kardoill, title of Thomas Lucy

*Priest*
William Burhend, title of William de Crakanthorp

**397**   Rose chapel, 21 February 1377.

*Acolyte*
Adam de Aglanby of Carlisle dioc.

*Subdeacons*
John de Penyton of York dioc., by letters dimissory, title of Furness [abbey]
John Mayson of Glasgow dioc., title of Thomas de Raghton, by letters dimissory

*Deacons*
John de Dufton of Carlisle dioc., title of William de Stapelton

---

[334] His possession was ratified by the king, 22 Jan. 1376 (*CPR 1374–7*, 216).

Robert de Arkylby of Carlisle dioc., title of John de Camerton
William del Wall[335], canon of Lanercost

**398**   Rose chapel, 14 March 1377.

*Deacons*
John Bery, canon of Carlisle
John Tinctor, canon 'there'
John Mayson of Glasgow dioc., title of Thomas de Raghton, by letters dimissory

*Subdeacon*
Roger de Morland, title of Hexham [priory]

*Priests*
Robert de Arkilby, title of John de Ca[m]berton
John de Dufton, title of William de Stapelton

**399**   [Place omitted], 28 March 1377.

*Subdeacon*
John de Bradlee of Carlisle dioc., title of Sir John de Derwentwater

*Deacon*
Roger de Morland of Carlisle dioc., title of Hexham [priory]

*Priests*
Thomas Kardoill, title of Thomas Lucy
John Mayson of Glasgow dioc., title of Thomas de Raghton

**400**   Rose chapel, 16 May 1377.

*Deacons*
John de Bradlee of Carlisle dioc., title of John de Derwentwater
John de Penyton of York dioc., title of Furness [abbey]

*Priest*
Roger de Morland, title of Hexham [priory]

**401**   [p.279] Rose chapel, 19 September 1377.

*Subdeacon*
Thomas de Raghton, title of Clement de Skelton

*Priests*
John de Bery, canon of Carlisle
William del Wall, canon of Lanercost

[335] Cf. 'William de Lanercost' (**393**, **396**).

Brother Richard de Kirkeby
John de Bradelee of Carlisle dioc., title of John de Derwentwater[336]

**402**   London, in the bishop of Durham's chapel, by commission of the bishop of London (**403**), 17 April 1378.

*Subdeacons*
John Mildenale, canon of hospital of St. Mary without Bishopgate, [London][337]
M. Richard Strensall of York dioc.

*Deacons*
Michael Hanham, canon of St. Mary without Bishopgate
Thomas Ayketon of Carlisle dioc.
Thomas Wergra of Lincoln dioc.
William Drapper, rector of Barnston (*Berneston*), London dioc.

*Priests*
John Wourth, OP
Elias Sutton of Salisbury dioc., rector of Bradford (*Braddeford*)
John Rough *alias* Albone of York dioc.
Richard Porter, rector of Quinton, Lincoln dioc.

**403**   Commission to Thomas, bishop of Carlisle, from William [Courtenay], bishop of London, to ordain to major and minor orders (on Easter Saturday, in any suitable place in his diocese) secular and regular clergy of his own or any diocese; dated at his palace in London, 16 April 1378.[338]

**404**   Dalston church, 18 December 1378.

*Acolytes*
John de Pykring', OSA
John Moscropp, OP

*Subdeacons*
John de Skelton, title of Sir John de Derwentwatre
William Teb, OSA
Adam de Aglenby, title of William Dengayne

*Priests*
John de Karlo', canon of Carlisle
John de Penyton of York dioc., title of Furness [abbey], by letters dimissory

[336] Followed by 4 cm space.
[337] Prior 1393 (*CCR 1392–6*, 40)
[338] Written across the bottom margin of p.279.

**405**    Rose chapel, 5 March 1379.

*Subdeacons*
John Moscropp, OP
John Pykryng', OSA

*Deacons*
John de Skelton, title of Sir John de Derwentrwatre
Adam de Aglenby, title of William Dengayne[339]

**406**    [p.280] Dalston church, 9 April 1379.

*Subdeacon*
Henry Y[er]mayne of Worcester dioc., title of William Dengayne

*Deacon*
John Pikring', OSA

*Priests*
John Skelton, title of Sir John de Derwentwatre, kt.
Adam de Aglenby, title of William Dengayne

**407**    Rose chapel, 4 June 1379.

*Subdeacon*
Adam de Culgayt, title of William de Crakanthorpe

*Deacons*
Henry Ymayne of Worcester dioc., by letters dimissory, title of William Dengayne,
by letters dimissory
William Brigham, OP
Richard de Otri[n]gton, OFM

**408**    Rose chapel, 24 September 1379.

*Deacon*
Adam de Calgayt', title of William de Crakanthorpe

*Priests*
William del Wall, canon of Lanercost
Henry Y[er]mayne of Worcester dioc., by letters dimissory, title of William
Dengayne

---

[339] Followed by space (7 cm) to head of **403**.

**409** Rose chapel, 11 December 1379.[340]

*Acolytes*
John de Penreth
Hugh de Kirkeby, canon of Carlisle
John de Blachall, canon of Carlisle
Thomas de Hoton, canon of Carlisle
John de Crosseby, canon of the same

**410** Carlisle cathedral, 17 December 1379.

*Acolytes*
William de Penreth, Cistercian monk [of Holm Cultram]
John de Stanewyg'

*Subdeacons*
John de Penreth, rector of Kirkland, title of his benefice[341]
Hugh de Kirkeby   )
John de Blachall   ) canons of Carlisle
Thomas de Hoton )
John de Crosseby  )

*Deacon*
William Teb, OSA

*Priest*
Adam de Culgay', title of William de Crakanthorpe

**411** Dalston church, 24 March 1380.

*Acolytes*
John de Appelby
John Cosure
Robert de Vampole

*Subdeacon*
William de Penreth, monk of Holm [Cultram], Cistercian order

*Deacons*
Hugh de Kirkeby   )
John de Blachall    ) canons of Carlisle
Thomas de Hoton )
John de Crosseby  )

---

[340] Sunday before St. Lucy.
[341] Collated 14 Apr. 1379, **515**; see Nicolson & Burn, II.443.

**412**   [p.281] Rose chapel, 9 March 1381.

*Acolytes*
Ralph Spuruer of Carlisle dioc.
William de Wedyrmelhok' of the same
John de Eberston of York dioc.
Thomas Spenser of Carlisle dioc.
William de Artureth of Carlisle dioc.
Thomas de Plumland, monk of Holm [Cultram], of Cistercian order
John Blythe, monk of Cistercian order

*Subdeacon*
William de Stirkeland, rector of Rothbury, Durham dioc., title of his benefice[342]

*Priests*
William Penhalwyn, Exeter (Oxon.) dioc., title of hospital of Longbridge by Berkeley (Langbryge juxta Berkeley), Worcester dioc.
Hugh de Kirkeby, canon of Carlisle

**413**   Rose chapel, 30 March 1381.

*Subdeacons*
Ralph Spuruer of Carlisle dioc., title of John de Dalston
John Makholme of Carlisle dioc., title of John de Dalston
Thomas Spenser of Carlisle dioc., title of William de Stirkland
William de Artureth of Carlisle dioc., title of William Dikson
John de Plomland, monk of Holm [Cultram]
Thomas de Blythe, monk of Holm [Cultram]
John de Eberston, title as above[343]

*Deacon*
William de Stirkeland, rector of Rothbury, Durham dioc., title of his benefice

**414**   Rose chapel, 13 April 1381.

*Acolyte*
Robert de Thoresby of Carlisle dioc.

*Subdeacon*
William de Wedermelhok of Carlisle dioc., title of Geoffrey de Thirlkeld

*Deacons*
Ralph Spuruer of Carlisle dioc., title of John de Dalston

---

[342] Admitted 7 Dec. 1381, according to *BRUO*, III.1806, which also gives dates for orders as in **413–15**.
[343] This line interlined. See Acolytes in **412**.

John Makholme of Carlisle dioc., title of John de Dalston
Thomas Spenser of Carlisle dioc., title of William de Stirkeland
William de Artureth of Carlisle dioc., title of William Dikson

*Priest*
William de Stirkeland, rector of Rothbury, Durham dioc., title of his benefice

**415**   Rose chapel, 8 June 1381.

*Acolyte*
Thomas de Ormesheved of Carlisle dioc.

*Deacon*
William de Wedermelhok' of Carlisle dioc., title of Geoffrey de Therlkeld

*Priests*
Ralph Spuruer of Carlisle dioc., title of John de Dalston
Thomas Spenser of Carlisle dioc., title of William de Strikeland
William de Artureth of Carlisle dioc., title of William Dykson
John Makholme of Carlisle dioc., title of John de Dalston
William de Stirkeland, rector of Rothbury [repeating **414**]
John de Blachall, canon of Carlisle

**416**   Rose chapel, 21 September 1381.

*Acolytes*
John Longe of London dioc., by letters dimissory
William Baty of Carlisle dioc.
William de Askeby of Carlisle dioc.
William del Holme of Carlisle dioc.
William de Morpath, canon of Shap
John de Morton, rector of Easton (Eston), Carlisle dioc.[344]

*Priest*
William de Wethermelhok', title of Geoffrey de Thirlkeld

**417**   [p.282] Rose chapel, 5 March 1382.

*Acolytes*
John de Skirwyth of Carlisle dioc.
Thomas Marshall of Carlisle dioc.
Richard de Aspatryk, monk of Holm Cultram

*Subdeacons*
William de Askeby of Carlisle dioc., title of Thomas de Blenkansopp

---

[344] Previous known rector John de Dalston, instituted 1354 (*Reg. Welton*, 9, no.41).

Thomas de Ormesheved of Carlisle dioc., title of the same Thomas [de Blenkan-sopp]
William de Morpath, canon of Shap

*Deacons*
Adam de Exsex, monk of Calder, by letters dimissory
John de Balne, rector of Crosby Garrett (*Crossebygarard*), title of his benefice[345]
John de Plumland, monk of Holm [Cultram]
John de Blyth, monk of Holm [Cultram]

*Priests*
Thomas de Hooton, canon of Carlisle
John de Crosseby, canon of Carlisle
John de Scrueton of York dioc., by letters dimissory, title of Easby abbey
(house of St. Agatha by Richmond)


**418**   Carlisle cathedral, 22 March 1382.

*Acolytes*
William de Hayton of Carlisle dioc.
Patrick de Karlo', OP

*Subdeacon*
Richard de Plumland, monk of Holm Cultram

*Deacons*
Thomas de Ormesheved, title of Thomas de Blenkensopp
William de Askeby, title of Thomas de Blenkensopp

*Priests*
John de Balne, rector of Crosby Garrett, title of his benefice
Adam de Exsax, monk of Calder
John de Ely, OP
John de Plumland, monk of Holm [Cultram]


**419**   Dalston church, 5 April 1382.

*Acolyte*
Richard de Whale, monk of Holm [Cultram]

*Priests*
William de Askeby of [Carlisle] dioc., title of Thomas de Blenkansop
Thomas de Ormesheved, title of the same


---

[345] Instituted 1381 after death of Henry Sandford (**576**; *Test. Karl.,* 147–8).

**420** Rose chapel, 31 May 1382.

*Acolytes*
M. John de Karlo'
John de Korkeby, OFM, Carlisle

*Subdeacons*
William del Holme of Carlisle dioc., title of St. Agatha's [abbey, Easby]
William de Hayton of Carlisle dioc., title of Walter de Bampton in Allerdale
William Batte of Carlisle dioc., title of Egglestone abbey
John Thomson de Skyrwith of Carlisle dioc., title of William de Lancastr'
David Syngcler', OFM, Carlisle

*Deacon*
William de Morpath, canon of Shap

*Priests*
William Teb, OSA, Penrith
William Brigham, OP, Carlisle

**421** [p.283] Brough (*Burgh subtus Staynesmor*) church, 20 September 1382.

*Deacons*
William Baty of Carlisle dioc., title of Egglestone [abbey]
William del Holme of Carlisle dioc., title of St. Agatha's [abbey, Easby]
John son of Thomas de Skirwyth of Carlisle dioc., title of William de Lancastr'

*Priest*
William de Morpath, canon of Shap

**422** Rose chapel, 1 February 1383.[346]

*Acolytes*
William de Camerton, canon of Carlisle
William de Burgham, canon of Carlisle
John Talbot', OFM, Carlisle

**423** Dalston church, 14 February 1383.

*Acolytes*
Richard de Colby of Carlisle dioc.
Thomas Faynte of Carlisle dioc.
John de Burgh, canon of Carlisle
Robert de Askeby, canon of Carlisle

---

[346] The Vigil of Purification, a Sunday.

*Subdeacons*
Robert Allale of Carlisle dioc., title of Robert Tailliour, rector of Scaleby[347]
Clement de Mylkyksthwayt of Carlisle dioc., title of William Byset'
Thomas de Egremond of Carlisle dioc., title of Thomas del Sandes
William de Camerton, canon of Carlisle
William de Burgham, canon of Carlisle
Thomas Quale, monk of Holm [Cultram]

*Deacons*
Thomas Castell, OFM, Carlisle
David Syngcler, OFM, Carlisle

*Priests*
William Baty of Carlisle dioc., title of Egglestone [abbey]
John Skirwyth of Carlisle dioc., title of William de Lancastr'

**424**   Rose chapel, 7 March 1383.

*Acolytes*
John Hawkyn
John de Derham of Carlisle dioc.

*Deacons*
William Burgham, canon of Carlisle
William de Camerton, canon of Carlisle
Robert Alladale of Carlisle dioc., title 'as above'
Clement de Milkykthwayt, 'as above'
Thomas de Egremond of Carlisle dioc, 'as above'[348]

**425**   Rose chapel, 26 September 1388.[349]

*Subdeacon*
John Hawkyn, title of 5 marks granted by John Hunter

**426**   [Fo.88; p.284] Writ *dedimus potestatem* ordering the bishop to receive the oath of John de Derwentwater as sheriff of Cumberland; he was appointed by letters patent, which are enclosed. Westminster, 6 October 1375.[350]
Form of oath (as in **320**) (in French). [Return omitted.]

---

[347] Previous known rector was John de Grandon, instituted 1362, and occurs 1364 (*Reg. Welton*, 83, no.460; **18**). Robert appears as a chaplain, in Carlisle, 1366, 1373 (**110, 308**).

[348] Followed by space 3.5 cm deep.

[349] This late insertion has headings for all 4 orders, with unfilled spaces following Acolytes (2.5 cm), Deacons (1.5 cm) and Priests (7 cm to the foot of the page).

[350] See *CFR*, VIII.297.

**427**   Mandate to the deans of Carlisle and Cumberland. The prior and convent of Carlisle have complained that unknown evildoers have taken and concealed lands and rents which they had peacefully possessed, with confirmations of popes and kings of England; and also felled and removed oaks and other trees in Inglewood forest. Being ready, as he is obliged, to defend the convent's rights, the bishop orders proclamation in all churches of the deaneries, as required by the convent, for restitution or compensation to be made within ten days; also reports of the names of offenders. Otherwise sentences of major excommunication are to be pronounced with bells etc. [unfinished].

**428**   [Fo.88v; p.285] Mandate to all rectors, vicars and parish chaplains of Carlisle deanery. Unknown satellites of Satan murdered Lord Ranulf de Dacre, a priest, in his bed at Halton, in York diocese.[351] They are to be denounced as excommunicate, together with their supporters etc., until they deserve absolution. Rose, 9 November 1375.
   Note of similar mandates to the deans of Allerdale, Cumberland and Westmorland.

**429**   Informal letter to [Simon Langham], cardinal of Canterbury. He will know that the diocese of Carlisle lies on the border between England and Scotland, which have long been at war; despite truces, they remain disturbed with many of their people permitting warlike behaviour, attacking rights of the Church, violating its liberties and spoliation of its possessions. There is great need of clerks, particularly of skilled lawyers, for the counsel of magnates and other councillors of both kings in the march; there are few of them in [the bishop's] country. He therefore asks [the cardinal] to advise the pope of these and other circumstances and allow [the bishop] to promote clerks to benefices in his gift who can give counsel in the business of his church, and also to create notaries and to dispense vicars of parish churches to be absent to attend a university, despite their oaths to reside; their [required] number will be furnished by his clerk and kinsman, M. Henry Bowet, licenciate in laws, the bearer of these letters.[352] With expression of [the bishop's] gratitude for the numerous honours and benefits received by his kindness. Rose, 4 July 1375.

**430**   Similar letter to the cardinal, with fulsome thanks for his favours, commending M. Henry Bowet as his representative. Rose, 4 July 1375.

---

[351] Printed thus far in *Complete Peerage*, IV.5, note 'a'. The text closely resembles the archbishop's mandate of 5 Oct. 1375 (**431**). In both texts, the address clause is followed by this preamble: 'Illorum merito prosequi digne severitas ulcionis qui divinorum preceptorum immemores proximorum suorum et presertim virorum ecclesiasticorum necem conjectarunt et ad id manus impias extendere non verentur.' Ranulf was killed on the night of 17–18 Aug. 1375. His brother Hugh was held as suspect in the Tower of London, until July 1376, when he was pardoned (ibid., IV.5; *CPR 1374–5*, 294). Hayton, Lancs., was in the diocese of York.
[352] See *Oxford Dictionary of National Biography* (2004), T.F. Tout, revised J.J.N. Palmer, 'Bowet, Henry'; *BRUO*, III.2154–5.

**431** [Fo.89; p.286] Mandate of Alexander [Neville], archbishop of York, exhorting the bishop to publish the excommunication of the murderers of Ranulf de Dacre [as in **428**], in accordance with the constitutions of the church of York. Cawood, 5 October 1375.

**432** Note of licence to Hugh de Yar[um], clerk, as questor for Saint-Antoine-[de-Viennois] for one year from 23 December 1375.

**433** Note of letters to [Thomas de Maltby,[353]] rector of Musgrave, to be absent for three years from Whitsun [10 June 1375], farming his church etc.

**434** (i) Institution of Robert de Kirkby, clerk, to Kirklinton church, now vacant; presented by Edward III in the minority of Robert Tilliol's heir.[354] He was admitted in the person of Thomas de Stirkland, clerk, his proctor.[355] (ii) Archdeacon to induct. Rose, 5 December 1375.[356]

**435** [Fo.89v; p.287] Will[357] of John Taverner of Penrith, dated 11 December 1375. Commends soul to God, Blessed Mary and all saints. Burial in Penrith church or its churchyard, with his best beast for mortuary, 5lb of wax, £3 for the poor and 12d. for every priest at the office for the dead. The vicar of Penrith, 6s. 8d. for forgotten tithes. The friars of Penrith, 6s.8d. A chaplain celebrating for his soul and the souls of the faithful for one year, 9 silver marks. Residue to his wife Mariota and his son John. Executors: Adam Curteys of Penrith and Mariota.
    [No notice of probate.]

**436** Note of licence to John de Northfolk', rector of Kirklinton,[358] to be absent, farming the church to laymen etc., for one year from 21 June 1376.

**437** Note of grant to Simon de Querton, rector of Ousby,[359] of letters as follow: licence for absence for 3 years from present day to study in an English university, provided he is ordained subdeacon within a year of entering the

---

[353] Instituted 29 May 1375 (**330**).

[354] By letters dated 6 Aug. 1375. The king had presented his clerk Thomas Maddyngle to this church on 26 June, but on 19 July to West Monkton church, Somerset (*CPR 1374–7*, 131, 112, 127).

[355] He probably was the rector of Lowther whom the king presented to Kirklinton in an exchange with John Bone in May 1373; which Thomas exchanged with Thomas Slegill for Bawtry hospital, Notts., 2 months later, again by royal presentation (*CPR 1370–3*, 281, 328); and cf. **436**.

[356] Followed by margin of 7 cm, cancelled.

[357] Printed in *Test. Karl.*, 109–10, which misreads the testator's name as 'Tanner': see *Reg. Welton*, 22, no.116.

[358] Presented by the king, 23 Apr. 1376 (*CPR 1373–6*, 264); cf. **434**.

[359] Probably in recent succession to John Wartreward (**147** and n.). Simon had royal letters of ratification dated 22 Jan. 1376 (*CPR 1374–7*, 216).

benefice; being excused absence from synods and chapters, and from further ordination. London, 6 June 1376.

**438** Note of licence to Robert Pay, rector of Thursby, to be absent from 29 August 1376.

**439** Memorandum of probate of the nuncupative will (made on the Sunday after Easter) of Agnes wife of Thomas Wylkynson of Skirwith (Skyrewith), with administration to Thomas. Rose chapel, 21 October 13[76].

**440** The same of the nuncupative will [not quoted] of Cecily wife of Robert Lander of Hawksdale (*Haukysdale*), with administration to Henry Waller (named as executor). 26 October 1376.

**441** The same of the nuncupative will [not quoted] of Robert Pynkinegh of Dalston, with administration to John de Herdendale and Robert's widow (named as executors). 23 October 1376.

**442** Memorandum that Robert de Merton, rector of Newbiggin, wishing to be free of the cure of souls etc., resigned his church to the bishop. Witnesses: John Mason, chaplain, and John Clerc. Rose chapel, 22 October 1376.

**443** (i) Institution of Thomas de Stirkland, clerk, to Newbiggin church, vacant by the resignation of Robert de Merton; presented by William de Crakanthorpp. [Fo.90; p.288] (ii) Archdeacon to induct. Rose, 24 October 1376.

**444** Memorandum of resignation by Thomas de Stirkland of Newbiggin church. Witnesses: John Mason, chaplain, and John Clerc. Rose (chapel), 26 October [1376].

**445** (i) Institution of John de Merton, chaplain, to Newbiggin church, vacant by the resignation of Thomas de Stirkland; presented by William de Crakanthorpp. (ii) Archdeacon to induct. Rose, 27 October 1376.

**446** Resignation by John de Merton of Newbiggin church, in an exchange to the church of Clifton.[360] Witnesses: M. John de Appelby, archdeacon of Carlisle, and Thomas de Ryggusby, rector of Cliburn.[361] Rose chapel, 30 October 1376.

**447** (i) Collation to Robert de Merton, chaplain, to Newbiggin church, vacant by the resignation of John de Merton, in an exchange of benefices, with Robert de Lonesdale, chaplain, acting as Robert de Merton's proctor;

---

[360] M. Thomas de Salkeld was rector in 1366 but presumably departed on becoming rector of Caldbeck (**54** and n.).

[361] Previous known rector of Cliburn was Henry Heynes *alias* de Rosse, died 1367 (**82**).

presented by William de Crakanthorpp. (ii) Archdeacon to induct. Rose,
31 October 1376.

**448**   Resignation (by his proctor, Robert de Lonesdale) of Robert de Merton,
rector of Clifton, in an exchange of benefices. Witnesses: M. John de Appelby,
archdeacon, and Thomas de Ryggusby, rector of Cliburn. Rose chapel,
30 October 1376.

**449**   (i) Collation to John de Merton, chaplain, to Clifton church, vacant by the
resignation (by Robert de Lonesdale, his proctor) of Robert de Merton, in an
exchange. [Fo.90v; p.289] (ii) Archdeacon to induct. Rose, 31 October 1376.

**450**   Resignation (by his same proctor) of Robert de Merton, rector of Newbiggin. Witnesses: Robert de Byx, vicar of Torpenhow, and John Mason, chaplain. Penrith church. 3 November 1376.

**451**   (i) Collation to Robert[362] de Merton, chaplain, to Newbiggin church,
vacant by the resignation of Robert de Lonesdale, chaplain, as proctor of
Robert de Merton, its last vicar; presented by William de Crakanthorpp.
(ii) Archdeacon to induct. Penrith, 4 November 1376.

**452**   Will[363] of John de Bryntholme of Crosthwaite parish, dated 14 September
1376. Commends his soul to God. Burial in Crosthwaite churchyard, with 6s.
8d. for oblations, 9lb of wax for lights, 12 dozen [ells?] of russet cloth for the
poor (viz. for 32 tunics), and 100s. for funeral expenses. Ellen, his mother, 40s.
Lawrence, his brother, 20s. with his usual tunic. Alice Mayden, 6s. 8d. John, her
son, 6s. 8d. John Alman, 10s. Sir Adam, parish chaplain of Crosthwaite, 20s.
Brother William de Goldesburgh, 25s. The friars minor, Carlisle, 3s. 4d. The
friars preachers there, 3s. 4d. The Carmelite friars, Appleby, 3s. 4d. 6lb of wax
before the image of the BVM and St. Kentigern.[364] To repair Derwent bridge,[365]
6s. 8d. Thomas the clerk, 3s. 4d. Robert Atkynknave, 6s. 8d. His wife, 6s. 8d.
Robert de Sponhowe, 10s. John Frankys, 3s. 4d. John del Bank' of Wythop,[366]
13s. 4d. Adam de Wakthwayt and Isabel his wife, 20s. John their son, 6s. 8d. The
poor of his burial-day, 60s. The keeper of St. Mary's light, for it and the light of
St. James, 3s. 4d. The vicar of Crosthwaite, for forgotten tithes, 6s. 8d. Sir Henry
Clerc, chaplain, 6s. 8d. Residue for the use of his wife and children. Executors:
Ellen his wife, William his son, and Thomas de Crosthwayt.
[Note of probate omitted.]

**453**   Commission to M. John de Appelby, archdeacon of Carlisle. John de
Horncastre, prior of Carlisle, has sought leave to resign because his age and

[362] *Sic.*
[363] Printed in *Test. Karl.*, 111–12.
[364] To whom Crosthwaite church was dedicated.
[365] In Cockermouth (*EPNS Cumberland*, II.309).
[366] In Allerdale (ibid., II.457).

infirmity make him unable to perform his duties.[367] As the bishop is too busy to receive his resignation, the archdeacon is empowered to act, during pleasure, except in related matters. Rose, 10 November 1376.

**454** Petition to the bishop by the subprior and convent of Carlisle for licence to elect a prior in place of John de Horncastre, whose resignation has been received by the bishop's authority. Under their common seal, 13 November 1376.[368]

**455** LICENCIA CONCESSA DICTIS SUPPRIORI ET CONVENTUI AD ELIGENDUM [PRIOREM.] Letter of the bishop to the subprior and convent. Their letters (brought by Robert de Edenhale, their fellow-canon) had certified the vacancy caused by the resignation of John de Horncastre and sought the bishop's licence to elect his successor; it had also been certified by John de Appelby [incomplete].[369]

**456** [Fo.92; p.290. Last 11 lines of mandate to execute writ **471**.]

**457** Note of probate of the will [not quoted] of William Artureth, rector of Orton.[370] Rose (chapel), 3 March 1377.

**458** Indictment[371] of William de Rouclyf, clerk, viz. that he and others burgled the house of Robert Watson of [Kirk] Bampton and stole gold, silver, goods and chattels worth 40 marks on 31 October 1375; he is a common thief and burglar (*deburgator*) of houses, and collaborates (*communicans*) with Scots to commit robberies in England.

**459** Commission to the official of Carlisle, John de Penreth, canon [of Carlisle],[372] and John de Midelton, rector of a mediety of Aikton, to receive the purgation of William de Rouclyf, clerk, in the parish church of St. Mary, Carlisle, on Monday next, by the hands of twelve rectors, vicars and clerks; he was lately charged in a secular court before Roger de Kirkton and Roger de Fulthorpp, justices of gaol delivery at Carlisle, in that [as in **458**], and thus defamed and committed to prison until he can be purged. Rose, 25 January 1377.

---

[367] He was ordained subdeacon in 1332 (*Reg. Kirkby*, I.16).
[368] MS Thursday after St. Martin: cf. 18 Nov. in *Fasti*, VI.106.
[369] The original following folio (numbered 91) is wanting. Obviously the text would have continued with the remainder of the licence, the bishop's subsequent confirmation of the election (or possibly with his provision of another as prior) and other contingent letters (e.g. as in *Reg. Welton*, 13–14); the priory was still vacant on 8 Apr. 1377 (**470**). The next known prior was John de Penreth, when he resigned in 1381 (*Fasti*, VI.100); he was vicar of Castle Sowerby from 1360 (*Reg. Welton*, 58, no.314; and see **322** below).
[370] Instituted 1337 (*Reg. Kirkby*, I.403, 406).
[371] Probably copy of the court of gaol delivery's record.
[372] Cf. **455**n..

**460**   (i) Institution of Richard de Langwathby, priest, to Orton church, vacant by the death of William de Artureth; presented by Clement de Skelton and his wife Joan. (ii) Archdeacon to induct. Rose, 17 March 1377.

**461**   (i) Institution of John Fox, chaplain, to Skelton church, vacant by the death of Adam de Armestrang';[373] presented by Ralph, Baron Greystoke. (ii) Archdeacon to induct. Rose, 23 March 1377.

**462**   [Fo.92v; p.291] (i) Institution of John Mason, chaplain, to Croglin (*Creglyn*) church, now vacant;[374] presented by Hugh de Querton. (ii) Archdeacon to induct. Rose, 27 March 1377.

**463**   Will[375] of John Pynknegh, senior, dated Good Friday [11 April] 1376. Commends soul to God, Blessed Mary and all saints. Burial in churchyard of St. Michael's, Dalston, with best beast for mortuary, 12d. for wax and 12d. for oblations. St. Wenem's bridge, 6d. Dalston bridge, 6d. The vicar of Dalston for altarage in that year, 4 stricks of oats. The friars minor, Carlisle, 12d. The friars preachers, Carlisle, 12d. A chaplain celebrating for his soul for one year, 8 marks. A wake for friends and neighbours, 12d. A dole for the poor, 6s. 8d. and beer from half a skep of malt. His wife, 10s. from his portion, and half his portion of his corn; the other part to be distributed among the poor in bread, beer and flour. Isabel his maid, [abraded] and a third-year heifer. Residue to his executors, viz. Alice his wife and John Ragstra. John Marche, vicar of Dalston, 3s. 4d. Thomas the clerk, 6d.
Note of probate. Rose (chapel), 16 March 1377.

**464**   [Nuncupative] will[376] of William de Wyllerdby, rector of Croglin,[377] dated Palm Sunday [22 March] 1377. He commended his soul to God, Blessed Mary and all saints. Burial wherever God disposes, as decided by John de Marche, vicar of Dalston, and Henry de Bewyke, his executors. A priest celebrating for his soul, 6s. 8d. A man visiting [obscured –possibly ? mon'] of Beverley,[378] 4s., *vel pro modo conduci poterit*. He bequeathed the residue to his [above] executors to pay his debts and dispense at their discretion. Witnesses: John de Kirkby, chaplain, and John Tayllor.
Note of probate. Rose (chapel), 3 April 1377.

**465**   [Fo.93; p.292] Will[379] of William de London, citizen of the city of Carlisle, dated 13 May 1377. Commends soul to God, Blessed Mary and all

[373] See **194** and n..
[374] See **464**.
[375] Printed in *Test. Karl.*, 112–13.
[376] Printed in *Test. Karl.*, 113–14.
[377] See **293** for previous known rector, and **462** for William's successor.
[378] 7 miles north of Willerby.
[379] Printed in *Test. Karl.*, 114–15.

saints. Burial in cemetery of the canons of St. Mary's, Carlisle, next to his parents; a stone of wax for 5 lights to burn round his body; 10s. for bread for the poor. Sir John de Midilton, 2s. The friars preachers and minor, Carlisle, 6s.8d. equally divided. The nuns of Armathwaite, 3s. 4d. Each priest of the town of Carlisle attending his exequies, 6d. John de Yarum, clerk, 6d. The nuns of St. Bartholomew, Newcastle upon Tyne, a psalter and 6s. 8d. Joan his wife, for her life, his 2 tenements lying between the tenements of John the clerk of Annan (Anand) and Edmund de Warton, to be held of the chief lords of the fees by the customary services; after her death they are to remain forever with Richard de London, his brother, their heirs and assigns, from the chief lords as above. Residue to Joan his wife. Executrix: Joan, by the view and ordinance of Richard de London, his brother, and William de Karlton, junior. [Dated] before many witnesses.

**466** Will[380] of Walter de Claxton, being of sound mind, dated 22 May 1376. Commends soul to God, Blessed Mary and all saints. Burial in the cemetery of St. Mary's [Carlisle], with his best horse and arms for mortuary; for lights round the feretory, 5s.; in oblations, 5s.; a wake for neighbours, and for the poor, 40s. The abbot and convent of Holm Cultram, 20s. Six chaplains celebrating and ministering at his exequies, 12s. The friars of Carlisle, 6s. 8d. equally divided. The friars of Penrith, 3s. 4d. The friars of Appleby, 40d. William his kinsman, clerk, 5 marks. Residue to a chaplain celebrating for his soul and the souls of all his parents and benefactors in Wigton church, for as long as it lasts. Executors: Adam [de Crosseby], vicar[381] of Bolton, John de Aykeheved, chaplain, and David de Stokdale. Witnesses: Adam del Hegborne and John Moreman.
Note of probate. Rose (chapel), 15 May 1377.

**467** Note of probate of will of William de London [**465**]. Rose (chapel), 22 May 1377.

**468** [Extracts from Exchequer rolls.] Thomas, bishop of Carlisle, owes the king for a pond called Linstockgarth in the River Eden, 6 acres of land in Skitby (*Scotby*) to the north of the river, and 12 acres in Langholm, which William de la Vale, escheator in Cumberland, seised for the king. Edward III granted their custody to the bishop on 5 November 1374.[382] Order to the barons to restore custody to him and suspend the suit in the Exchequer.

**469** Commission of John [Buckingham], bishop of Lincoln, appointing Bishop Thomas to consecrate the numerous altars, some of them new, in Tattershall (*Teatishale*) church.[383] Liddington, 20 March1376.

---

[380] Printed in *Test. Karl.*, 115–16.
[381] *Recte* rector.
[382] See *CFR*, VIII.263.
[383] 13 miles from Horncastle, Lincs., the bishop of Carlisle's manor.

**470** [Fo.93v; p.293] Certificate to Alexander [Neville], archbishop of York, acknowledging receipt on 21 March of his mandate (dated at his manor near London, 2 March 1377) which quotes Edward III's writ (dated at Westminster, 16 December 1376) ordering the archbishop to call his clergy to York as soon as possible to grant a subsidy for the defence of the Church and realm;[384] the archbishop, being anxious to assist, orders the bishop and prior of Carlisle etc., to assemble on 15 April 1377.

The bishop reports that he has cited the abbots of Holm Cultram and Shap and the prior of Lanercost in person. As the priory of Carlisle was vacant, he has cited the archdeacon to attend in person. The convent of Carlisle is to send a proctor, as are the convents, chapters and colleges of Holm, Shap and Lanercost: their names are M. Hugh de Fletham (Carlisle chapter), M. John de Norton (Holm chapter), Brother William de Sotton, canon of Shap (for its convent),[385] William de Ulnsdale, clerk (Lanercost convent), and M.William de Bownes, rector of the same,[386] and Robert de Bys, vicar of Torpenhow.[387] Rose, 8 April 1377.

**471** Mandate to official to execute writ of Edward III summoning the bishop to attend a parliament at Westminster on 27 January 1377, with *premunientes* clause for the clergy; dated Havering atte Bower, 1 December 1376.[388] [Fo.94; p.294]. Order to cite prior and archdeacon in person, chapter and clergy by proxies. Rose, 6 January 1377.

**472** Certificate of Ralph [Erghum], bishop of Salisbury, that he has executed the bishop of Carlisle's commission (dated Carlisle, 18 December 1377) for an exchange of benefices between John Marsshall, rector of Warfield (*Warefeld*, dioc. Salisbury), and John de Bouland, rector of Arthuret; the king presented Marsshall to Arthuret.[389] London, 4 February 1377.

**473** Memorandum that on Monday, 26 January 1377, in the presence of M. William del Hall, official of Carlisle, and John de Midelton, rector of Aikton, William de Rowclyf, clerk, charged *ut superius in registro* [**459**], was purged by the oaths of the following, in St. Mary's church, Carlisle:

Hugh de Lameslee, rector of Stapleton
Richard Hog', vicar of Walton

| | |
|---|---|
| John Strakour | Thomas Kardoill, deacon |
| John Colt | William Rudd |
| Robert de Rossgill | John de Yarum |
| William Freman | William de Kerby |

---

384  *CCR 1374–7*, 469.
385  Ordained subdeacon, 1361 (*Reg. Welton*, 117).
386  *Alias* William del Hall, rector of Bowness on Solway, official of Carlisle (**473**).
387  See his will, *Test. Karl.*, 129.
388  See *CCR 1374–7*, 466–7.
389  By letters dated 2 Dec. 1376; a previous presentation for this exchange had been revoked in July 1376 (*CPR 1374–7*, 302, 406).

| William de Kirkbride | William Rome |
| John de Galwidia | William Cullerdof |
| Alexander de Burgh | William Belron |
| Thomas de Wygton | Alexander del Vale |
| and Adam Kardoill, chaplains | and Thomas del Mane, clerks |

**474**  To King Edward. The bishop is unable to attend Parliament on 27 January because of bodily infirmity and business about his cathedral church, and therefore appoints as his proctors M. Walter Scirlawe[390] and Sir John Marshall,[391] clerks, and John de Kirkby, Thomas de Skelton and William de Stirkeland. Rose, 8 January 1377.

**475**  (i) Institution of John de Culwen, chaplain, to Newbiggin church, vacant by the resignation of Robert de Merton; presented by William de Crakanthorpp. (ii) Archdeacon to induct. Rose, 30 July 1377.

**476**  [Fo.94v; p.295] Presentation to Thomas [Hatfield], bishop of Durham, or his vicar-general, of M. John de Appelby, canon of Norton collegiate church (dioc. Durham),[392] to Rothbury church, now vacant. Rose, 20 July 1377.

**477**  Resignation [quoted] of Robert de Merton, rector of Newbiggin. Witnesses: John Mason, rector of Croglin, and John de Morton, clerk. Rose chapel, 26 July 1377.

**478**  (i) Resignation [quoted] of William de Culwen as proctor of Roger de Kirkeoswalde, vicar of Bromfield,[393] in an exchange for the rectory of Newbiggin. Witnesses: John Mason, rector of Croglin, and John de Morton, clerk.
(ii) Note of resignation of John de Culwen, rector of Newbiggin, in the same exchange.
(iii) Collation of John de Culwen, chaplain, to Bromfield vicarage, vacant by the resignation of William de Culwen as proctor of Roger de Kirkoswalde.
(iv) Archdeacon to induct.
(v) Institution of Roger to Newbiggin church, vacant by the resignation of John de Culwen as William's proctor; presented by William de Crakanthorpp'.
(vi) Archdeacon to induct. Rose, 6 August 1377.

**479**  [Fo.95;[394] p.296] Will[395] dated 1 March 1377 of John de Warthecopp, being of good memory. Commends soul to God, Blessed Mary and all saints.

---

[390]  See *BRUO*, III.1708–10; *Oxford Dictionary of National Biography* (2004), M.G. Snape, 'Skirlawe, Walter'.
[391]  A king's clerk, and see **472**.
[392]  He was canon of Norton and archdeacon of Carlisle in 1366 (**56**).
[393]  Instituted 1344 (*Reg. Kirkby*, I.158–9).
[394]  From here foliations given in arabic numerals, possibly in the same hand as the pagination.
[395]  Printed in *Test. Karl.*, 116–17.

Burial in Kirkby Stephen churchyard, with best beast for mortuary; for light to burn round body, 3s. 4d.; oblations, 6s. 8d.; the high altar, 13s. 4d.; dole for the poor, 5 marks; a wake for neighbours, 5 marks. The church fabric, 60lb of lead. For services celebrated in the church for his soul, £10 13s. 8d. Sir John Yve, 6s. 8d. Thomas Lambe, chaplain, 6s. 8d. William Clerc, 3s. 4d. Roger his [testator's] son, 40s. John de Merton, chaplain, 6s. 8d. The four orders of friars, 26s. 8d.; in equal portions. Margaret del Hall, a good cow with a stirk. Henry Henryson, 20s. Residue to his and his wife Mariota's children. Executors: Mariota, his son Thomas and Henry Henryson. Witnesses: Gilbert Henryson and John Yve, chaplain.

Sentence of probate, with administration to executors named. Rose (chapel), 15 September 1377.

**480**  Letter to Katherine, widow of Thomas Smert of Kirkby Stephen; as he died intestate, without appointing executors, the bishop grants her administration of his goods in the diocese. Rose, 15 September 1377.

Note of similar grant to Marg[aret], widow of Hugh de Querton of Kirkby Stephen. Same date.

**481**  Sentence[396] of probate of nuncupative will of William del Banks of Kirkby Stephen made on 23 November 1376. After his canonical burial and payment of his debts, he gave his goods to his wife Maud and his children. Executor: Simon Kelay. Witnesses: Robert Henryson and Simon's wife Alice. Administration granted to the executor. Rose, 15 September 1377.

Note that the bishop also proved the will of Anabel, wife of John Murolf' of Kirkby Stephen, who was granted administration. Same date.

**482**  Writ of King Richard II ordering the bishop be present in person at his coronation in Westminster on 16 July 1377. Kennington, 26 June 1377.

**483**  [Fo.95v; p.297] Letters of Richard II requesting prayers and processions to assist his defence of the kingdom from its invasion by the French and their adherents. Westminster, 1 July 1377.[397]

**484**  Letters patent. The bishop has received letters (dated Avignon, 20 January 1375) of John, cardinal-priest of Saints Nereus and Achilleus, papal penitentiary, on behalf of Nicholas de Stapilton, clerk (dioc. Carlisle); who was dispensed despite being the son of unmarried parents to be promoted to all orders and to hold a benefice. Afterwards he was promoted to the church of Ousby which he held peacefully for two years,[398] despite not being ordained priest within one year, for which he sought dispensation. By the pope's verbal

[396]  Printed in *Test. Karl.*, 117.
[397]  Similar letters were sent to the archbishops, all other bishops and the two universities (*CCR 1377–81*, 82). Rye was sacked on 29 June.
[398]  Collated, as clerk, 1365; exchanged to Stapleton church, 1368 (**20, 132**).

command, Nicholas may be dispensed for his disability after resigning the church to Bishop Thomas and accounts for his receipt of its revenues. The bishop accordingly certifies that Nicholas has resigned the church, an enquiry has found that he has spent the revenues for its benefit and otherwise at the bishop's discretion, and has been absolved after doing penance so that he may have a benefice. Date omitted.

**485** MONICIO ET CITACIO CONTRA VICARIUM DE GILCROUCE. Mandate to the dean of Allerdale. Parishioners of Gilcrux have complained that their vicar, Richard [de Irland],[399] contrary to his oath to reside, has been absent overseas for a long time. . . .[400]

**486** [p.298] NOTA HIC MAGISTER WILLELMUS BOWNES VICARIUS IN SPIRITUALIBUS GENERALIS.[401]

**487** Letters of William, rector of Bowness, commissary *in hac parte* of Bishop Thomas, instituting John de Alanby, chaplain, to the vicarage of Dalston, in the bishop's collation and by his authority; vacant by the death of John del Marche. Under the seal of the officiality, Carlisle, 25 June 1378.

**488** Mandate of William, rector of Bowness, vicar-general *in spiritualibus* of Bishop Thomas (absent *in remotis*), to the dean of Westmorland and vicar of Shap. John [de Bampton], vicar of Bampton,[402] has been absent for a long time, despite his oath to reside, neglecting the cure of souls and exercise of hospitality; he has not applied for a licence, and has wasted the revenues in distant places. He is to be cited in church before his parishioners, friends and proctors (if any): if he does not return within six months, proceedings will be taken for his deprivation. [The vicar-general] is to be sent a certificate of execution within two months. Under the seal of the officiality (as he does not have one for the vicariate), Carlisle, 20 June 1378.

**489** Mandate of the same to the dean of Carlisle. John [Marshall], rector of Arthuret,[403] Elias, rector of Scaleby,[404] and John de Northfolk, rector of Kirklinton,[405] have for long been absent without cause or licence, wasting their

[399] Instituted 1371 (**261**); see also **493**.
[400] Continuation missing. The next page, only paginated as 298, is the first of a quire of 4 openings.
[401] With a large pointing hand from the inner margin. The last commission for vicars-general in the register is **217**, dated 1371, appointing the prior and archdeacon. William is named 'del Hall' from his institution as rector of Bowness on Solway, in 1354 (*Reg. Welton*, 8, no.36). He occurs as official of Carlisle from 1369, and from then tends to be named 'William de Bowness'.
[402] Instituted 1369 (**139**).
[403] Instituted 1377 (**472**).
[404] The last-known rector was John de Grandon, instituted 1362 (*Reg. Welton*, 83, no.460); licensed absence, 1364 (**18**).
[405] Instituted 1376 (**436** and n.).

revenues and giving none to the poor as they should. [p.299] They are to be cited in their churches and return to serve their parishioners within six months, otherwise proceedings for their deprivation will be initiated. [The vicar-general] is to be certified within two months. Under the official's seal, Carlisle, 20 June 1378.

**490**   Letter of William de Crakanethorpp to Bishop Thomas or his vicar-general presenting Robert de Merton, chaplain, to Newbiggin church, vacant by the resignation of Sir Roger, the last rector. Carlisle, 26 May 1378.

**491**   Letters patent of Roger de Kirkossewald, rector of Newbiggin in Westmorland,[406] resigning the church to Bishop Thomas or his vicar- or vicars-general, and appointing William de Culwen as his proctor. Under the seal of the dean of Allerdale, who confirms its use, Bromfield, 13 January 1378.

**492**   Licence of William, rector of Bowness, vicar-general of Bishop Thomas in his absence, to Robert Paye, rector of Thursby, at the request of Lady Maud de Clifford, for him and another chaplain she chooses to celebrate divine services in her presence in Brougham church and in any other suitable place; valid until Martinmas [11 November]. Under the official's seal, Carlisle. n.d.

**493**   Certificate of the dean of Allerdale to the bishop, acknowledging receipt of a mandate of William, rector of Bowness, vicar-general, showing that Richard de Ireland, vicar of Gilcrux, has deserted [Fo.98; p.300] and neglected his cure for a long time [etc., with orders as in **489**]; under the official's seal, Carlisle, 12 July 1378. The dean reports that on the feasts of Saints Margaret [20 July] and Thomas the Martyr after Christmas [29 December], he had solemnly (*cruce erecta*) in the presence of Richard's parishioners in Gilcrux church cited him to return within six months. Aspatria, 29 January 1379.

**494**   Letters patent testifying that William de Colwen, proctor of Roger, rector of Newbiggin,[407] resigned the church to John de Penrith, prior of Carlisle, and William, rector of Bowness, vicar-general. Under their seals, Carlisle, 22 [omitted] 1378

**495**   [Fo.98v; p.301] Will[408] of Joan de London dated 29 October 1378. Commends soul to God, Blessed Mary and all saints. Burial in churchyard of St. Mary's, Carlisle, with best beast for mortuary; 16lb of wax for light; 13s. 4d. for bread to the poor. The four orders of friars, 13s. 4d. in equal portions. Her parish chaplain, 12d. The parish clerk, 6d. St. Mary's light, 3s. 4d. St. Alban's light, 3s. 4d. Joan wife of William del Cote, a set of silver beads with a gold clasp. Isabel Marchaell, a set of amber beads. Edmund de Warton, 10s. William de Carleton, 26s. 8d. Joan wife of Edmund de Burton, cloth for a tunic and a

---

[406]   Instituted 6 Aug. 1377 (**478**).
[407]   See **491**.
[408]   Printed in *Test. Karl.*, 117–19.

melde hood with her best silk veil. Robert de Rosgyll, chaplain, to celebrate for her soul for a year in the chapel of St. Alban, 7 marks. The dau. of John de Daker, once wife[409] of John de London, 2 beds, 2 hangings, 2 towels and 2 copper pots and a basin with a jug. The said John de Daker's dau. and her heirs forever, 2 tenements in Botchergate between those of John de Denton and Nicholas Alaynson; but should she die without legitimate issue, the executors are to sell them for celebrations for her soul and those of William de London and William Sleht. Richard de London and his heirs for ever, a tenement in Fisher Street between those of Robert de Strayt and William de Stirkeland. Joan de London, nun, a hood of black cloth. Ellen dau. of Thomas de London, 2 copper pots pledged [to Joan]. John Howeth, 24s.; also a surcoat with a melled tunic. The wife of John Paytfine, a rose-coloured tunic. Joan de Halton, a tunic of the same cloth. Margaret wife of John Halden, a silk kerchief and a linen veil with a hood. The wife of Robert Barbour, a silk kerchief. Alice Otere, a blanket tunic. William Swaene, a tunic and 8s. Thomas de London, 40s. for the marriage of his dau. Ellen. Residue for her executors to spend for her soul. Executors: William de Carlton, junior, and Richard de London. Witnesses: Thomas de London, John Halden and Joan Paytfin.

**496** Letters of William, rector of Bowness etc., instituting John de Kerby, chaplain, to a mediety of Aikton church, vacant by the death of John de Mydylton; presented by Hugh de Dacre, lord of Gilsland, kt. Under the official's seal, Carlisle, 25 November 1378.

**497** Sentence[410] of the official of Carlisle proving the nuncupative will of Hubert de Knaton, chaplain, dated 24 November. He commended his soul to God and all saints, and burial in the churchyard of Morland or elsewhere if God provided that he died elsewhere. He gave all his goods to John del Pray, vicar of Morland, and Thomas the clerk, to spend for his soul, appointing them his executors. Witnesses: Nicholas Carpenter, W. chaplain of Bolton and John de Tesdale. Penrith church, 9 February 1378.

**498** Letters patent of Bishop Thomas appointing Isabel widow of John del More, Henry de Threlkeld and Roland Armestrange to administer the goods of John, who died intestate; relaxing his sequestration. Under his seal. Date omitted.

**499** [Fo.99; p.302] Will[411] of John Marshall of Carlisle, being healthy in mind and memory, dated 25 May 1378. Commends soul to God, Blessed Mary and all saints. Burial in churchyard of St. Cuthbert's, Carlisle, with best beast and cloth as mortuary; for light then, 5lb of wax; in dole for the poor, 40s. The parish altar in the church for forgotten tithes, 6s. 8d. £10 in silver to buy a vestment with apparel, viz. a chasuble with an alb, amice, embroidered stole and maniple, with

---

[409] MS *filie.*
[410] Printed in *Test. Karl.*, 119–20.
[411] Printed in *Test. Karl.*, 120–2.

a cloth hanging before altar, a frontal, 2 napkins, a cloth on the altar and 2 curtains of the same suit; this vestment with all its apparel is to stay on St. Mary's altar in St. Cuthbert's church; the £10 is to remain in the executors' hands to be spent for this purpose as soon as it can be fitly spent, with any remainder given to the keepers of St. Mary's said light. To the prior and convent of 'our' cathedral church, 26s. 8d. for a pittance, and the friars preachers and minor, 26s. 8d. in equal portions. His sister, 20s. Thomas Doget, chaplain, 7 marks to celebrate before the cross in St. Cuthbert's for a whole year. A friar chosen from the preachers and minorites by the prior, 7 marks to celebrate for his soul for a year. The parish chaplain of St. Cuthbert's, 6s. 8d. John Statore, William Rider and Thomas Doget, 10s. in equal portions. The parish clerk, 18d. Each chaplain coming to his exequies, 12d. Emma, his servant, 6s. 8d. Brand, his servant, 40d. Robert, his servant, 40d. John de Appelby, archdeacon of Carlisle, 20s., and Richard de London, 20s. Isabel, his wife, the tenement he lives in with the tenement once Henry de Malton's, with all appurtenances, for her life, with remainder to his son John and the lawful heirs of his body; with successive remainders to his son Thomas and dau. Joan. All his tenements in St. Cuthbert's venell are bequeathed [as above] to his said son Thomas, with successive remainders to John and Joan. The tenements in Rickergate once Peter Spicer's are bequeathed to Joan, with remainder to Isabel for her life, with successive remainders to John and Thomas.

Should his children John, Thomas and Joan all die without legitimate issue, all these tenements are to remain with Isabel, if she and her heirs survive; but if none of them survive, the tenements are to be disposed of as seems best for their (nostrum) souls. Residue of all goods not bequeathed left to Isabel and [testator's] children. Executors: John de Appelby, archdeacon of Carlisle, Richard de London and the said Isabel. Witnesses: Sir Thomas del Overend, Thomas Doget 'and others'.
[No note of probate.]

**500**  [Fo.99v; p.303] Memorandum of enquiry before the bishop into an exchange of Croglin church and Dalston vicarage. The witnesses said that its cause was that John Mason would prefer (*melius placet*) to have the vicarage than the church while John de Alanby would prefer the church, to which Hugh de Querton last presented;[412] William [Beauchamp], rector of Kirkoswald, is now patron. The church is not vacant, pensionary or portioned, assessed at £9 15s. 4d. and worth 10 marks p.a. The presentee [. . .].[413] Rose chapel, 7 February 1379.

**501**  Citation of the prior and convent of Carlisle to attend visitation by the bishop or his commissaries in their chapter house on 11 January [as in **36**]. Rose, 2 January 1379.

**502**  Mandate to the dean of Carlisle to cite clergy and lay representatives to attend visitation by the bishop or his commissaries [as in **304**]. Rose, 2 January

---

[412]  See **462**.
[413]  Incomplete, partially erased.

1379. [Postscript.] Parishioners are to be ordered by their priests to bring their children for confirmation on the days and places listed in the schedule.

**503** Will[414] of Robert Goldsmyth of Carlisle. Commends soul to God, Blessed Mary and all saints. Burial in churchyard of St. Mary's, with best beast and cloth for mortuary; a stone of wax to burn round his body; 10s. for dole for the poor. The parish priest, 12d. The parish clerk, 6d. Richard Orfeure, a protective jacket and maple sleeve. John Cardoill, a hauberk. John [Robert's] son and heir, a basinet with a visor, a pair of plate gloves, a protective jacket, 2 *pesaynes*, a silver-plated axe and a trenchant sword. Thomas Goldsmyth, his son, and Agnes de Bowatby, his yearly terms in a messuage with garden in Caldewgate, which he has by demise of the prior of Hexham, now held by John de Fournes, smith; also his yearly terms in a grange with a toft which he has by demise of William [Fo.100; p.304] de Yarum, chaplain; also to Thomas, half his tools for a goldsmith's art, with silver and cutlery. Alice, sister of Thomas, 2 pairs of beads with clasps and hanging rings once the wife of William de Dundrawe's; also 3s. owed by Adam Blistblod or a brass pot and [. . . . pledged] for them. Robert his servant, a good new tabard with a tunic of the same colour. Richard de Haverington, half a skep of barley and a skep of oats. St. Mary's light, a gold ring. John Austyn, 7s. John de Dundrawe's wife, a gold ring with a sapphire stone. John de Dundrawe, his silver baselard. The friars minor, 2s. The friars preachers, 2s. John Austyn, a pair of plate. Ellen, [Robert's] dau., 3s. annual rent from a tenement next to St. Alban's church, to her and her legitimate heirs, with remainder to his heirs.The inner Eden bridge,[415] 6s. 8d., and Caldew bridge, 18d. Priests celebrating for his soul, 5s. Residue to Margaret, his wife, and their dau.s. Executors: Margaret, John Cardoill and John Austyn. Dated Carlisle, 31 January 2 Richard II [1379].
    Note of probate. Rose chapel, 10 February 1379.

**504** Will[416] of John del Marche, vicar of Dalston, being healthy in mind and memory, dated 16 May 1378. Commends soul to God, Blessed Mary and all saints. Burial in Dalston churchyard or wherever else God disposes, with best beast for mortuary. A cow with calf to the light of the Blessed Mary and St. Michael in that church. A cow with calf to Joan dau. of Thomas de Stirkland. A two-year-old colt to John son of John de Penreth. To John son of Robert Blome, a cow with calf. Half the acre of oats at Jopcroft to Thomas called Clerc. To John son of Thomas Sympson, a stag. Hugh Porterman, a colt. Residue to John de Dalston and Thomas de Stirkland, to spend by their ordinance, appointing them executors. Witnesses: Thomas called Clerc and Roger Baynes. Under his seal.
    Note of probate. Rose chapel, 6 February 1379.

**505** Will[417] of Roger de Salkeld. Commends soul to God and Blessed Mary. Burial where God pleases, with his best beast there; 6s. 8d. for wax and 40s. for

---

[414] Printed in *Test. Karl.*, 123–4.
[415] See ibid., 124, n.; also *EPNS Cumberland*, I.43.
[416] Printed in *Test. Karl.*, 124–5.
[417] Printed in *Test. Karl.*, 125–6.

oblations. 13s. 4d. to each order of friars. The canons of Carlisle, 20s. The nuns of Armathwaite, 6s. 8d. 6 marks to celebrate for the souls of Eudes Russell and Margaret his wife, Alexander Blaber, Adam Russell and all deceased whose goods he has. 100s. to a priest to celebrate for his soul. Robert del Hall, 3s. 4d. Richard Bowman, 6s. 8d. Hugh Hardyng, 40s. John Fecher, 6s. 8d. John Smith, 40s. Robert Baker, 6s. 8d. Thomas de Malton, 12d. William Shirlok, 40s. John de Canesby, 6s. 8d. William Cowper, 2s. John Baty, 6s. 8d. John Stanehaus, 12d. John Hyme, 12d. William Colt, 6s. 8d. Thomas Baker, 40d. John Bryscow, 2s. Thomas de Wedrall, 10s. Simon Baty, 6s. 8d. [. . . .], 12d. Alice Vedue, 12d. Alice Rowese, 12d. Henry Pety, [. . . .]. The children of William the cobbler, 6s. 8d. John de Clifton, 6s. 8d. John Mewros, 10s. Roger son of Robert Carpenter, 10s. St. Mary's light, Salkeld, 13s. 4d. The bridge there, 6s. 8d. Every servant in his house at his death, 2s. The two sons of his brother Hugh, 20s., and Hugh, all his arms. [Roger's] dau. Margaret, 40s. The poor on his burial day, 40s. Brother Thomas, 6s. 8d. His wife and Alice his dau., his chamber and all the utensils of his house. Half the residue of all his goods to his dau. Alice, the other half to be spent for his soul at his executors' discretion. Executors: William Bowcham,[418] rector of Kirkoswald, Hugh [Roger's] brother and Joan his wife.

Note of probate. Rose chapel, 16 January 1379.

**506**    [Fo.100v; p.304] Will[419] of Thomas Spenser, living in Botchergate in the city of Carlisle, being sound in mind and memory, dated 13 January 1379. Commends soul to God, Blessed Mary and all saints. Burial in St. Cuthbert's, Carlisle, or its churchyard, with best beast for mortuary. His dau. Maud de Kokirmuth, a lead cistern with a mash tub and trough, a copper pot, a pitcher, a coverlet with 2 sheets and 2 blankets. His servant Agnes, a green gown. His servant William, a russet doublet. John Cow, a double hood. Robert de Kokirmuth, all his other tailor-made clothes. The friars preachers, Carlisle, 40d. The friars minor, 40d. His dau. Maud, a skep of pure malt barley, and a saddle with a pair of boots and pair of hose. Thomas del Hall, his silver-plated knife, and Maud a salt cellar. His wife Agnes, residue of his goods to be spent for his and her souls and the souls of the faithful departed, as seems best. Executors: Agnes his wife and Thomas del Hall. Sealed with his seal. Witnesses: William Spencer, Thomas his son and Maud [the testator's] dau.. Dated as above at Carlisle.

Note of probate. Rose chapel, 24 February 1379.

**507**    (i) Collation of John Mason, chaplain, to Dalston vicarage, vacant by the resignation of John de Alenby in an exchange of benefices.
(ii) Collation of John de Alenby, chaplain, to Croglin church, vacant by the resignation of John Mason in this exchange. Rose, 8 February 1379.[420]

---

[418] Cf. 'Bowetham' in *Test. Karl.*, 126; usually 'Beauchamp', e.g. **14, 551**.
[419] Printed in *Test. Karl.*, 126–7.
[420] Cf. **500**.

**508** Letter to John Fox, rector of Skelton. The bishop received a plea that John was an absentee and neglected his parishioners. He appeared on citation before the bishop, excused his absence and was absolved. Rose, 4 March 1379.

**509** Mandate to the official to execute writ of Richard II (quoted; dated Westminster, 16 February 1379) summoning the bishop to attend a parliament at Westminster on 24 April, with *premunientes* clause for the clergy.[421] [Fo.101; p.306] Order to cite the prior and archdeacon in person, chapter and clergy by proxies. Rose, 17 March 1379.

**510** Mandate to the prior and chapter of Carlisle. Many wrongdoers injure the church of Carlisle and its subordinate churches, infringing its liberties [etc.] and thus incurring excommunication; all violators are to be solemnly warned of these sentences by bell, book and candle. Carlisle, 1 March 1379.

**511** Mandate to all parish clergy of the deanery of Westmorland. The master, brothers and sisters of St. Leonard's hospital, York, have informed the bishop that unknown persons of the deanery have taken rents and thraves called St. Peter's corn, and other goods belonging to the hospital. Order to warn all those keeping corn commonly called thraves of St. Nicholas (granted to the hospital by kings of England) to make restitution under pain of excommunication. Rose, 18 March 1379.

**512** Certificate of John de Penreth, prior of Carlisle, and William de Bownes, official of Carlisle. They received the bishop's mandate on Wednesday, 17 February 1378, viz. Ralph, Baron de Graystok, has told him that Greystoke church is very rich (*opulenta*), with ample revenues and fruits which could support more ministers. It often happens, however, that rectors responsible for the cure of souls, visitation of the sick, and other duties, have been absent, depriving parishioners of services and the church of ministers.[422] The baron has submitted to the bishop's ordinance for reform.[423] He therefore orders the [prior and official] to enquire [Fo.101v; p.307] in Greystoke or Carlisle church (or another suitable place in the diocese, at their discretion) by rectors, vicars, other clergy and laymen, into the annual value of the church and its charges, the present and customary numbers of its ministers, the size of the parish and other relevant circumstances, certifying [the bishop] or his commissary or commissaries their findings and the names of the jurors. London, 25 January 1378.

---

[421] *CCR 1377–81*, 235.

[422] For M. Ralph Ergum, rector 1316–57, see *Reg. Welton*, xvii, 36, 37, nos.196; 204.

[423] Ralph's father William was licensed to endow and establish a college in Greystoke church by Edward III and Bishop Welton in 1358, but died in 1359. Ralph was a minor until 1374 and revived his father's intention in 1377 when he obtained Richard II's confirmation of the original royal licence (*Reg. Welton*, 49; *CCR 1374–7*, 20; *VCH Cumberland*, II.204–8; R.L. Storey, 'Chantries of Cumberland and Westmorland, Part I', *CWAAS*, 2nd ser. 60 (1960), 91–3).

The enquiry was made on Saturday, 20 February in Carlisle cathedral by the oaths of:

John de Dacre, rector of Dacre[424]
John Bon, rector of Lowther
Robert de Louthre, rector of Hutton [in the Forest]
John Cole, vicar of [Castle] Sowerby[425]
Thomas Hayton, vicar of Edenhall
Thomas de Lowthre, Thomas de Overton and Thomas del Dale, chaplains
John Belsow and John Clerk' of Skelton, clerks of Dacre and Skelton
William Johnson, John Wylkynson, John Bowett', Norman Walkar, John Tailour, John Post, John de Madirdale and Adam Wrigthson, laymen.

They said that the church was worth £100 in annual rents and fruits; £80 after deductions for charges. It was customarily served by a parish chaplain in the church and a clerk and a holy water clerk. Another chaplain and his holy water clerk served in Watermillock (*Wethirmelok*) chapel which is 3 miles from the church on one side. Another chaplain and holy water clerk serve in Threlkeld chapel, 7 miles from the church on the other [i.e. west] side. No clerks are required [in these chapels], and these are the usual number of ministers and hitherto they have been sufficient for the church's cure of souls. The parish is ample, being 7 miles long and 6 wide. There are no ordinary charges except for procurations of legates and visitations by archbishops and bishops according to the customs of the English church. Dated as above [Carlisle, 20 February 1378].

**513**  Letters patent. For various reasons the bishop is unable to attend the provincial council to be held by Alexander [Neville], archbishop of York, on 29 April next, and therefore appoints M. Thomas de Salkeld, rector of Caldbeck, and M. Hugh de Fletham, advocate of the court of York, as his proctors to consent to its measures for the defence of the church. Rose, 21 April 1379.

**514**  [Fo.102; p.308] Certificate to the archbishop quoting his mandate [dated Cawood, 30 March 1379; received 8 April]: in compliance with the king's writ [dated Westminster, 16 March 1379] ordering him to call the bishops and clergy of the province at an early date to grant a subsidy for the defence of the realm against French invasion.[426] The archbishop therefore summons a

---

[424]  Previous known rector was John de Ingelby, instituted 1370 (**246**).

[425]  John Penreth, canon of Carlisle, was instituted 1360 (*Reg. Welton*, 58, no.314); elected prior of Carlisle, 1376 (**455** and n.) and presumably succeeded at Castle Sowerby by John Cole, canon of Carlisle, ordained subdeacon, 1370 (**364**).

[426]  *CCR 1377–81*, 234. Printed also in *Records of the Northern Convocation*, ed. G.W. Kitchin, Surtees Society 113, 1907, 105–6, from 'Reg. Appleby, Carl. fo.308' as part of a letter of Archbishop Neville replying to this writ of 16 Mar. 1379. From this point, however, its text continues (ibid., 106–8) with a reply by the archbishop to an earlier writ and reports two subsidies granted on 22 Mar. for payment on 1 May and 20 July 1378 (confirmed in *CFR*, IX.97–8). There is no notice of this previous convocation of Dec. 1378 – Jan. 1378 (*HBC*, 597) in Appleby's Register.

provincial assembly to meet in York on 29 April, citing the bishop, prior [etc., as in **259**]. [Fo.102v; p.309] The bishop has cited John [de Penreth], prior of Carlisle; Robert [de Rabankes] and Lambert [de Morland], abbots of Holm Cultram and Shap; John [de Appleby], archdeacon of Carlisle; and, as proctors of the clergy, Masters Thomas [de Salkeld] and Adam, rectors of Caldbeck and Bolton.[427] Dated 'in April'.

**515**  (i) Collation to John de Penreth, clerk, of Kirkland church, vacant by the death of John de Langholme.[428] (ii) Archdeacon to induct. Rose, 14 April 1379.

**516**  Certificate of the official of Carlisle quoting the bishop's mandate [addressed only to the official but otherwise similar to the mandate in **512**, *mutatis mutandis*], and [Fo.103; p.310] dated Rose, 10 April 1379]. The enquiry was made on Tuesday, 26 April in Penrith church by the oaths of:
John [de Dacre], rector of Dacre
Thomas [de Derby], rector of Brougham
William [de Neuton],[429] vicar of Barton
Thomas de Hayton, vicar of Edenhall
John [Cole], vicar of [Castle] Sowerby
Gilbert Bowet, Hugh de Yarum and Thomas de Lowthre, chaplains
William del Brygges and John de Belsow, clerks of the parish churches of Penrith and Greystoke
William Jhonson, John del Bek, Robert del Grarthouse, John Tailor, William Slegh, John de Madirdale, Adam Wrigthson and John Bowet', laymen.
    They said that the church was rich, but although its revenues had fallen in recent days, they sufficed to support many ministers; they were now worth £100 after being £120 in past years. It would honour God and increase the devotion of people and clergy if there were more priests and clerks officiating in the church. It was ruled by three chaplains and three holy water clerks, with a chaplain and clerk in the parish church and the same numbers in the chapels of Threlkeld and Watermillock; but its revenues would support a provost and five chaplains. There are no other charges save for *sinodalia* and procurations of ordinaries visiting the church, according to customs of the English church. The parish is large, being 7 miles long and 6 wide. Carlisle, 30 April 1379.

**517**  Mandate to the dean of Carlisle to cite clergy and lay representatives to attend visitation by the bishop or his commissaries, who are to be certified before the first days listed in the schedule [as in **304**. Fo.103v; p.311]. Rose, 8 May 1379.

**518**  Citation of the prior and chapter of Lanercost to attend the bishop's visitation on 17 May. Rose, 8 May 1379.

---

[427]  Cf. list in 1371 (**259**).
[428]  Rector since 1350? See *Reg. Welton*, 9–10, no.44 and n.
[429]  Ratified 1373 (*CPR 1370–4*, 251) and feoffee 1393 (*CPR 1391–6*, 268).

**519**   Mandate to the dean [of Westmorland] to go to Bampton and enquire by rectors, vicars, clerks and laymen into defects in the manse and other buildings which should have been repaired by John [de Bampton[430]], late vicar, the predecessor of William [de Wicliff[431]], now vicar, and estimate their cost. n.d.

**520**   Licence to Robert de Lowther, rector of Hutton [in the Forest], to be absent for a year from this day while in the service of the prior and convent of Carlisle, excusing him from personal attendance of synods and chapters; but to be void if he fails to provide a proctor answering for ordinary charges or neglects the cure of souls. Rose, 28 May 1379.

**521**   Letters patent of Bishop Thomas announcing an indulgence of 40 days for contributions to repair of the bridge of Stramongate (*Strowemondgate*) over the River Kent beside Kendal (*Kirkbykendale*) town in York diocese; valid for one year. 1379.

**522**   [Fo.104; p.312] Licence for one year to Hugh de Yarum, chaplain, as questor for the hospital of Saint-Antoine-de-Viennois, with preference before other quests except that for the fabric of Carlisle cathedral. Rose, [. . .] 1379.

**523**   Mandate to the dean of Cumberland to cite all persons named in the attached schedule to pay *sinodalia* due from their benefices within 20 days from the date of [the dean's] monition, under pain of excommunication. n.d.

**524**   Writ of Richard II ordering the bishop to appoint collectors of the graduated poll-tax granted by prelates and clergy in convocation in St. Peter's, York, for defence of the English church and realm, due on 1 August. [Fo.104v; p.313] Westminster, 8 July 1379.[432]

**525**   INHIBICIO CONTRA TENENTES FORA DIEBUS DOMINICIS ET FESTIVIS. Mandate to the dean of Westmorland. Many incumbents and other clergy have complained that, despite canonical sanctions, crowds of people from within and outside the diocese gather in churchyards and hold markets on Sundays and festivals, disturbing divine service, often quarrelling among themselves and frightening parishioners. [The dean] is to go to the places concerned in person and publicly announce in churches and their churchyards that all those engaged in such business will incur sentence of excommunication; anyone found disobeying these monitions are to be cited before the bishop or his commissaries in Dalston church and their names reported to the bishop. n.d.

---

[430]   See **488**.

[431]   Full name provided from **593**.

[432]   See *CFR*, IX.158–9, for detailed rates; also J.L. Kirby, 'Two Tax Accounts of the Diocese of Carlisle, 1379–80', *CWAAS*, 2nd ser. 52 (1953), 70–81.

**526** Note that Simon de Querton, rector of Ousby, has letters of absence for 3 years while studying in the schools and remaining subdeacon. 6 June 1379.

**527** Mandate to the dean 'etc.'. The bishop has received the king's writ to collect the subsidy last granted by the clergy and to explain it, as he intends to do in a meeting and discussion (*colloquium et tractatum*) with the prelates and his other clergy, for their assistance (*utilitatem*) and expedition of this business. [The dean] is therefore to summon [Fo.105; p.314] all abbots, priors, rectors, vicars and other beneficed clergy of the deanery to appear before the bishop in the chapter house of Carlisle cathedral on 3 August to counsel and consent to these matters for the common benefit of the clergy and expedite the said business by common consent.

**528** Commission to John de Penreth, prior of Carlisle, Robert de Rawebankes, abbot of Holm Cultram, and Lambert de Morland, abbot of Shap, ordering them to collect the graduated poll-tax [as in **524**].[433]

**529** [Fo.105v; p.315] Probate[434] of the will of John Clerk of Annandale, as follows:
Commended soul to God, Blessed Mary and all saints. Burial in church of friars minor, Carlisle. Bequeathed his tenement in Carlisle city (between the tenement of Richard de Loundon and the tenement which John de Dalton holds of Lord Dacre) to his wife Isabel and her heirs and assigns, to be held of the chief lord for the customary services. He also left her all his goods to pay his debts and for disposal at her discretion. Executors: W. Henryson of Annandale and John Bell. Witnesses: Richard chaplain of Sebergham, John Clerkson of Edenhall and others.
Sentence of probate before the bishop. Rose, 22 August 1379.

**530** Collation to M. William del Hall, official of Carlisle, of Caldbeck church, vacant by the death of M. Thomas de Salkeld.[435] Rose, 24 August 1379.

**531** Return to the treasurer and barons of the Exchequer. In response to the king's writ ordering the bishop to collect the subsidy granted by the last convocation in York,[436] he has appointed the prior of Carlisle and abbots of Holm Cultram and Shap; they have sworn to secure this subsidy from parsons and ecclesiastics of the diocese, without favour to anyone. n.d.

---

[433] The text of this commission is tightly compressed, leaving no space for the date at the foot of the folio; for which see **524**. The margin has these notes: '*Malum subsidium concessum regi*'; '*sed non fuit levatum*'. In fact, it was paid into the Exchequer in Nov. 1379 (F.P. Mackie, 'The Clerical Poll Tax of 1379 in the Diocese of Carlisle, a reassessment', *CWAAS*, 2nd ser. 100, 152). See also **531, 533**.

[434] Printed in *Test. Karl.*, 128.

[435] Cf. **534, 573**.

[436] See **524, 528, 533**.

**532**  Note of licence to Robert Paye, rector of Thursby, to be absent for one
year from Michaelmas. [29 September] 1379.

**533**  Letters appointing the dean of Carlisle as collector of the subsidy volun-
tarily granted to the king by the prior and chapter of Carlisle and all abbots,
priors and clergy with benefices in the diocese, to be paid in equal portions on
8 September and 2 February [1380], under pain of spiritual penalties; [Fo.106;
p.316] he is to provide the bishop with accounts of receipts and names of non-
payers. Rose, 6 September 1379.
   Note of similar letters to the deans of Westmorland, Cumberland and
Allerdale.

**534**  (i) Collation to John de Appelby, archdeacon of Carlisle, of Caldbeck
church, vacant by the death of M. Thomas de Salkeld.[437] (ii) Commission to
John Mason, rector of Croglin, and Adam Burell, chaplain, to induct Sir John
de Appelby, late archdeacon of Carlisle, to Caldbeck church, vacant and in
the bishop's collation, as the bishop has no archdeacon to officiate. Rose, 24
September 1379.

**535**  Certificate to M. Cosmatus Gentilis of Sulmona, licenciate in decrees,
provost of Valva (*Valuen'*), papal nuncio and collector in England, quoting his
mandate, viz. letters of M. Laurence de Negris, the previous collector, had
ordered the bishop to cite listed persons in debt to the chamber to appear
before him or his deputies; they have incurred excommunication for contumacy. [The bishop] is ordered to denounce them in his cathedral and other
churches; they may not be absolved without the collector's order [Fo.106v;
p.317]. Their benefices, as listed, are to be sequestrated until debts to the
chamber are paid. They are to come to his house in the parish of St. Stephen
Walbrook, London, on 11 October. Under his seal, London, 5 July 1379.
   [Schedule] The bishop has accordingly denounced Thomas de Kirkeby, who
once occupied Clifton church by collation.[438]
   Simon de Querton still occupies Ousby church; he was cited but cannot be
found.[439]
   Robert de Louther, collated to Musgrave church.
   M. Thomas de Eskheved, vicar of Crosthwaite.[440]
   The bishop certifies that they have been cited to the collector's house; their
benefices will be sequestrated. John de Penreth, prior of Carlisle, has also been
cited for the same date. n.d.[441]

**536**  [Fo.107; p.318] LITTERA GENERALIS SENTENCIE. To all rectors, vicars
and parish chaplains of the deanery of Allerdale. Despite canonical prohibition,

---

[437] Cf. **530**.
[438] *Recte* Thomas de Salkeld? (**57**; *Reg. Welton*, 10–11, no.51, and index).
[439] Cf. **437, 526**.
[440] See **57**, n.
[441] Followed by space of 7 cm cancelled.

parishioners of Aspatria are reported to have dared to prevent the collection of tithes of sheaves due to the bishop in Allerby (*Crosseby Aylward*);[442] mandate to pronounce sentence of excommunication of all such offenders and discover and report their names. n.d.

**537** Memorandum that John de Appelby, rector of Caldbeck, resigned the archdeaconry of Carlisle to the bishop, saving his right to re-enter the archdeaconry. Rose chapel, 21 October 1379.

**538** (i) Note of institution of Robert Barnet to St. Lawrence's vicarage, Appleby.[443] (ii) Archdeacon to induct. 21 October 1379.

**539** Mandate to the abbot of Shap and official of Carlisle to execute a grace of Pope Urban VI to Robert Spaldyng, a poor clerk (dioc. York), providing him to a benefice in the gift of the prior and chapter of Carlisle; the bishop is himself too busy to act as its executor. Rose, 31 October 1379.

**540** [Fo.107v; p.319] Dispensation to John Mariounson of Hawksdale, clerk (dioc. Carlisle) as the son of unmarried parents, to be promoted to all orders and hold a benefice, if he resides; by authority of letters (quoted) of Elziarius, cardinal-priest of S. Balbina, papal penitentiary, dated at S. Maria in Trastevere (*Transtiberim*), Rome, under his seal as bishop of Chieti, 24 November 1378. n.d.

**541** (i) Undertaking by John de Penreth, prior of Carlisle, to accept the bishop's award to end the dispute arising from his removal of Robert de Clifton, canon of Carlisle, from the office of cellarer; renouncing all his appeals and taking an oath on the Gospels.
(ii) Corresponding undertaking, *mutatis mutandis*, by Robert de Clifton. [Fo.108; p.320]
(iii) Following this submission to the bishop, he enquired into the matter with the counsel of experts. He ordains that the prior should restore Robert to the office of cellarer because he had removed him within the first half-year without the counsel and assent of the greater and wiser part of the chapter. Subsequently, after the bishop had received and accepted Robert to the office, the prior and chapter had not admitted him, as was customary. The bishop therefore ordered the prior to admit him according to custom and to minister in the office as freely as other cellarers had done, nor should he be removed from office without the counsel and consent of [the above majority].[444] The bishop will consider the other grievances as soon as he is able. n.d.

---

[442] See *Reg. Welton*, 19 (no.99).
[443] Previous known vicar was William Colyn, in 1370 (**205** and n.). St. Mary's, York, was the patron (Nicolson & Burn, I.321–4).
[444] See *VCH Cumberland*, II.146.

**542**   Will[445] of the vicar of Crosby,[446] knowing himself too weak to remain long on earth, dated 29 October 1379. Commends soul to God, Blessed Mary and all saints. Burial with the friars preachers, Carlisle, with 2½ pounds of wax to burn round his body in their church. A skep of barley and a skep of oats to the said friars. Half skeps of barley and oats to the friars minor, Carlisle. Two oxen to celebrate 4 trentals for his soul. Hugh son of Robert, 2 cows. The same Hugh and Emma his dau., a cow and a stott (*bovettum*). Thomas Sparow, a coulter with a ploughshare, yokes and pole. Residue to Richard de Histon, his executor.

   [Fo.108v; p.321] Probate, with grant of administration. Rose, 21 December 1379.

**543**   (i) Note of institution of Robert Tayllor to the vicarage of Crosby [on Eden] (ii) Archdeacon to inuuct. 2 January 1380.

**544**   Note that John Bone, rector of Lowther, was licensed to be absent for one year from 1 January 1380. He was released from all impeachment for non-residence since he became rector.

**545**   Licence to John de Penreth, rector of Kirkland, to study in a *studium generale* in England or elsewhere from the date of his institution,[447] farming his benefice and not being ordained beyond the subdiaconate for 7 years. n.d.

**546**   Note of licence to John de Claston, rector of Greystoke,[448] to be absent for two years following. 12 February 1380.

**547**   Oath of Robert Mareschall, abbot of Shap, Premonstratensian order, to be obedient to the bishop and his successors. n.d.[449]

**548**   Note of licence to Robert Jardyn as questor[450] for one year from 18 April 1380.

**549**   Note of indulgence for Cocker (*Cokir*) bridge[451] for one year from 15 April 1380.

**550**   (i) Collation of Robert Tayllior, chaplain, to Scaleby church, vacant by the resignation of Sir Elias[452] in an exchange of benefices. (ii) [Fo.109; p.322]

---

[445]   Printed in *Test. Karl.*, 128–9.

[446]   As in margin, but in the will as 'John de Crosseby, chaplain'; probably Crosby on Eden, 4 miles north-east of Carlisle.

[447]   See **515**. The king ratified his title, 13 Feb. 1380 (*CPR 1377–81*, 440).

[448]   Presented by the king, 1369 (*CPR 1367–70*, 233). Also canon of Salisbury; died 1382 (*Fasti*, III.63).

[449]   Presumably in succession to Lambert de Morland, who first (probably) occurs as abbot in 1354 and last in April 1379 (*Reg. Welton*, 101, no.544 and n.; **514**). Robert was ordained subdeacon in 1370 (**366**).

[450]   See **229**.

[451]   See **65**.

[452]   See **489**.

Collation of Sir Elias [. . . .] to Crosby [on Eden] vicarage in the same exchange. (iii) Archdeacon to induct to both benefices. Rose, 14 April 1380.

**551** (i) Institution of William de Hoton, chaplain, to Croglin church, vacant by the resignation [of John Mason]; presented by William Beauchamp, rector of Kirkoswald.[453] (ii) Archdeacon to induct. n.d.

**552** (i) Collation of John Mason, chaplain, to Torpenhow vicarage, vacant by the death of Robert de Byx. (ii) Archdeacon to induct. 'Same date'.

**553** Resignation by John Mason, vicar of Torpenhow, of Croglin church, which he had previously held.[454]

**554** [Fo.109v; p.323] Will[455] of Robert de Bix, clerk of Carlisle diocese [and] Oxford,[456] being sound of mind but weak of body, 20 March 1380. Commends soul to God, Blessed Mary and all saints. Burial in porch of St. Peter in the East [Oxford], with a mark for its repair if he is buried there. For wax round his body in *Dirige* and exequies, 12½ pounds in 10 candles. 20s. in oblation and among 4 chaplains serving in the church, and the remaining pence or half-pence to distribute for his soul on his burial day. Each of the four orders of friars, 6s. 8d. Brother Stephen, 6s. 8d. The college common room, 13s. 4d. for burial-day expenses. The manciple, 2s. 6d. for his service. The cook, 18d. for his service, and the kitchen boy, 6d. Boys in Queen's Hall saying a psalter for his soul, 4d. each. All his clothes and any in Oxford except those given to William Rudde, Nicholas de Skelton and Sir William de Kirkebride, chaplain, which are to be sold for the support of William de Byx at the discretion of Brother William de Penreth, BTh., Sir Thomas de Slegill[457] and John de Penreth. Brother William de Penreth, a grey cloak, new pair of sheets and the 12 remaining red bankers and cushions. Sir Thomas de Slegill, a red cloak. Thomas de Skelton, his black belt with its dagger. Four curtains with a cover for the orna-ments of his altar in his church. The high altar of Torpenhow church, a napkin with a towel, and for the 2 altars of this church, similar napkins and towels in his chest with the official [of Carlisle]; Robert Byx has its key. To decorate the nave of his church, a red cloth with *trewloves* bought in Newcastle upon Tyne, with red bankers. Little[458] William Byx and William Rudde, his bed in which he lies. John Penreth, a blue piece of bankers. M. Adam de Crosseby, rector of Bolton, a basin with a jug. The rectors of Bowness and Bolton, Clement de Skelton [and] John de Crofton, 4 dozen pewter dishes of which 3 dozen are in

---

[453] Cf. **500**.

[454] Incomplete? Followed by space.

[455] Printed in *Test. Karl.*, 129–32.

[456] As 'Byx' in *BRUO*, I.336, which shows him as rector of Wardley, Rutland, in 1369, and otherwise notices only his association with Queen's College, 1379–80. For numerous Carlisle references, see Index below.

[457] *Sic* in MS and below; cf. 'Stegith' regularly in *Test. Karl.*, 130–2.

[458] MS *parvo*; *Test. Karl.*, 131, *puero*.

a chest with M. William de Bownes,[459] to be equally divided between him, Clement and John; the rector of Bolton is to have the fourth dozen which is at Torpenhow with Richard Cokks, who is to have the remaining old pewter dishes. The official, another basin with a jug; a stenyd linen cloth with 6 hangings; a napkin with a towel. The rector of Bolton, another napkin and towel. The official, new red fittings for a saddle; the best bed of his choice. Sir Thomas de Slegill, a pair of linen sheets. John de Morton, a curtain with half a tester. The college of Queen's Hall, Oxford, 12 silver spoons for daily use in hall. Robert de Skelton, 6 silver[460] spoons of the same set. The library of St. Mary's, Carlisle, two books, viz. a set of Clementines and a set of Decretals which the lord official has in his custody. The said[461] church, a copper cauldron. Sir John Swan, his breviary. Richard Cokks, the old ornaments of his hall. William de Bix, Richard Coks, John and Robert de Bix, 4 beds: William is to choose after the official and to have 2 [Fo.110; p.324] sheets with 2 blankets, the best after the official. William de Bix, if he should stay in England, all his beasts in Westward except the black ox [the testator] bought from Robert de Bix, who is to have it again; but if [William] does not stay in England, all these beasts are to be consigned to Richard Cokks and [the testator's] sister. Adam Jonson, an ox he has. John de Bix, 2 oxen he has. Sir William de Wandethwayt', 50s. to celebrate for his soul. Sir Stephen, as much to celebrate instead for half a year in his church of Torpenhow. The four orders of friars in Carlisle diocese, 40s. (10s. each). Residue to his executors: Brother William de Penreth, BTh., M. William de Bownes, official of Carlisle, John de Penreth, rector of Kirkland, Sir Thomas de Slegill, canon, Sir William de Wandethwayt', chaplain, and Richard Koke, to dispose for his soul and perform his will as they would [answer] to God. Witnesses: John de Morton, William Rude and Robert de Collerdowe, clerks. Dated at Oxford as above.

Sentence of probate before M. Henry Fowler, official of the chancellor of the university, with commission of the goods in his jurisdiction to William and John de Penreth, reserving their commission to other executors. Under his seal of office, St. Mary's church, Oxford, 31 March 1380.

Similar commission to Richard Koke, 2 April [1380].[462]

**555** [Fo.110v; p.325] Will[463] of Richard de Brysseby, dated 28 May 1380. Commended his soul to God, Blessed Mary and all saints. Burial in [Castle] Sowerby churchyard, with best beast for mortuary. Alice dau. of Edmund[464] and John son of the same, 4 cows, 4 oxen, 12 sheep and half his corn in Sowerby fields. Alice dau. of John Bell of Sebergham, 2 oxen and 2 heifers. William de Docwra, a cow. Alice dau. of William de Hoyrys, a stott. John Slayw[r]ight, an ox, and

---

[459] The official of Carlisle.

[460] Omitted in *Test. Karl.*, 131.

[461] MS *primam*.

[462] Leaving a space (14 cm, cancelled) for the bishop's sentence of approval.

[463] Printed in *Test. Karl.*, 132–3. Not described as nuncupative although all the bequests are expressed in the third person (see *Reg. Welton*, xxi).

[464] With surname (?) deleted.

Nicholas de Brysseby, an ox. Emma wife of Ralph Smyth, an ox. William Slaywright and John his brother, 2 stotts in equal shares. Alice dau. of John de Bowaldeth, a stott. Joan widow of William Baron, an ox. Howath[465] bridge over the Caldew, 20s.

Residue to his executors to dispose for his soul, viz. John Bell, Nicholas de Brysseby and William Slaywryght. Witnesses: John Bell and John Slaywryght. Note of probate. Rose, 10 June 1380.

**556**  Will (in French)[466] of William de Stapilton [knight].[467] Commends soul to God. Burial in Edenhall churchyard if he dies in Carlisle diocese or within a day's journey, with mortuaries to churches where they are reasonably due, but no arms are to be offered to the church; nor does he wish anything to be provided at his burial except viands for those wishing to attend, poor as well as others; 15 pounds of wax are to be provided, 5 for 5 candles burnt at *Dirige* and 10 for 5 candles before high mass at his interment; also 1d. each to the poor. The nave of Edenhall church is to be repaired at his expense, with 4 or 5 beams, as necessary, and 2 windows, one towards the south, the other to the north, with the northside *coverer de spune*. The belfry [is to be repaired?] as had been planned by the vicar and himself. The 4 orders of friars are to have £4, 4 skeps of corn and 8 of barley, in equal portions. His goods are to be sold. If Laurence lives, he is to have a bay hackney gelding and 40s. Denis Drases, a gown of London russet and other cuts, as suit him; if he behaves himself and helps [William's] wife and executors, he is to have 40s. in the second year and 2 marks in the third. William [William's son], his blessing, the habergeon he had from Richard de Brysbye,[468] the basinet darrayn set, his short sword, a pair of plate gauntlets, a shield and his great silver saltcellar (*sautre*?). His son John, his blessing, the habergeon [the testator's] father[469] gave him, and the basinet in which he was armed, if [John] reaches the age of 18. Roland Vaux, the basinet in his keeping, a jackman breastplate, a pair of plate gauntlets. To John de Dalton.[470] n.d.

**557**  [Fo.113; p.326] Will[471] of John de Dundrawe of Carlisle, being sound of mind and memory, dated 16 July 1380. Commends soul etc. (*sic*). Burial in

---

[465] Perhaps Howk, in Caldbeck (*EPNS Cumberland*, II.279).

[466] Printed in *Test. Karl.* 133–5.

[467] His death was reported to Chancery by 12 Mar. 1380 (*CFR*, IX.205).

[468] See **555** above.

[469] See *Reg. Welton*, 82, no.452.

[470] Lost, with the following opening (fos.111–12). In a pardon dated 8 Apr. 1383, William's executors are named as Robert de Hormesheved, William del Hall, late rector of Bowness (see **573**), and William's widow Mary. The pardon was for escapes from Carlisle castle when he was sheriff of Cumberland; he was appointed 25 Nov. 1378 (*CPR 1377–83*, 240; *CFR*, IX.113).

[471] Printed in *Test. Karl.*, 135–8. Both this and the next will (his wife's) have notes *compotus re'* under their marginal notices in a smaller (but same?) hand. Neither, however, nor the 7 following wills (**559–64**) are followed by the usual entries recording probates and grants of administration.

church of friars minor, Carlisle, with best beast as mortuary to his parish church, St. Cuthbert's, Carlisle; a stone of wax to burn round his body; 4 marks for the poor; £4 in silver for his funeral expenses, a wake for his friends and 12d. for each chaplain coming for his exequies. Two minorite chaplains of Carlisle celebrating for his soul and those of the faithful departed in the minorites' church at [Our] Lady's altar for one year, or one [friar] for 2 years, 15 marks. The friars preachers of Carlisle, 6s. 8d. The parish chaplain of St. Cuthbert's, 40d. John Stracore, chaplain, 40d. The parish clerk of that church, 12d. Its light of the Blessed Mary, 10s. The fabric of St. Mary's, Carlisle, 6s. 8d. The clerks of its choir, 2s. His sister Alice, 20s. John de Dundrawe, his kinsman and executor, 20s. for faithfully executing his will and testament. John Austyn, on the same condition, 20s. William de Dundrawe, his kinsman, 20s. and his best haketon with an armed basinet. Walter, his kinsman, 20s. and a suit of plates with an armed basinet. Agnes wife of Nicholas Mariman, 13s. 4d. John son of Robert Goldsmith, 20s. Petterill bridge by Harraby and Botcherby bridge, 6s. 8d. equally divided. Magota Graye, his servant, 6s. 8d. Salkeld bridge, 6s. 8d. The friars of Penrith, 6s. 8d. The friars minor of Richmond, 6s. 8d. Emma widow of John de Hornby, 10s. Gilbert Grute, chaplain, 40d. Eden bridge, 10s. His godsons, 10s. Margot dau. of John Austyn, 20s. Ellen dau. of Robert Goldsmith, 20s. Thomas Doget, chaplain, 13s. 4d. Two chaplains (beside the said 2 friars) to celebrate for his and all souls in St. Cuthbert's, Carlisle, for one year, or one for 2 years, 13 marks. The friars minor, Carlisle, to celebrate for his soul on his burial day and for his obit, 17s. 4d. Sir Thomas Doget, to celebrate for him for a year at the Blessed Mary's altar in St. Cuthbert's; for his salary, he is to have 7 of the above 13 marks. William de Kyrkeby, 20s. William de Dundrawe and his heirs, the whole tenement he lives in, freely from the chief lords of the fee by the due services, for ever. John de Galway, chaplain, 6s. 8d. and a pound of cumin annually from that tenement. John son of Robert Goldsmyth and his heirs, [the testator's] tenement in Baxter's Row, freely from the chief lords of the fee by the due services, for ever. Richard Orfeur, 20s. John Kardiole, 20s. The friars minor of Carlisle, a water jug and murrey cup. John Austyne and his legitimate male heirs of his body, the whole tenement in Botchergate [the testator] lives in, freely from the chief lords of the fee by due services and customary right; if he dies without an heir male, it shall revert to Margaret Goldsmyth and the legitimate male heirs of her body, [with successive remainders to the lawful female heirs of John Austyne; Margaret's female heirs; and the rightful heirs of Joan the testator's wife; all from the lords of the fee etc.].

Residue to the following, to dispose for his and his wife's souls, and the souls of all the faithfully departed, at their discretion. Executors: John de Dundraw, his kinsman, John Austyn, Joan [the testator's] wife, Richard Orfeur, John Kardell, Sirs Thomas de Overende and Thomas Doget, chaplains. Witnesses: Sir William, vicar of Stanwix, William de Dundraw and William de Glentona.

**558** [Fo.113v; p.327] Will[472] of Joan, wife of John de Dundrawe, dated 20 July 1380. Commends soul etc. Burial in church of friars minor, Carlisle, with

---

[472] Printed in *Test. Karl.*, 138–40.

customary mortuary to her parish church; a stone of wax; the poor, 40s.; funeral expenses, 4 marks. Each acting executor, 6s. 8d. Her parish chaplain, 40d. Her parish clerk, 2s. The friars minor, Carlisle, 20s. The friars preachers, 6s. 8d. The prior and convent of Lanercost, 13s. 4d. for a pittance. William Henrison, canon, 6s. 8d. Each chaplain at her exequies, 12d. A friar minor celebrating for her soul for a year, £4. Eden, Caldew and Petteril bridges, 6s. Blessed Mary's light in St. Cuthbert's, Carlisle, 6s. 8d. The prior and convent of Carlisle, 20s. for a pittance. Maud de Boyse, a kirtle with a murrey hood. John Austyne's wife, a kirtle and coats with a red hood and a honey[-coloured] hood. Marjory her dau., a switely with a red hood and a honey[-coloured] kirtle. Margaret Graye, 6s. 8d. Ellen Stacy, a violet gown. Alice servant of William del Sandy, a murrey gown. Emma de Tyby, a black gown. Margaret Goldsmyth, 3 stones of wool, all her coverchiefs, a cup worth 4 marks, 7 cows, 2 skeps of pure malt, a skep of malt oats, 2 beds, 3 brass pots, a little brass pot, a cistern, a cow called 'Coll', 2 cloths, 2 towels, and her terms in a place near Carlisle called 'Paradyse'. Margaret Prestmanwyff, a white kirtle with a hood and 2 veils. Pama Fleshewer, a honey[-coloured] hood, 2 veils and a long gown. Marjory de Byrkynside, a gold ring. The image of Blessed Mary in Carlisle church, a silver-plated belt. Richard Orfeour, 6s. 8d. John Austyn and his lawful heirs, all her tenement she lives in in Botchergate [continuing in almost identical words with the entail in **557** save that the final remainder is to Joan's rightful heirs, in perpetuity]. Adam Parvyng junior, 28s. Maud dau. of Richard Waren, 6s. 8d. Sissota wife of John de Spence, 6s. 8d. Joan Goldsmyth, a mark. Marjory Austyne, a mark. Ellen Goldsmyth, half a mark. Magota Austyne, half a mark. Magota Gonson, 40d. John Austyne, 7 sacks, 3 skeps of malt oats and a skep of malt barley, 3 or 4 beds, 2 brass pots, a chest, a cistern, 2 cloths and 2 towels. Emma de Tyby, half a skep of corn, a posnet, a pan, a skep of coal and half a stone of wool. John Kardoll, half a mark. The said Sir Thomas, half a mark. Alice servant of William del Sandys, 6s. 8d. John Jakson of Brunstock (*Brunthnaye*), half a mark. John Austyne and Margaret Goldsmyth, all her 'brewing vessales', equally divided with John having the larger. Residue to her executors to dispose for her soul and her husband's at their discretion. Executors: John Austyn, John Kardell and Sir Thomas Doget, chaplain. Witnesses: Joan del Sandys, Marjory de Byrkynside, Joan Tayliour.

**559** [Fo.114; p.328] Will[473] of Robert Pay, rector of Thursby, dated 6 August 1380. Commends soul to God, Blessed Mary and all saints. Burial where God pleases; 6 pounds of wax to be burnt in 5 candles; for the poor on that day, a mark; each priest coming to his exequies, 12d. The friars preachers, minor, Austin and Carmelite, equal portions of half skeps of barley and oats. Five skeps of oatmeal to be distributed among his poor parishioners by his executors. [. . .] de Layland, 8 skeps of oatmeal. Sir Richard de Bolton, a breviary which is at Skipton. A priest to celebrate for his soul in Thursby church for a year, 100s. Robert son of William Clerk, 40s. William Clerk, 5 marks. Robert Allale, 4 skeps of oatmeal. Margaret Allale, 3 skeps of oatmeal. Residue to his executors, viz.

---

[473] Printed in *Test. Karl.*, 140–1.

John de Crofton, Sirs Thomas de Lowther and John de Kirkanders, chaplains, and William Clerk. Witnesses: Richard de Bolton, Robert de Crofton, John Layland, and others.

**560** [Fo.114v; p.329] Nuncupative will[474] of William del Schamb,[475] rector of Aikton' dated 6 August 1380. Commended soul to God, Blessed Mary and all saints. Burial in choir of this church. To Blessed Mary's light, a surcoat. Richard, chaplain of Thursby, a breviary. Thomas [de Bampton], rector of [a mediety of Kirk[bampton[476]], a pair of millstones. Thomas de Clyfton, a red horse. John de Wellys, a stott aged 3 years. Nicholas, a cow, a russet tabard and a brass pot. His niece Agnes, a coverlet with a pair of sheets, a blanket, a brass pot with a pan, a winnowing fan, a sack and a half part of a cow. His servant John, a cow with a calf, a heifer, a bed, a brass pot with a cauldron. His servant Katherine, a half part of a heifer. His servant Mariota, a green gown and a griddle. Executors: John Willyson of the Dowhyll and William Atkinson. Witnesses: Thomas, rector of [Kirk]bampton, Richard, chaplain of Thursby.

**561** Will[477] of John, vicar of Ainstable,[478] dated 5 September 1380. Commended soul to God, Blessed Mary and all saints. Burial in Ainstable churchyard; for oblations, 18d.; for a wake for neighbours, 26s. 8d. Executors: John de Wyndschale and his son John. Witnesses: William de Hayton and Margaret wife of John Person.

**562** Will[479] of Thomas de Sandforth, being sane in mind and memory, 29 August 1380. Commends soul to God, Blessed Mary and all saints. Burial in St. Columba's, [Warcop]; its costs, 100s.; in dole to the poor, 100s. The Carmelite friars, Appleby, 20s. The [Austin] friars, Penrith, 20s. The friars minor, Carlisle, 13s. 4d. The friars preachers, Carlisle, 13s. 4d. To repair the bridges of Warcop, [Temple] Sowerby, Salkeld and between Tebay and Roundthwaite, 13s. 4d. [each]. The vicar of Warcop, 20s. for forgotten tithes. William de Sandeforth, parson of Mareham [le Fen],[480] his waterpot made of stone called 'Beryle', the rest silver and gold. His son, his armour; a piece of silver called 'Boll' which he had made, with a cover; a cup made with an egg called 'Grypeks', the rest silver, with a cover; one of his better mazers; 6 of the better spoons; and a little primer. His son's wife, another primer. Alice Birde, 40s. Isabel de Newby, 20s, and Joan

---

[474] Printed in *Test. Karl.*, 141–2. Thus described in margin.

[475] Margin extended to 'Schamb(les)'. Cf. William de Chaumbrelayn in his institution to a mediety of Aikton in 1364 (**16**).

[476] See *Reg. Welton*, 48, no.258.

[477] Printed in *Test. Karl.*, 142. Expressed in third person etc., as with **558**.

[478] Last known vicar was Eudes, 1372 (**293**); probably the same as Ives, 1377 (*CPR 1374–7*, 443).

[479] Printed in *Test. Karl.*, 143–5.

[480] Ordained acolyte, 1357 (*Reg. Welton*, 116, no.614). As 'William Sandford, parson of Marham, Lincoln dioc.', presented in exchange to Thornton in Lonsdale church, Yorks West Riding, 1382 (*CPR 1381–5*, 176).

her sister, 20s. David son of John Watson, 6s. 8d. William de Thornburgh, 40s. [Thomas's] sister, 10 marks. William Birde, 5 marks. Each chaplain celebrating in Westmorland ward, 2s. Isabel dau. of Henry de Warcopp, junior, the marriage of her brother Henry de Warcopp, if both live until he is married or his marriage is sold to another. Thomas Skayffe, £3 lent to him. The prior and convent of Carlisle, £3 which he lent them, and £4 which they owe from his fee. His lesser tenants and others, 20 marks to be distributed by his executors. Half his wool, to be distributed among his lesser kinsmen and other needy people. £40 to chaplains celebrating for his soul and the souls of his father, mother, his brother William, his wives and all faithful departed; each chaplain is to be charged to celebrate a trental at the due feasts every year; and 100s. for 30 trentals in all possible haste after his death. The new bridge in Kendal, 13s. 4d. John del Bank of Bleatarn, 6s. 8d. of the 10s. he owes [Thomas]. Robert his son, his coral rosary with a gold clasp having 4 corals. Mary his wife, his carriage and the household utensils in his mansion in Carlisle city, [and] his knife with appurtenances. William de Sandforth, parson of Mareham, a ring with a sapphire - 'the stone of truth' - and a silver cup with cover which he bought from the executors of Robert Tylieff. Robert his son, his long knife and all his books. Residue after payment of debts to be faithfully divided between Mary his wife and Robert his son. Executors: Robert de Ormysheved and William de Thornburgh.

**563** [Fo.115; p.330] Will[481] of William de Arthuret, vicar of Aspatria,[482] dated 1 September 1380. Commended soul to God, Blessed Mary and all saints. Burial in Aspatria churchyard. Joan Walas, 4 oxen, 4 stotts (*bov'*), 6 silver spoons and a murrey cup. Gilbert son of Mariota de Sostele, 100s. silver and 6 silver spoons. Thomas Walas, 20s. and a white horse. Sir John de Arthureth, his kinsman, a breviary, a bed, 4 silver marks and all his pewter vessels. Joan dau. of John Bouescharlet, a calf and 2 brass pots. Thomas son of the same John Bouescharlet, a 'graye' horse and a silver mark. Adam Walas, an ox, a cow and his vestments. To celebrate masses, 20s. The friars preachers and minor of Carlisle, 2 cows. Adam Hird, 12d. John Tabard, 12d. Adam Hamlyn, 12d. John Alanson, 12d. John son of Ebote, 8s. John son of Alice de Brantyngham, a white horse and a mark. Residue after payment of debts: John Walas, Gilbert son of Mary de Sostele and Sir John de Arthureth. Executors, appointed before [unnamed] witnesses, the above Sir John, John Walas and John Boneskarlet.

**564** [Fo.115v; p.331] Will[483] of Thomas de Karlton, rector of Castle Carrock,[484] dated 1 September 1380. Commended soul to God, Blessed Mary and all saints. Burial in chancel, Castle Carrock [church]. John his brother, 3 oxen, 3 cows, 10 sheep, 10 lambs and a horse. Isotte and her dau. Maud, 2 cows and 8 stones of wool. John Raynaldson, 2 oxen. Patrick Rychell's wife, 3 stones of wool. John le

[481] Printed in *Test. Karl.*, 145. Expressed in third person etc., as with **558**.
[482] Last known institution was of Adam de Alanburgh, 1358 (*Reg. Welton*, 41, no.223).
[483] Printed in *Test. Karl.*, 146–7. Expressed in third person etc., as with **558**.
[484] Previous known rector was Thomas Gerrard, 1374 (**317**).

Parsonman's wife, 2 stotts, a cow, a calf, 2 stones of wool and a copper pot. The vicar of Edenhall, a book called 'Placebo dirige'. William Bell, 12 lambs. John de Hill's wife, a stone of wool. A chaplain celebrating for his soul for a year. Sir William de Hill, chaplain, a bed and overtunic with hood. John Kardoll's wife, a bed, tabard and 2 stones of wool. John Raynaldson, a cow, bed and a [. . .] with [. . . . .].[485] John le Parsonman and his wife, 2 sheep, a chest, and a cloth with a towel. Thomas [. . .], a cow, a heifer, a tripod, 3 cushions, 2 canvas [. . .] with a silk [. . . . .]. Thomas Clerk, 2 stones of wool. Isotte, a horse with reins and saddle and a winnowing fan. The vicar of Edenhall, a saddle and bridle. William Tayliour, a horse. John his brother, a bow with arrows and a sword. Residue to be divided among his poor kinsmen. Executor: Thomas de Hayton, vicar of Edenhall.[486] Witnesses: John his brother, William Bell, Thomas Shapman and John Raynaldson.[487]

**565**  [Fo.118; p.332] Letter of William [del Hall], rector of Bowness, vicar-general in the absence of Bishop Thomas, to Robert Crofft, chaplain, instituting him to Beaumont church, vacant by the death of Walter de Ormesheved;[488] presented by Hugh de Dacre, lord of Gilsland. Carlisle, 1 October 13[80].

**566**  Letter of the same to John de Marton, canon, instituting him to Askham vicarage, vacant by the resignation of Sir Henry;[489] presented by prior and convent of Warter. Carlisle, 6 September 13[80].

**567**  Letter of the same to Peter de Derlyngton, canon, instituting him to Bridekirk vicarage, vacant by the death of Brother William de Crathorne; presented by the prior and convent of Guisborough. Carlisle, 25 October [13]80.

**568**  Letter of the same to John Colt, chaplain, instituting him to Castle Carrock church, vacant by the death of Thomas [de Carleton];[490] presented by the prior and convent of Carlisle. Carlisle, 15 October [13]80.

**569**  Letter of the same to John de Stapilton, chaplain, instituting him to Bew-castle (*Bithcaster*) church, vacant by the death of Robert;[491] presented by the prior and convent of Carlisle cathedral. Carlisle, 12 November 1380.

**570**  [Fo.118v; p.333] Will[492] of Andrew de Laton, dated 10 July 1380. Com-mended soul to God, Blessed Mary and all saints. Burial in Dacre churchyard,

---

[485]  Illegible.
[486]  Previous known vicar John de Kerby, by exchange, 1369 (**181**).
[487]  Followed by a space of 9 cm.
[488]  Instituted 1366 (**45**).
[489]  Previous known vicar was Robert de Feryby, 1367 (**155**).
[490]  See **564**.
[491]  Otherwise the previous known rector was Adam Armestrang, 1362 (*Reg. Welton*, 77, no.427). In 1395, John was presented to St. Peter the Great, Chichester, in a proposed exchange with Richard Baker (*CPR 1391–6*, 569).
[492]  Printed in *Test. Karl.*, 147. Expressed in third person.

with best beast. Beatrice de Butycome, 12 cows. Residue for services for his soul in [Dacre] church. Executors: William [de Neuton], vicar of Barton,[493] and Richard Ellotra. Dated at Dunmallard (*Dunmallet*).[494]

Sentence of probate by the bishop, with grant of administration to Richard de Ellotson; reserved to the other executor. Rose, 14 February 1381.

**571** LITTERA GENERALIS. Those who prevent the execution of a will incur sentence of excommunication. Richard Ellotson, executor of Andrew de Laton, has complained that many persons unknown have removed and hidden various goods he had at the time of his death. They are to be ordered by proclamation to restore them, under pain of excommunication. Dated as above.

**572** (i) Institution of Richard Hogges, chaplain, to Carlatton (Karlaton) vicarage;[495] presented by the prior and convent of Lanercost. (ii) Archdeacon to induct. 1380.

**573** [Fo.119; p.334] 'Proceedings in the exchange of Caldbeck and Bowness churches.'
(i) Letter of John Broyne, lord of Drumburgh, to Bishop Thomas. M. William del Hall, rector of Bowness, and Thomas de Barton, rector of Caldbeck (both in dioc. Carlisle), wish to exchange their benefices. Subject to the bishop's approval (as patron of Caldbeck), John presents Thomas to Caldbeck. Carlisle, [.....] 1381.
(ii) Mandate to the dean of Carlisle to enquire into Thomas's presentation, without waiting for a full chapter, provided that there are sufficient rectors, vicars and chaplains; certifying by letters patent. Rose, 6 April 1381.
(iii) Resignations (quoted) to the bishop by William and Thomas. Rose chapel, 6 April 1381.
(iv) Letter of the bishop collating William to Caldbeck. [Fo.119v; p.335] Rose, 15 April 1381.
(v) Mandate (quoted) to the archdeacon to induct William. Same date.
(vi) Letter of the bishop instituting Thomas to Bowness. Same date.
(vii) Note of mandate to the archdeacon for his induction. Same date.
(viii) Memorandum that after a short interval the same William del Hall read a protestation before the bishop and witnesses that he had resigned Bowness in an exchange, but if it should happen that he was unable to thus obtain possession of Caldbeck, he would sue for recovery of Bowness: it was not his intention to surrender his title to this church. [Not completed.][496]

---

[493] Instituted 1362; still in 1393 (*Reg. Welton*, 77, no.427; *CPR 1391–6*, 268).
[494] In Dacre (*EPNS Cumberland*, 187).
[495] Previous known institution was of William de Stokdal, 1344 (*Reg. Kirkby*, I.156, no.752.
[496] Leaving a space of 8 cm, cancelled by crosses. The exchange was reversed in 1387, when the king presented Thomas to Caldbeck and William to Bowness (*CPR 1385–9*, 270).

**574**   [Fo.120; p.336] Will[497] of Henry de Sandford, rector of Crosby Garrett,[498] in good memory, dated 23 December 1380. Commended soul to God, Blessed Mary and all saints. Burial in the said church; 13lb of wax to be burnt around body; 6s. for oblations; 5 marks for paupers; wake for neighbours, 100s. The fabric of the church, 20s., and 20s. to make it a bell. The four mendicant orders, 2 marks equally divided. The friars preachers, Carlisle, all his books. Thomas Lambe, chaplain, to celebrate for his soul and the souls of the faithful departed, for 4 years, £22. Thomas Skayffe's children (*liberos*), 10 marks. John Bowesfeld, 20s. Sisot' dau. of Henry, 20s. Adam Burcy, 24s. 8d. John de Musgrave, 20s. 4d. Alice Browne and Alice Spurner, 3s. equally divided, 3s. John Robynson of Crosby Garrett, 3s. 4d. Joan widow of William de Soulby, 22s. William Watson, 6s. 8d. Residue to be disbursed among his poorest acquaintance and friends, at his executors' choice. Executors: John Wilson and John de Gryndon of Crosby Garrett. Witnesses: John de Bousfeld and William Dobynsson.
    Note of probate before the bishop, Rose chapel, 27 March 1381.

**575**   (i) Institution of Robert de Cestria, chaplain, to Walton vicarage, vacant by the resignation of Richard Hogg'; presented by the prior and convent of Lanercost. (ii) Archdeacon to induct. Rose, 9 March 1381.

**576**   (i) Institution of John de Balne, clerk, to Crosby Garrett church, vacant by the death of Henry de Sandford; presented by Thomas de Musgrave, kt. (ii) Archdeacon to induct. Rose, 27 March 1381.[499]

**577**   [Fo.120v; p.337] (i) Institution of Richard Gudrych, chaplain, to Burgh by Sands church, vacant by the resignation of John de Kave;[500] presented by abbot and convent of Holm Cultram. (ii) Archdeacon to induct. n.d.

**578**   (i) Collation to Robert de Lowther, priest, to Wigton vicarage,[501] vacant by the resignation of John de Welton[502] in [the following] exchange. (ii) Archdeacon to induct. n.d.

**579**   (i) Institution of John de Welton, priest, to Hutton [in the Forest] church, vacant by the resignation of Robert de Lowther in the above exchange. (ii) Archdeacon to induct. 'Same date.'

**580**   Petition of the subprior and convent of Carlisle cathedral. Their prior, John de Penereth, has resigned his office to the bishop, who accepted the

---

[497]   Printed in *Test. Karl.*, 147–8. Expressed in third person.
[498]   Entitled rector and master in licences for absence and study, 1353–62 (*Reg. Welton*, xvii, and index).
[499]   Followed by gap (7.5cm), cancelled.
[500]   See **199** for previous known institution, of John Lukesson, 1369.
[501]   Still vicar of Wigton 1392, 1400 (*CPR 1391–6*, 195; *CPR 1399–1401*, 6).
[502]   Vicar from 1369 (**167**); ratified by the king, 1373 (*CPR 1370–4*, 245).

resignation. They therefore send their canons William de Dalston and John de Boury to ask the bishop for licence to elect. As the priory seal is not available, this letter is under the seal of the official of Carlisle, as he has confirmed at their request. 9 August 1381.

**581** [Fo.121; p.338] Repetition of the above, as a notarial instrument appointing the two proctors under the chapter's common seal, dated in the chapter house, 26 August 1381.

**582** Decree by the bishop pronouncing that he has waited long enough for the persons cited; they will be declared contumacious if they object to the election of William de Dalston, canon of Carlisle, as prior.[503] n.d.

**583** Decree. The subprior and convent presented William de Dalston's election to the bishop. He proclaimed for objections, but none were made. After he considered the business with counsel, with Brother John de Byry acting as proctor, the bishop declared that all was in order; he committed charge of the priory to William and ordered his induction.[504] n.d.

**584** Note against those disturbing or impeding the collection of tithes, reference being made to their incurring excommunication in accordance with a Durham synodal constitution. n.d.[505]

**585** [Fo.121v; p.339] (i) Collation of John de Morton, clerk, to Easton church, vacant by the death of John de Dalston.[506] (ii) Archdeacon to induct. Rose, 22 September 1381.

**586** Licence to John Bone, rector of Lowther, to be absent for one year from 1 January 1381

**587** Mandate of Cosmatus Gentilis of Sulmona, papal collector and nuncio. He had written to the bishop ordering him to publish the excommunication of cited persons for their contumacy in not appearing before him.[507] Their benefices are to be sequestrated and they are cited to the collector's house in London on 24 Oct. [incomplete].

**588** [Fo.123; p.340][508] List of *synodalia* [as in *Reg. Kirkby*, II.842, save that for Westmorland deanery the figures are 2s. for Musgrave, 3s. for Clifton, and 12s.

---

[503] The election was disputed: see Summerson, *Medieval Carlisle*, I.353. William's rival was Thomas de Warthole, ordained priest in 1342 (*Reg. Kirkby*, I.133), who was subprior in 1369 (**170** below). William was ordained priest in 1354 (*Reg. Welton*, 114).

[504] Followed by space of 1.5cm. The next entry in another hand.

[505] This memorandum added at the bottom of a folio probably relates to the tithe problems at St. Nicholas, Newcastle, dioc. Durham (see **594**).

[506] Collated by lapse, 1354 (*Reg. Welton*, 9, no.41).

[507] See **535**.

[508] Start of new quire continuing to fo.130v.

for the total; while the figures for pensions are clearer, viz. Burgh [by Sands], 20s., Crosby [on Eden], 2s., Stanwix, 6s. 8d., Scaleby, 20s., Warcop, at Martinmas and Pentecost, £4; [Newton] Arlosh (*Arloske*), 6s. 8d.; Greystoke, 40s.].

**589**   [Fo.123v; p.341] Licence for John Bone, rector of Lowther, to be absent for one year from 1 January 1382.

**590**   Similar licence to the vicar of Irthington[509] for 2 years from 24 May 1382.

**591**   Will[510] of Thomas de Derby, rector of Brougham, dated 1 April 1382, sane in memory while lying in his sickbed. [*in egritudinis sue loco*][511] Commended soul to God. Burial in St. Wilfrid's, Brougham. Bequeathed a red bed to the said church, 12lb[512] of wax to be burnt at his burial, 20s. for the poor and for exequies and a wake for neighbours at his executors' discretion, and likewise for chaplains. His son Thomas, a black horse with saddle. Ellen de Coundall and her 2 boys, 12 marks. His servant Agnes and her 2 boys, 12 marks. John de Oxsthwayt, 20s. John Dikenson, 20s. His 2 nephews, 40s. His servant Elizabeth, 10s. From the residue, for 2 chaplains to celebrate for his soul in Brough under Stainmore and Brougham churches; with similar employment of any remaining residue. Executors: Thomas de Lowther, chaplain, and Ellis de Bradley. Witnesses: Thomas de Derby and John Merisson.
    Sentence of probate by the bishop, Penrith church, 14 June 1382.

**592**   ARTICULUS *ex officio*. A. de K., a priest of the diocese, is commonly reputed to have kept Alice, a woman of the diocese, as his concubine in his house in a town in the bishop's jurisdiction, which they have inhabited for a long time, committing fornication. The bishop intends to take canonical proceedings against him for the salvation of his soul.

**593**   (i) Institution of William de Sutton, canon of Shap, to the vicarage of Bampton in Westmorland deanery, vacant by the resignation of William de Wicliff; presented by the abbot and convent of Shap. (ii) Archdeacon to induct. [13]82.

**594**   [Fo.124; p.342] Mandate of John [Fordham], bishop of Durham, to the vicar of St. Nicholas, Newcastle upon Tyne, upon the complaint of Bishop Thomas and the prior of Carlisle, to excommunicate all those who have disturbed the collection of tithes in the parish, the church of which is appropriated to the bishop and Carlisle cathedral priory. Dated Durham, 22 September 1382.

**595**   Mandate of Bishop Thomas to the parish chaplain of Greystoke and chaplains of the chapels of Threlkeld and Watermillock. In a recent visitation of the

---

[509] None known by name 1337–1567 (Nicolson & Burn, II.485–6).
[510] Printed in *Test. Karl.*, 148–9. Expressed in third person.
[511] As in MS, said to be 'much rubbed' in *Test. Karl.*, which supplies asterisks.
[512] MS *iij libras*.

diocese, the bishop found large defects in the walls of the nave of Greystoke church, with glass windows covered with wood, and the belfry wholly ruined and falling down. He ordered repairs by a certain date. He has learnt, however, that certain inhabitants of Greystoke and Watermillock have been negligent in their attendance and refused to contribute to the repairs. They are to be admonished to comply within 15 days, or else to appear before his official in Penrith church on 24 November 1382, under pain of excommunication. n.d.

**596** Note of licence to M. Robert de Marrys, rector of Uldale, to be absent to study for one year from Michaelmas 1382, according to the constitution [*cum ex eo*].

Note of similar licence to John de Kerby, rector of Aikton, for 3 years. n.d.

**597** Admission of Richard de Appilton, monk of St. Mary's, York, to Wetheral priory and the cure of its parishioners, presented by the abbot of St. Mary's; reserving the bishop's rights and all processes, etc. in litigation against the abbot by the bishop and his predecessors concerning Wetheral and Warwick churches. The bishop has received his obedience and institutes him.[513] n.d.

**598** [Fo.124v; p.343] Note of licence for John Bone, rector of Lowther, to be absent from next Christmas until 24 June [1383].

**599** Licence of Pope Urban VI to Alexander [Neville], archbishop of York. According to a petition of Ralph, Baron Greystoke of Carlisle diocese, Greystoke church, of which he claims to be patron, is rich enough to support seven parsons celebrating offices. The parish is 20 English miles in width and length. Its rector is often absent and the church thus defrauded of divine services. He therefore seeks the goodwill of the pope to create a collegiate church with seven chaplains and other necessary officers. If the archbishop, whom the pope trusts, approves of this proposal, the church is to be erected as a college, receiving all the church's revenues by papal authority and compelling their payment by ecclesiastical censures. St. Peter's, Rome, 8 May 1380.

**600** Commission of Archbishop Alexander as the pope's executor in this business to Henry Bowett', DCnL, dean of Dublin.[514] The following appointments have been made in Greystoke college by papal authority:

Gilbert Bowet, priest, as master or warden

John Lake, priest (dioc. Lichfield), to the perpetual chantry at the altar of St. Andrew the Apostle

Thomas Chambirleyne, priest (dioc. Norwich), the like at the altar of St. Mary the Virgin

John Alne, priest (dioc. York), at the altar of St. John the Baptist

Richard Barwell, priest (dioc. Lincoln), at the altar of St. Katherine the Virgin

Robert Newton, priest (dioc. Lichfield), at the altar of St. Thomas the Martyr

---

[513] Cf. *Reg. Welton*, 8, no.35.
[514] *BRUO*, II. 2154.

John de Harum, priest (dioc. York), at the altar of the Apostles Peter and Paul
    They have been admitted and instituted by the archbishop, who now orders
[Henry Bowet] to receive their oaths to the bishop of Carlisle and church of
York, and have them or their proctors inducted. Cawood, 22 December 1382.

**601**  [Fo.127; p.348]$^{515}$ Memorandum of probate before the bishop with grant
of administration of the deceased female's (*dicte defuncte*) goods to her executors. Rose, 4 June 1384.

**602**  Memorandum of the [1291] assessments of the churches of Newburn
(£62), St. Nicholas, Newcastle upon Tyne (£39 13s. 4d.) and Warkworth (£90);
and of the new rates [1318] of half of St. Nicholas's church (100s.) and the
whole of Newburn church (66s. 8d.).$^{516}$

**603**  Mandate to Thomas Doget, parish chaplain of the cathedral church of
St. Mary, Carlisle. William de Dalston, its prior,$^{517}$ was lately summoned to
appear before the bishop sitting formally in the chapter house, in order
to take the oath of obedience due to the bishop; nor has he complied with the
bishop's order not to leave without his licence, thus incurring sentence of
excommunication. He is therefore to be denounced in St. Mary's church, on
Sundays and feast-days, until he seeks and deserves to be absolved. Rose,
12 August 1385,

**604**  Mandate to the same chaplain, quoting the above mandate, which he has
not obeyed. He is to obey this command within 8 days, under pain of excommunication. Rose, 19 August 1385.

**605**  [Fo.127v; p.349] Further mandate to the same. The bishop recently
ordered him and the parish chaplain of St. Cuthbert's, Carlisle, to denounce
certain persons as excommunicate for contumacy. Unknown evildoers in large
number, however, came to these churches, laying hands on these chaplains and
threatening to injure them, seizing the bishop's letters and preventing their
execution. All such transgressors, lay as well as clerical, even chaplains assisting
them, are to be admonished in the cathedral to make satisfaction within ten
days, under pain of excommunication, reserving their absolution to the
bishop; their names are to be reported to him. Rose, 23 August 1385.

**606**  Mandate to Thomas de Barton, rector of Bowness. Scandalous rumour
has recently informed the bishop that William de Dalston, prior of Carlisle, has
frequently committed adultery. [Thomas] is ordered, under pain of excommunication, to cite the prior to appear before the bishop or his commissaries, or

---

$^{515}$ The '8' is written over another '4'. Fos. 125 and 126 are missing.
$^{516}$ All in Northumberland, Durham diocese. See *Taxatio Ecclesiastica Angliae et Walliae,
auctoritate Papae Nicholai IV*, circa 1291, ed. S. Ayscough and J. Caley, Record Commission, 1802, 316–17.
$^{517}$ For his election, in 1381, see **582–3**.

commissary, in the cathedral on Friday 25 August to answer appropriate articles; the date may be moderated. Rose, 13 August 1385.

**607** Writ [of Richard II] under the privy seal (in French). He has written to the prior and convent of Carlisle (*Kardoill*) about their disputes, charging them to submit to the bishop's ordinance for the welfare of the priory, which is a royal foundation in the king's patronage. He wishes and beseeches the bishop to examine the causes of this dissension and bring it to a befitting end, for their ease and quiet, and to save the priory from wasting its goods and resources. Newcastle upon Tyne (*Noefchastell sur Tyne*), 21 August [1385].[518]
[Postscript] In case the prior and convent are unwilling to agree and accept the bishop's ordinance, he is to certify the king by sealed letters sent to the office of the privy seal, showing where the fault lies, so that the king may ordain further by his council's advice as seems best.

**608** [Fo.128; p.350] Mandate to John de Penreth, canon of Carlisle.[519] The bishop recently ordered him to admonish all those who came to the churches of Saints Mary and Cuthbert, Carlisle, and forcibly prevented the execution of his mandates to give compensation. n.d.

**609** Mandate of Alexander [Neville], archbishop of York, to the official of Carlisle or his commissaries. He has learnt that William, prior of Carlisle, Richard Orfeur, John de Kerby, rector of a mediety of Aikton, and Thomas Doget, chaplain of Carlisle, are accused of various crimes which the bishop has neglected to correct. Lest a bad example be given, the archbishop orders that the prior and Richard be cited before the archbishop or his commissaries in the collegiate church of St. John, Beverley, on Monday, 2 October, and John and Thomas on 9 October, to answer for their offences. Beverley manor, 28 August 1385.[520]

**610** [Fo.128v; p.351] Mandate to the vicar of Bridekirk to order the people of Isel to attend only their parish church, under pain of excommunication, and not Bridekirk and other adjacent churches; reporting offenders to the bishop. Rose, 24 September 1383.

**611** Commission to M. William de Bownes, rector of Caldbeck,[521] Sir William de Stirkeland, rector of Rothbury, and M. John de Southwell, skilled in law. A majority of the canons of Carlisle have told the bishop that the priory is in great need of reform in spiritualities and temporalities, and have asked him to come to exercise the office of visitation. Heeding their requests, the bishop ordered the prior and all members of the cathedral priory then in the chapter house on 14 September,[522] *viva voce*, that all canons (including absentees obliged to

---

[518] On the king's return from his expedition into Scotland.
[519] Prior 1376–81 (**454n.**, **580**).
[520] Followed by a cancelled space (7 cm).
[521] *Alias* William del Hall, formerly rector of Bowness.
[522] MS *die mensis subscripti.*

attend) should appear before him or his commissaries in the chapter house on
Monday, 25 September and following days for his visitation, to receive his com-
mands, corrections and injunctions. He will not, however, then be able to take
part in person, being detained on the cathedral's business. The commissaries
are therefore appointed, singly or collectively, to deputise for the bishop in this
visitation, with canonical powers. Rose, 24 September 1385.

**612**  LITTERA GENERALIS SENTENCIE. Mandate to Brother William de Dalston, prior of Carlisle. The bishop has learned that many leading clergy and citi-
zens of Carlisle, variously armed, with a crowd of worthless people, have entered
the buildings of the cathedral and the parish churches of the Blessed Mary and
St. Cuthbert of Carlisle, particularly during masses on feast-days; they have
attacked the bishop's ministers, robed as priests, seizing and removing letters
with his orders [Fo.129; p.352]. They later expelled various priests, his ministers
wearing vestments for a solemn occasion. The bishop, with paternal affection,
admonished their leaders to mend their ways, and also all who gave the evildoers
counsel, favour or friendship, that they should admit their wickedness and make
amends. As they have contumaciously scorned his monitions, they have incurred
sentence of excommunication. Rose, 21 September 1385.[523]

**613**  Notice to the chapter of Carlisle that Brother William de Dalston, formerly prior, humbly sought the bishop's permission to resign the priory, for
good reasons. The bishop has accepted the resignation and approves of it, as
he now tells the chapter so that they cannot plead ignorance ('*ne in eventu super
facto hujusmodi ignoranciam pretendere valeatis*'). Rose, 28 September 1385.

**614**  Petition of the chapter for the bishop's licence to elect Brother William's
successor as prior; under its seal. 29 September 1385.

**615**  Licence for the election, in response to the chapter's letters brought to
the bishop by Brother John de Bury, fellow canon.[524] Rose, 30 September 1385.

**616**  [Fo.129v; p.353] Memorandum that Brother William de Dalston, prior of
Carlisle, took an oath of obedience to Bishop Thomas, his successors and ministers (quoted), in the priory's chapter house in the presence of the priory's
convent, William de Stirkeland, William de Bounes, rectors of Rothbury (dioc.
Durham) and Caldbeck (dioc. Carlisle), M. John de Southwell, skilled in law,
and William de Ulnedale and Thomas Davison, notaries. 14 September 1385.

**617**  Certificate of the official of Carlisle quoting the bishop's mandate to cite
any objectors to the election as prior of Robert de Edenhall, canon OSA of
Carlisle.[525] They are to appear in Dalston church on Tuesday, 8 October[526] to

---

[523] See Summerson, I.352–4; *VCH Cumberland*, II.134.
[524] Ordained priest, 1377 (**401**).
[525] Ordained acolyte, 1361 (*Reg. Welton*, 117); priest, 1365 (**342**).
[526] Interlined over August (cancelled).

show, if they can, why the bishop should not confirm the elect [etc.]. Dated as above.

**618** Letters patent of John de Bury, precentor, and the chapter of Carlisle, [Fo.130; p.354] appointing [John] de Overton[527] and Richard de Everwyk,[528] canons of Carlisle, to act as proctors for the chapter in seeking the bishop's confirmation of Robert de Edenhall as prior and in any arising litigation. Dated in the chapter house, 7 Oct. 1385.

**619** Decrees by the bishop.
(i) As objectors to Robert's election were called, and none appeared, the bishop declares anyone objecting to be contumacious and precluded from making any form of objection.
(ii) As any possible objectors had been cited, but had not appeared, the bishop discussed the business with legal counsel and pronounced Robert to have been elected; he was presented by the chapter's proctor, Brother Richard de Everwyk, admitted to its temporalities and spiritualities, and his induction and installation ordered.

**620** Mandate to the archdeacon of Carlisle[529] to install [etc.] Robert de Edenhall as prior of Carlisle, being elect and confirmed. 10 Oct. 1385.[530]
[Fo.130v; p.355] ROUTHBURY[531]

**621** Copy of charter of liberty of Rothbury church (dated Rothbury, St. Barnabas' day, 1275), made as amicable settlement of dispute between Robert son of Roger and Richard of Thenfield, rector of Rothbury.[532]

**622** [Fo.131; p.356] (i) To the subprior and canons of Carlisle. The bishop has confirmed their election of Brother Robert de Edenhall as their prior and orders them to obey him. (ii) To Robert de Edenhall. Following his election and presentation, the bishop admits him as prior; he will supplement any defects in the process. Rose, 30 September 1385.[533]

**623** Mandate to the official[534] of Carlisle. Prelates, rectors etc. of parish churches are obliged to reside unless licensed by the bishop to study or for

---

[527] Ordained acolyte, 1361 (*Reg. Welton*, 117).
[528] Ordained acolyte, 1370 (**364**).
[529] His identity uncertain (see *Fasti*, VI.102).
[530] Followed by space of 4.5 cm, cancelled.
[531] Centred in large hand.
[532] Printed in J.H. Hodgson, *A History of Northumberland*, 7 vols., Newcastle, 1820–58, part 3, vol.2, 139–41. For an ample summary, see Northumberland County History Committee, *A History of Northumberland*, 15 vols., Newcastle upon Tyne, 1893–1940, 15.311.
[533] Cf. later dates **617–18**.
[534] MS *dilecto filio officio nos.tro Karl'*.

other good reasons, so that church services, hospitality and other works of charity are performed. J. de K., T. de D. and other vicars and rectors, however, are absent from the diocese, their cures neglected and revenues not given to the poor. He is therefore charged to cite [absentees] in churches where they have parishioners and friends, to bid them return within six months, otherwise the bishop will proceed against them; he is to be certified. n.d.[535]

**624**   [Fo.131v; p.357] Mandate to unnamed [ministers?] following closely **612**. Date omitted.[536]

**625**   Institution of John de Karlio', [canon,] as vicar of [Castle Sowerby]. 5 January 1386.[537]

**626**   (i) Note of institution of Adam Stuward[538] as vicar of Aspatria in an exchange from Gilcrux. (ii) The like of Robert de Ponte Fracto as vicar of Gilcrux in the above exchange. (iii) Mandates to archdeacon to induct both vicars. 18 January 1386.

**627**   Note of licence as questor to Robert [Jardyn][539] for one year from 25 January [1386].

**628**   Note of licence to John Frysell, rector of Uldale, to be absent for three years. 10 December 1385.

**629**   [Fo.132; p.358] Will[540] of Adam Tailliour of Carlisle (being well in mind and memory), dated in his house in Castle Street, 5 January 1386. Commends soul to God, Blessed Mary and all saints. Burial in the churchyard of the parish church, with 6s. 8d. for mortuary and a stone of wax worth 4s. for a light burning round his body; 40s. for the poor at his burial; 13s. 4d. for a pittance to the canons of Carlisle cathedral serving God there; 6s. 8d. for its fabric. Blessed Mary's light in the parish church, 6s. 8d.; the light of the cross there, 12d.; St. Sitha's light there, 12d.;[541] Blessed Catherine's light there, 12d.; Blessed Trinity's light there, 6d. The friars preachers, Carlisle, 6s.8d. The friars minor there, 6s. 8d. Caldew bridge, 6s. 8d. His parish chaplain, 2s., and clerk, 6d. Each secular chaplain coming to his exequies in a surplice, 6d. Residue to his executors to provide for his soul and souls of his benefactors and all the faithful departed, as they consider fitting, except for all his grants which he made and

---

[535] Followed by space (10 cm), cancelled by crosses.
[536] Marginal note, partly lost, ends with *littera non emanavit*.
[537] Omissions supplied from margin. Previous known vicar was John Cole, a canon of Carlisle, 1378 (**512**); probably still in 1386 (*CPR 1385–9*, 157).
[538] Not 'Fouward' as in Nicolson & Burn, II. 117, 156.
[539] Supplied from margin.
[540] Printed in *Test. Karl.*, 149–51.
[541] See Summerson, I.359.

confirmed by charter to Thomas Boget,[542] William de Tuxforth [and] Robert de Musgrave, chaplains, their heirs and assigns, of all his lands, tenements, rents, services and reversions with their appurtenances in Carlisle city and out-side in the county of Cumberland, for the same to hold of the chief lords of the fee by services due for ever. Executors: Joan his wife, Thomas Boget, William de Tuxsforth [and] Robert de Musgrave. [Witnesses:] Richard Martyn, Thomas Taillour, Adam Malsor and others.

[Second will, repeating his name and the above date]. As Adam clearly fore-saw that his goods and estates would not suffice to perform his will, he declared on 20 January that his wife and other executors named above should, at their discretion, reduce or cancel bequests of money specified therein. Witnesses: Stephen de Karlo, John del Bakehaus and others.

Sentence of probate before the bishop, with commitment of goods in the diocese to above executors. Carlisle cathedral, 20 January 1386.[543]

**630** (i) Collation to John Mason, chaplain, to Isel vicarage, vacant by the death of John Baynard;[544] in the bishop's collation this turn by gift of the prior and con-vent of Hexham, the patrons. (ii) Archdeacon to induct. Rose, 28 February 1386.

**631** (i) Note of collation to Richard de Brorton, chaplain, to [Nether] Denton.[545] (ii) Archdeacon to induct. 23 March 1386.

**632** [Fo.132v; p.359] (i) Institution of Adam de Aglynby, chaplain, to the chantry at the altar of Blessed Mary in Greystoke collegiate church; presented by Ralph, Baron Greystoke. (ii) Archdeacon to induct. Rose, 10 May 1386.

**633** General sentence against violators of the liberties of the Church. Mandate to [the dean of Carlisle?][546] to publish the sentence of excommunication against unknown evildoers who came armed and broke into a place in the town-ship of Hayton belonging to the bishop and cathedral of Carlisle, removing goods of John de Thurstanefeld, the bishop's tenant and man. Their absolution is reserved to the bishop, who is to be informed after enquiry etc. n.d.

**634** Appointment of John Halswayne and John Leynard, clerks, and Robert de Haryngton, layman, as the bishop's proctors to appear before Walter [Skirlaw], bishop of Coventry and Lichfield or his commissaries in visitations and other convocations of clergy, taking part in making statutes, etc., concerning the parish church of Melbourne (*Melburn*) and Chellaston (*Chelaston*) in Lichfield diocese, 'long' held by bishops of Carlisle. n.d.[547]

---

[542] *Recte* Doget?

[543] Margin: *Non red' compotum.*

[544] Instituted 1362 (*Reg. Welton*, 95, no.515).

[545] The previous known rector was Stephen de Cumquinton, murdered by Oct. 1383 (*CPR 1381–5*, 353; see also **121** below).

[546] MS *dilecto filio etc.*

[547] Skirlaw held the see of Lichfield from Jan. to Aug. 1386; and cf. *Reg. Kirkby*, I.123, no.607.

**635**   [Fo.133; p.360] Warrant of Richard II under the privy seal (in French) to the treasurer and barons of the Exchequer. He had ordered William Walworth and John Philippot, war-treasurers, to make payments for their attendance of the king's council to the earl of March (300 marks), the bishops of Salisbury (500 marks) and Carlisle (400 marks)[548] and Henry Scrope, banneret (200 marks). Dated 2 August 1378.

**636**   Similar warrant (in French) ordering the treasurer and chamberlains, by the advice of the council, to pay Bishop Thomas £100 for attending the council, by parliament's order; and also for spending some time with men-at-arms and archers in Carlisle city for its defence when John [of Gaunt], king of Castille and Leon and duke of Lancaster, with his army, was raiding Scotland in the 7th year of the reign;[549] also for various march days he and his deputies had held in Scotland; and for payment above £20 due to him from the king for being a deputy at a treaty of truce made last January with deputies of the king of Scots. Westminster, 23 March 1385.

**637**   Similar warrant (in French) to the treasurer and barons of the Exchequer, fully repeating the above details; the king therefore orders that the bishop be discharged for the said £20, so that he is now quit for these costs. Westminster, 26 March 1386.

Note [in another hand] that this letter was enrolled in the Exchequer among the *Brevia directa* for the Hilary term for the 9th term, rot. 30.

Note in margin [partly illegible]: this and the 2 other letters *habende . . . memoranda propter exoneracionem.*

[Also in margin: Stirkeland, and drawing of a pointing hand and glove with cuff.]

**638**   [Fo.133v; p.361] Indenture notifying all that Thomas, bishop of Carlisle, has granted to Thomas Smyth, his wife Serota and their heirs and assigns, the farm for 60 years of a tenement with a garden in Horncastle which he now holds at will, lying between the tenements of Thomas de Thymylby and Walter de Ebor', paying the bishop and his successors 11s. in equal parts at Easter, St. Botolph's [17 June], Michaelmas and Christmas; they will make necessary repairs. Carlisle, 24 June, 9 Richard II [1386?].[550]

Sealed notice of their confirmation by Robert de Edenhall, prior of Carlisle, and the convent. Dated 25 June.

**639**   Mandate to the dean [of Carlisle?]. Rectors and vicars of his deanery, or their parish chaplains, are bound by custom and law to come in procession to

---

[548] Appleby was one of the 3 bishops appointed to the 'council of nine' in Richard II's first parliament, Oct. 1377 (*Select Documents of English Constitutional History 1307–1485*, ed. S.B. Chrimes and A.L. Brown, London, 1961, 115–16). For his salary of 400 marks, see J.F. Baldwin, *The King's Council in England during the Middle Ages*, Oxford, 1913, 121.

[549] About Easter 1384 (G. Ridpath, *The Border-History of England and Scotland*, (London, 1776), 244).

[550] The regnal year dated from 22 June.

the cathedral church on the fourth week in Pentecost and make oblations at the high altar as a token of their subjection to the cathedral. Many listed in a schedule have contumaciously failed to comply. They are to be cited to appear at a set day etc. Dated 'etc'.

**640** Letter of the abbot and convent of St. Mary's, York, presenting John de Bruddeford, chaplain (dioc. York), to Kirkby Stephen vicarage, vacant by the death of Peter [de Morland];[551] saving an annual pension of 20s. due to them from ancient times, and without prejudice to the rights of the apostolic see, its legates etc. 28 June 1386.

**641** [Fo.134; p.362] Certificate to M. Cosmatus Gentilis of Sulmona, DCnL, papal nuncio and collector in England, quoting his mandate (dated London, 20 May 1385) to cite the following listed persons in debt to the chamber to appear in his hospice in the parish of St. Margaret, London, on 12 August to show why they should not be excommunicated, viz.:

Robert de Lowthir, vicar of Dalston, who was provided; he has been excommunicated and denounced in the vicarage and neighbouring churches, which will not cease without further order, and the fruits of the church sequestrated.

The prior of Carlisle as also been cited in respect of Peter's Pence.

Robert Taillior, once rector of Scaleby,[552] who is blind

Robert Carter and John de Ingilby cannot be traced.

**642** Admission of Thomas Pygott', monk of St. Mary's, York, to the priory of Wetheral and the cure of its parishioners, presented by the abbot of St. Mary's; reserving the bishop's rights and all processes, etc. in litigation against the abbot by the bishop and his predecessors. The bishop has received his obedience and institutes him. Rose, 12 Oct. 1386.

**643** Will[553] of John de Dounthwayt, dated 8 December 1386 Commends soul to God, Blessed Mary and all saints. Burial in churchyard of St. Andrew's, Penrith, with best beast for mortuary, 5lb of wax for burning on burial day, and 100s. for a wake for friends and the poor. Each priest celebrating in this church, 6s. 8d.; its clerk, 6s. 8d.; its fabric, 20s. The light of Blessed Mary, 6s. 8d. The lights of the Crucifix, Saints James and Nicholas, and St. Katherine, 10s. equally divided. Brother Thomas de Warchop, 6s. 8d.; also for him to celebrate for the soul of William del Gill, 8 marks. Sir John Penymayster, to complete his term celebrating, 36s. The 4 orders of friars in Carlisle, Penrith and Appleby, 20s. each. To repair the bridges at Eamont, Lowther, Sowerby, Appleby, Salkeld, Warwick, Eden, Caldew, Cocker, Derwent, Isel and Waterouse, 40s. in equal portions. The nuns of Armathwaite, 40s. Sir John Garou, 13s. 4d.; also for him to celebrate for the soul of Agnes de Welton, 4 marks. Brother Thomas de Warthcop, to celebrate 13 masses, 6s. 8d. Sir William de Stirkeland, 12 silver

---

[551] See as executor, **11**.

[552] Instituted 1380 (**550**).

[553] Not printed in *Test. Karl.*

spoons. Sir Thomas Boget, a pair of tablets with *les menyle*. Diot' Hyll, 10s. Item
. . . .[Fo.134v; p.363] John Michelson's wife, 13s. 4d. Joan Shephirdoghter and
her dau. Marjory, 13s. 4d. Joan Emdoghter, 10s. Mariota de Barneby, 6s. 8d.
Ellen dau. of Mariota, 40d. William Garard, 40d. John Boste, 2 silver spoons.
Andrew Marschall, a spoon. Two hermits of Cockermouth, 6s. 8d., divided. Sir
John Penymaystr', 7 ells of linen cloth to make a surplice. Thomas de Barneby,
student (*scolarizanti*), a breviary, a book called *expositorem* and a surplice. John
de Barneby, chaplain, to celebrate for [the testator's soul] a missal; likewise a
missal to John de Morland; and to both, a red vestment to be given to Penrith
church after their deaths. John Colby, 10s. Christine, wife of Thomas de
Barneby, and their children, 40 marks. John de Barneby, chaplain, 40s. John de
Morland, chaplain, 40s. Brother John de Dunthwayt, £4. Maud Schort, 40d.
Serota the weaver (*textrici*), 40s. Christine de Barneby and her children, all
utensils of the hall and kitchen, with corn, hay, meat, fish, pigs and all other
fuels. Residue: John de Barneby and John de Morland, chaplains, appointed
executors ordaining celebrations for his soul. Witnesses: Brother Thomas de
Warthcop, John de Skelton, chaplain, Sir William del Pek, Sir John Penymayster, John Bost, Andrew Marschall, John Coke, Thomas de Barneby and
many more. Dated as above, at Penrith.

Note of probate, granted to above executors, 5 January [1387].

**644**   (i) Note of collation to John de Southwell, priest, to Kirkcambeck (*Cambok*)
church.[554] (ii) Archdeacon to induct. 12 January 1387.

**645**   (i) Collation to William de Kirssall, priest, to Kirkcambeck church, vacant
by the resignation of John de Southwell; presented by the prior and convent of
Carlisle. (ii) Archdeacon to induct. Rose, 22 February 1387.

**646**   Mandate of the bishop to the archdeacon of York or his deputy, quoting
a commission of Alexander [Neville], archbishop of York (dated [King's] Langley, 3 February 1387) to effect an exchange of benefices between John Suth-
well, rector of Kirkcambeck, and William de Kirssall, rector of a mediety of
Burnsall (*Brynsall*) church (dioc. York), following John's presentation to Burnsall by Joan, widow of Richard de Hebden, kt.; the archbishop is detained on
business of the king and kingdom. [Fo.135; p.364]. Mandate for John's induction dated Rose, 12 February 1387.

**647**   Warrant of Richard II under the privy seal (in French) to the treasurer
and barons of the Exchequer. With the assent of prelates, lords and commons,
the king appointed Bishop Thomas to attend the king's council continually to
ordain for wars and the estate of the realm, for which he received £266 13s.
4d. by a prest from the king on 12 August 1377. He is due to reimburse the
Exchequer, but the king has pardoned him for this sum. Westminster, 25 April
1392.

Enrolled among the writs to the barons, Easter 15 Richard II.

---

[554] For previous known rectors, see *Reg. Welton*, 31, no.174.

**648** Letters patent of the bishop certifying that when he was celebrating orders in the chapel at Rose on 3 April 1389 John Davison, acolyte (dioc. Durham), was ordained subdeacon on the title of Richard Louthre; and likewise on 19 March 1390 as deacon, and on 2 April 1390 as priest. Rose, 2 April 1390.

**649** [Fo.135v; p.365] Appointment by Thomas, abbot, and the convent of St. Mary's, York, as appropriators of Bromfield church (dioc. Carlisle), of their brother, Thomas Pygott, prior of their cell at Wetheral, and M. Alan de Newerk, advocate of the court of York, as their proctors in causes concerning this church. 24 November 1392.

**650** Mandate to the dean of Allerdale. The chancel of Bromfield church, which is appropriated to St. Mary's, York, is in so ruinous a condition that divine services cannot be celebrated in it. The abbot and convent assert that John de Culwen, its vicar, is responsible for its repair. [The bishop] wishes to perform his pastoral duty, avoid expense and ensure that repairs will be made by the person responsible. Order to cite them, John de Culwen or their proctors to appear before the bishop or his commissaries on 11 December to answer on this matter, certifying him, etc. Rose, 21 November 1392.

**651** [Fo.136; p.366] Commission to Masters Alan de Newerk, advocate of the court of York, Adam de Bolton, official of Carlisle, William de Bowness, rector of Bowness, and M. John de Karlio', vicar of Torpenhow. John de Culwen, vicar of Bromfield, has been cited to appear before the bishop or his commissaries in Carlisle cathedral on 11 November to answer in person why he should not be excommunicated for his violation of the bishop's sequestration of the church and its vicarage. As the bishop is absent for various reasons, they are to proceed in the cause as is just, with canonical powers [etc.]. Rose, 9 December 1392.

**652** Mandate to the dean of Allerdale. In his recent visitation of the city and diocese of Carlisle, the bishop discovered that the choir or chancel of Bromfield church was ruinous in its timber and roof, so badly that masses and other services could not be celebrated. He therefore issued monitions there that repairs should be made by the abbot and convent of St. Mary's, appropriators of the church, and its vicar, or by whichever of them had this duty. Being unable to find who was responsible, he orders the dean to go to Bromfield and sequester - as the bishop does - all sources of income and keep them in custody as he would answer for them, providing that the church was served until further order, certifying under his seal of office. Date omitted.

**653** Mandate to the same. The bishop was learnt that John de Culwen, vicar of Bromfield, has violated the sequestration, incurring excommunication. He is to be cited before the bishop or his commissaries in Carlisle cathedral on Wednesday 11 December to show why he should not be excommunicated. Rose, 21 November 1392.

**654** [Fo.136v; p.367] Commission to M. Adam de Bolton, the bishop's official of Carlisle, M. William de Bownes, rector of Bowness, Sir William de

Stirkeland, rector of Horncastle (dioc. Lincoln), and M. John de Karlio', vicar of Torpenhow. The bishop has cited the abbot and convent of St. Mary's, York, appropriators of Bromfield church, and Sir John de Culwen, its vicar, to appear before him in Carlisle cathedral on Wednesday 11 December to answer certain articles concerning the repair of the notoriously ruinous chancel of Bromfield church. As the bishop is prevented from taking part in this matter, the commissaries are to enquire and discuss who is responsible for these repairs, by the bishop's authority, compelling performance by ecclesiastical censures. Rose, 9 December 1392.

**655**  Statement by the proctor of the abbot and convent of St. Mary's, York, for the information of the bishop and his commissaries. He says that the monks have had sufficient and canonical title for 10, 20, 30, 40 and 60 years and held the church peacefully from time beyond mind, wholly free from any ordinary charge and particularly from the burden of repairs of the chancel. By the terms of the appropriation, John de Culwen, the vicar, is bound to meet all ordinary charges.[555] He and his predecessors had borne the costs of books, vestments, sacred ornaments etc.; also repair of the chancel, whenever it was necessary. They had provided bread, wine, lights. etc., and all other costs and expenses except those pertaining to the parishioners. To meet his costs, he has the greater part of the revenues of the church assigned to him, from which John had sufficiently met the charges of his incumbency, as is publicly known, which the proctor testifies.[556]

[555] Bishop Halton authorised the appropriation of the church in 1302, requiring vicars to meet all ordinary charges, but without mention of repairs to the chancel (*Reg. Halton,* I.203–5).

[556] The record ends here, with the bottom margin measuring 4 cm There may have been further entries in the cahier about this cause, lost with the remainder of the register.

# INDEX OF PERSONS AND PLACES

References in arabic numerals are to the numbered entries and their foot-notes; those in Roman numerals to the Introduction. The word 'WILL' is given in capital letters when transcripts of these documents occur in the register.

In the ordination lists (nos. 338–425), third and fourth notices of an individual's ordination are given in abbreviated form with a cross-reference to the previous full details. Place names are followed by examples of their original spellings, and next by abbreviated forms of their pre-1974 counties, with YER, YNR and YWR for the Yorkshire ridings. Compound place names are shown under their names of substance.

St. Mary in the North Bailey, rectors
    of, 126, 153–4
St. Mary in the South Bailey, rector
    of, Reginald, 153
St. Nicholas, 153
St. Oswald, parish chaplain, Thomas,
    153
  dean of Christianity of, 153
  diocese of, 279, 349–50, 367–9, 371–2,
    375–6, 388, 412–15, 648; clergy
    of, 98, 274
  constitution of, 584
  official of, 190; *and see* Farnham,
    William
  subsidy in, 274
Durisme, *see* Dunolm
Dyghton, *see* Dighton
Dykson, *see* Dikson
Dyssington, *see* Dissington
Dyx, *see* Bix

Eamont, in Barton, Westm., bridge, 317,
    643
Easby, St. Agatha's YNR, Prem. abbey, tit.,
    417, 420–1
Easingwold, Esyngwald, YNR, vicar of,
    Henry, and parish chaplain, 151;
    *and see* Esyngwad; Esyngwald
Easton, Eston, Cumb., church, 585
  rectors of, *see* Dalston, John; Morton,
    John
Eberston, John de, of York dioc., ords.,
    412–13
Ebor', *see* York
Ebote, John son of, 563
Eccleston, Heclyston in Laylandechyr',
    Lancs., 246
Eden, river, Cumb., benefices beyond,
    275
  fishery in, 468
Edenhall, Cumb., 184, 529
  church, repair of, 556
  churchyard, 556
  vicarage of, ordinance for, 170
  vicars of, 556, 564; *and see* Hayton,
    Thomas; Kerby, John;
    Marshall, John; Ravenstandale,
    Eudo
Edenhall, Edenhale, Robert de, canon of
    Carlisle, 106, 338, 342, 455;
    prior, 617–20, 622, 638
Edenham, John de, tit., 346–8

Patrick de, rector of Croglin, 293n.
    rector of Kirkborthwick, dioc.
    Glasgow), ord., 338–40
Edmund, Alice daughter of, 555
  John his son, 555
Edward II, king (1307–27), 98
Edward III, king (1327–77), 8, 71, 98,
    100–5, 109, 119, 131, 172, 176,
    179, 185–6, 207, 209–14, 221–3,
    226, 228, 230–6, 249–59, 274,
    276, 278, 281, 285, 287–8, 294,
    296–7, 301–2, 307, 320, 337,
    395n., 426, 434, 436n., 468,
    470–2, 474, 512n.; appoints
    wardens of marches, 72, 105,
    223, 235; order for array and
    residence in king's absence, 234,
    287; repair of truce, 236;
    planning expeditions abroad,
    179, 222, 226, 231, 234, 296–7,
    301–2, 310; attempts to raise
    loans, 232, 249–55, 257; treaty
    with king of Navarre, 251–2; visit
    by papal legates, 265; queen of,
    *see* Philippa; treasurer of, *see*
    Brantingham, Thomas
Edward, prince of Aquitaine and Wales,
    son of Edward III, 174, 301
Egglestone, YNR, Prem. abbey, tit., 360,
    420–1, 423
Egleston, Egelton, Egilston, William de,
    canon of Shap, ord., 366, 368–9,
    371
Egremond, Thomas de, of Carlisle dioc.,
    ord., 423–4
  William de, of York dioc., ord., 378,
    381–2
Eland, John de, of York dioc., ord., 366–8
Elias, rector of Scaleby and Crosby on
    Eden, 489, 550
Elizabeth, servant [of Thomas de Derby]
    591
Ellarle, John, 142
Ellerton, William de, rector of Musgrave, 8
Ellotson, Ellotra, Richard, 570–1
Ely, diocese of, 279; notary of, 265
Ely, John de, OP, priest, 418
Elziarius, cardinal priest of St Balbina, 540
Emdoghter, Joan, 643
Emma, servant of John Marshall, 479
Englys, *see* Lenglys
Epworth, *see* Hepworth

Lanercost, William de, *alias* William del
    Wall, canon of Lanercost, ord.,
    393, 396–7, 401, 408
Langbryge, *see* Longbridge
Lange, Alice wife of Stephen, 215
Langewatby, *see* Langwathby
Langham, Simon de, archbishop of
    Canterbury (1366–8), 51n.,
    115n., 192n.; chancellor, 98n.;
    cardinal-priest, papal nuncio,
    265–6, 268, 282–4; *alias* cardinal
    of Canterbury, 429–30
Langholm (in Kirklinton, Cumb.?), 468
Langholm, Langholme, John de, rector of
    Kirkland, 62, 262, 275, 289, 291,
    293, 515
Langlee, Langle, Walter de, OSA, ord.,
    369, 371, 375, 377
Langley, King's, Herts., 98, 100, 646
Langton, John de, OP, ord., 357–8
Langwathby, Langewatby, in Edenhall,
    Cumb., 170, 184
Langwathby, Richard de, chaplain, 293
    William de, ord., 368–70; rector of
    Great Orton, 460
Laton, Andrew de, 290, WILL of, 570–1
    Andrew, brother of William, 137
    John de, brother of William, 137
    Margaret, wife of William de, 137
    Thomas de, 137
    William de, of Newbiggin, WILL of, 137
Laverok', John, ord., 338; rector of
    Penersax, 339–41
Layalton, William, chaplain, 290
Layland, John, 559
Laysingby, Laysyngby, Leisingby,
    Leysyngby, John de, 122
    William, OFM, ord., 368, 370
    William de, rector of Welbury, vicar of
    Morland and Helmsley, 3, 150–1,
    155
    servant of, Robert, 77
    handmaid of, Joan, 77
Lazonby, Cumb., church, churchyard, 81,
    122, 175
    vicars of, 81n., *and see* Castro Bernardi,
    John; Otteley, Adam; Threlkeld,
    William; Witton, Richard
Ledale, Ledell, Lydell, Nicholas de, ord.,
    377, 391–3
Leeson, John, of Kirkbyth[ore?], 77
Legh, Lady del, 85

Leisingby, *see* Laysingby
Lekyl, John de, 137
Lenglys, Englys, Lenglise, Alice, 140
    Elizabeth, sister of Margaret, 142
    Isabel, daughter of Margaret, 142
    Margaret, widow of William, kt., WILL
    of, 142
    Margaret, widow of John de Hoton, 140
    Thomas, ord., 361, 363–5
    Thomas, kt., brother of William, 140n.
    William, kt., 86, 142, 233n., WILL of,
    140
Leventhorpe, Leventhorpp, John de, of
    Durham dioc., ord., 368–70
Leversdale, Robert de, burgess of Carlisle,
    WILL of, 112
    sister of, Elizabeth, 112
Levyngton, John de., tit., 371–2, 381
Lewes, Lowon', Sussex, prior of, 262
Leynard, John, clerk, 634
Leysyngby, *see* Laysingby
Lichfield, diocese, 279
Liddington, Rutland, 135, 159, 188, 241,
    469
Lincoln, archdeacon of, official of, 135
    bishop of, *see* Buckingham, John
    canons of, *see* Chesterfeld, Richard;
    Power, Walter
    cathedral, fabric of, 180
    diocese, ord., 279, 402, 654
Linstock garth, in Stanwix, Cumb., fishery,
    468
Lionel, son of Edward III, duke of
    Clarence, 214
Lismore, Ireland, bp of, *see* Reve, Thomas
Littestter, Lyster, Lytster, Laurence, of
    Carlisle dioc., ord., 369–71
    Philip, 77
    William, ord., 351–3
Llandaff, diocese, 279
Lodelowe, Loudelowe, Thomas de, chief
    baron of the Exchequer, 131,
    240, 260
Loeson, Maud daughter of Henry, 160
Loksmyth, Agnes, 77
Lombardy, Italy, 214
London, acta dated at, 17, 87–9, 96, 251,
    267–72, 282, 284, 289, 291, 403,
    437, 512, 535, 641
    bishop in, 512
    bishops of, 402 *and see* Bintworth,
    Richard; Courtenay, William

Newby, Neuby, Isabel and Joan, 562
  John de, monk of Holm Cultram, ord.,
    338, 342, 348
Newcastle upon Tyne, 317, 554
  burgesses (named), 149
  church of St. Nicholas, 584n., 602;
    building works at, 149
    vicar of, 195, 594, *and see* Bolton,
      Matthew
  nuns of St. Bartholomew's, 465
  Richard II at, 607
  *See also* Novo Castro
Newerk, M. Alan de, advocate of court of
    York, 649, 651
Newton, Neuton, YNR, parish chaplain,
    151
Newton, Neuton, Robert, chantry chap-
    lain in Greystoke college, 600
  Thomas de, ord., 340–1; chaplain, 153
  William de, vicar of Barton, 145, 516, 570
Newton Arlosh, Arloske, in Holme East
    Waver, Cumb., 77
  church, 588
Newton Reigny, Neuton, 34
Nicholas, 560
Nicholas son of Alan son of Walter, 308
Nonyngton, Nunyngton, John, monk of
    Holm Cultram, ord., 364, 368,
    382
Norfolk, Northfolk, John de, rector of
    Kirklinton, 436, 489
North, Richard, of Wold Newton, notary,
    157
North Collingham, *see* Collingham, North
Northcave, *see* Cave
Northfolk, *see* Norfolk
Northumberland, archdeacon of, 153
  array in, 287, 296
  escheator of, 520
  sheriff of, 236n.
Norton, co. Durham, collegiate church,
    canon of, *see* Appleby, John
Norton, M. John de, proctor of Holm
    Cultram, 470
Norwich, diocese, 279
Notyngham, John de, canon of Shap,
    ord., 366 (William), 368–9, 371
Novo Castro, M. Adam de, 269
Nunyngton, *see* Nonyngton

Ogle, Robert de, kt., 44
  Thomas de, kt., 12, 43

Old Ford, Oldforth, Middlesex, 50
Orchard, William del, rector of Dacre and
    Whitburn, 242–7
Orewell (Harwich), Suff., 234
Orfeur, Orfeor, *see* Goldsmith
Ormesby, John de, 11
Ormesheved, Hormesheved, Robert de,
    317, 556n., 562; tit., 370–2, 382,
    386, 389
  Thomas de, ord., 415, 417–19
  Walter de, rector of Beaumont, 45, 565
Ormside, Ormesheved, Westm., church,
    117
  rectors of, *see* Bix, Robert; Grete, John
Orton, Great, Orreton, church, 460
  rectors of, *see* Arthuret, William;
    Langwathby, Richard
Otere, Alice, 495
Otford, Kent, 166n.
Otrington, Richard de, OFM, deacon,
    407
Otteley, Adam de, vicar of Lazonby, 81n.
Ottobuono, *see* Fieschi
Ousby, Ullasby, Ulnesby, Cumb., church,
    20, 132–4, 147, 484
  rectors of, 437n.; *and see* Overton, Simon;
    Stapelton, Nicholas; Strickland,
    William; Waterward, John
Overend, Overende, Thomas del, chap-
    lain, 499, 557
Overton, Querton, Hugh de, 462, 500
  John de, canon of Carlisle, 106, 618
  John de, tit., 339–41
  Margaret widow of Hugh de, of Kirkby
    Stephen, 480
  Robert de, OFM, ord., 377–9
  Robert de, canon of Conishead, ord.,
    364
  Simon de, rector of Ousby, 395, 437,
    526, 535
  Thomas de, ord., 338–41; chaplain, 512
Overton, Everton, YNR, 151
  Robert, vicar of, 151
Overton, *see* Wharton
Oxendene, Thomas de, OP, ord., 357–8
Oxford, 554
  Austin friars, 336
  chancellor of, 336, 554
  church of St. Mary, 554
  church of St. Peter in the East, 554
  Queen's Hall/College, 205–6, 336,
    554

# INDEX OF SUBJECTS

Cross-references to persons and places are to those names in the preceding index.

into revenues of church, 512, 516

Installation, mandate for, 620

Institution to benefice, 12, 14, 16, 19, 32–3, 41–2, 44–5, 52, 78, 107, 139, 144, 175, 199, 261, 263, 298, 300, 311–14, 319, 434, 443, 445, 460–2, 475, 478, 487, 496, 538, 543, 551, 565–9, 572–3, 575–7, 579, 593, 600, 625–6, 632; *see also* collation; exchange

Institution, letters of, 304

Interdict, 326

Intestates, goods of, 116, 187, 480, 498

Invasion, 176, 234, 254, 275, 294, 296–7, 310, 483, 514

Inventory, 138

Jack, 138; *see also* paltock

Jacket, protective, 503

Jewel(s), 142, 215

Journal, 11

Judgment, court, 43

Jug, 113, 136, 495, 554, 557, *and see* pitcher

Jurors, jury, 191

Justices, of assize, 43; of Common Pleas, 128; of gaol delivery, 207, 212, 335, 459

Kerchief, 495; *see also* coverchief

Key, 554

Kiln, 191

Kirtle, 558

Kitchen, 191

Kitchen boy, 554

Knife, 148, 506, 562

Knight, 80, 124, 140, 142, 155, 167, 556, 646

Lambs, 137, 143, 315, 564

Lawyers, scarcity of, 429

Lead, 479

Legates, papal, 265, 267–9

Letters dimissory, 59, 168, 171, 203, 338–40, 344–6, 349–50, 354, 360–1, 363–4, 366–9, 376, 393, 396–8, 404, 407–8, 416–17

Liberties, of bishop, 207, 209, 211; of cathedral, 510

Licence(s) as confessor and penitentiary, 35

for absence, 5–7, 9, 15, 17–18, 38, 47, 68, 79, 191, 331–2, 433, 436–8, 520, 526, 532, 544, 546, 586, 589–90, 596, 598, 628

for non-attendance at synods, 10, 437, 520

for oratory, 24, 67, 84–6, 233

for questor/collector, 39, 65, 115, 201–2, 229, 432, 522, 548, 627

to celebrate sacraments and services, 34, 492

to elect, 454–5, 580–1, 614–15

to establish collegiate church, 599

to study and farm benefice, 545

Light(s) in church, 29, 50, 113, 138, 143, 145, 148, 183, 189, 308–9, 315, 317, 452, 465–6, 479, 495, 499, 503–4, 557–8, 560, 629, 643, 655

Linen, 30, 643

Litany, 25

Loan(s), 249–53, 255, 257, 562

Magic, 218

Maid, handmaid, 77, 114, 143, 463; *and see* servant

Malt, 69, 315, 463, 506, 558

Manciple, 554

Mandate(s), 40, 48, 60, 88–9, 107, 116, 151, 153, 155, 163–4, 169, 187, 191, 196–7, 205, 218–20, 224–5, 227, 248, 263, 265, 271–2, 275, 282, 289, 291–3, 304, 310, 322, 325–7, 333, 427–8, 431, 456, 470–1, 485, 488–9, 502, 509–12, 514, 516–17, 519, 523, 525, 527, 535, 539, 573, 587, 594–5, 603–6, 608–10, 617, 620, 623–4, 633, 639, 641, 646, 650, 652–3

Maniple, 499

Manor, 84, 101, 155, 218, 334

Manse, 191, 225, 308, 519

Market Place, 169

Markets in churchyards, 525

Marriage cases, 26, 76, 160; *see also* appeal; commission; divorce

Marriage, non-consummation of, 76

Marriage portion, 122, 308, 495

Mass(es), 113, 166, 183, 214, 254, 323, 556, 563, 612, 643, 652; provision made for celebration of, 11, 29, 50, 64, 81, 113–14, 122, 136–8, 140, 142–3, 145, 183, 189, 215, 290, 308–9, 317, 336, 435, 463–4, 466, 479, 495, 499, 503, 505, 542, 554, 556–9, 562–4, 570, 574, 591, 643

Matins, 308

Mazer, 145, 215, 562

Meat, 643

Thraves, 219, 511
Tithe case, 239
Tithes, 304; forgotten, 112, 137, 189,
    435, 453, 499, 562; impeding
    collection/non-payment of, 163–4,
    536, 584, 594
  of calves, 164
  of corn, 27, 163
  of hay, 163–4
  of lambs, 164
  of multure, 60
  of pasture, 239
  of peas, 27
  of sheaves, 162, 536
  of wool, 164
Title, for ordination, letter of, 204; to
    benefice, 304, 321, 655; for orders,
    338–425 *passim*
Toft, 503
Tools, goldsmith's, 503; for husbandry, 11
Torches, 122
Towels, 495, 554, 558, 564
Treaty, 251–2; *see also* peace treaty; truce
Trentals, 542, 562
Tripod, 564; *see also* brandreth; gridiron
Trough, 506
Truce, 70, 223n., 236–7, 296, 429, 636
Tub, mash, 506
Tunic(s), 215, 315, 317, 452, 495, 503

University, attendance of clergy at, 429,
    437; *see also studium generale*
Utensils, 122, 137, 505, 562, 643

Vacancy of see, 128
Veil, silk, 495, 558
Vestments, 11, 148, 499, 563, 612, 643,
    655; *see also* alb; amice; chasuble;
    maniple; stole; surplice
Vicar-general, 1, 111, 175, 217, 259, 265,
    310, 486, 488–94, 565–9
Vicarage, ordination of, 170; *see also*
    appropriations
Violence, 169

Visitation, bishop's, 36, 106, 177, 303–5,
    321, 501–2, 512, 517–18, 595, 611,
    634, 652
Visor, 138, 503

Wagon, 11, 114, 309, 315
Wake, funeral, 137–8, 140, 189, 309, 317,
    463, 466, 479, 557, 561, 574, 591,
    643
War-treasurers, 635
Wardens of the marches, appointment of,
    72–3, 105, 213, 223, 235
Wardship, 185n., 194, 319, 434
Warrant, 635–7, 647
Wax, 50, 64, 81, 113–14, 136–8, 140,
    145–6, 290, 308, 317, 435, 452, 463,
    465, 495, 499, 503, 505, 542, 554,
    556–9, 574, 591, 629, 643; *see also*
    candles; light(s)
Weather, 25; *see also* drought; flood; rain
Whipping of penitents, 169
Will(s) (full text given), 11, 30, 50, 64,
    80–1, 112–14, 122, 124, 136–8, 140,
    142–3, 148, 180, 183, 189, 215, 290,
    308–9, 317, 435, 452, 463, 465–6,
    479, 495, 499, 503–6, 529, 542,
    554–9, 561–4, 570, 574, 591, 629,
    643; nuncupative, 29, 69, 145, 315,
    318, 336, 439–41, 464, 481, 497,
    555(?), 560; impeding execution
    of, 571; insufficient goods for
    bequests in, 629; will mentioned
    but not recited, 28, 75, 82; *see also*
    administration, grant of; intestates;
    probate; testamentary
Windows, church, 556, 595
Wine, 655; cooler 11
Wool, 137, 240, 558, 562, 564
Writ(s), 8, 40, 43, 119, 131, 172, 178, 207,
    209, 211–12, 221–2, 228, 230, 240,
    259–60, 307, 310, 320, 426, 470–1,
    482, 509, 514, 524, 527, 531, 607

Yokes, 542